Hellcat:
The F6F in World War II

By Barrett Tillman

NAVAL INSTITUTE PRESS
Annapolis, Maryland

Third printing with corrections, 1988

Library of Congress Catalog Card Number: 78-58824
ISBN: 0-87021-265-6

Printed in the United States of America

To my valued friends of
The American Fighter Aces Association

These were honored in their generations
and were the glory of their times.

Ecclesiasticus XLIV, 7

Legends for chapter opening photographs follow:

Page 2: An F6F-5 of a carrier training unit aboard the USS *Puget Sound* (CVE-113).

Page 26: A lineup of F6Fs at the Munda airfield in the New Georgia island group in September 1943. Among land-based Hellcat squadrons in the Solomons were VF-33, VF-38, and VF-40.

Page 50: The end of a working day aboard an *Independence*-class light carrier as F6F-3s of the combat air patrol are recovered at dusk, February 1944.

Page 70: A division of Fighting One F6Fs. Flying from the the USS *Yorktown*, VF-1 saw heavy combat in the Bonins and Marianas during June and July of 1944.

Page 94: An F6F-5 of VF-74 aboard the escort carrier *Kasaan Bay*, ready to launch on a strike mission against southern France on 15 August 1944. Photo: R. M. Hill

Page 120: Catapult crewmen prepare a VF-29 F6F-3 for launch from the light carrier *Cabot* during operations against Formosa in early October 1944. Photo: R. M. Hill

Page 148: Lieutenant Charles R. Stimpson, top scorer of VF-11. He was one of only four fighter pilots to achieve ace status in both the F4F Wildcat and the F6F Hellcat. On 14 October 1944, he shot down five Zekes in one mission. Photo: R. M. Hill

Page 168: An F6F-5N night fighter with mixed armament of two 20-mm cannons and four .50-caliber machine guns. The -5N was by far the most numerous version of all Hellcat night fighters. Photo: R. P. Gill

Page 196: An F6F burns on the *Lexington*, 25 February 1945. The pilot escaped safely.

Page 218: Six aircraft of VF-88 off the *Yorktown* in August 1945. This squadron fought the last Hellcat combat of W. W. II on August 15 shooting down nine Japanese fighters for the loss of four F6Fs.

Contents

Foreword

It is a distinct honor and pleasure for me to have been asked to write the foreword to such an outstanding, well-organized, and expertly written book. I must admit, however, that it is difficult to do when one is personally mentioned in the manuscript.

This book is much more than just an account of actions and recorded events in which the Hellcat participated. It is also a dedicated memorial, not only to the combat pilots who flew the F6F so gallantly, but also to the designers, draftsmen, and test pilots who brought this plane on when our country was in desperate need of it to counter the opposition. And it is also a memorial to the thousands of people who kept these planes flying, often under the most adverse conditions of war.

No aircraft company can be more proud of the products produced, developed, and delivered than Grumman Aircraft of Bethpage, Long Island, and Pratt and Whitney Engines of Hartford, Connecticut. Their executives, many of whom I knew personally, were without doubt the best in the field. But a special vote of thanks is also due the American public, without whose funds the Hellcat would not have been available when needed.

It would be a serious omission not to mention that Barrett Tillman has spent countless hours and much effort putting together this book. He has carefully and diligently researched the historical files for combat action reports of the various fighter squadrons, and interviewed numerous people who were involved with or flew the F6F in combat.

I can truly recommend this book, both for the accuracy of what is recorded and for the enjoyment that a reader will reap by being able to identify with the persons and events described.

David McCampbell
Captain, U.S. Navy (Retired)

Preface

The Grumman F6F Hellcat was the U.S. Navy's air superiority fighter of the Second World War, just as its lineal descendant, the F-14 Tomcat, performs that role today. And though it may seem anachronistic to refer to the F6F as an air superiority fighter, it is nevertheless appropriate. For in spite of the fact that terminology as well as technology have changed in three decades, the nature of the mission has not.

Fighter-versus-fighter combat is what air superiority is all about. The combatant best employing his fighters will ultimately control the sky, allowing his own strike aircraft to do their work while denying such use to the enemy. Therefore, when two hostile fighters engage one another, the strategic implications transcend the tactical solution as to which opponent finally flies home.

According to the official record, 19 out of 20 times it was the Hellcat which flew home. The F6F made its combat debut in the early fall of 1943, at the beginning of the long Pacific offensive. But the Hellcat was not only in the spearhead of the thrust which led to Tokyo Bay; it was the tip of the lance. In 24 months of combat the angular fighters from Long Island were credited with over 5,000 Japanese aircraft destroyed in aerial combat, gaining outright air supremacy over invasion beaches. This success helped make possible the imaginative series of amphibious conquests which marked the Central Pacific campaigns.

The Pacific War was fought by identifiable stages, and each stage saw one aircraft which was instrumental during that period. The first, as described in my previous book, was the Douglas SBD Dauntless dive bomber which in 1942 may not have actually won the war, but most certainly shaped its course and prevented defeat at Midway and Guadalcanal. In 1945 the most influential aircraft was the Boeing B-29 strategic bomber, which literally burned out the heart of Japanese industry. Combined with the U.S. Navy's submarine campaign against Japan's merchant marine, Superfortresses crippled the enemy's ability to sustain aggressive war and helped render a bloody invasion unnecessary.

In between was the Hellcat, which was largely responsible for subduing Japanese air power wherever the Fast Carrier Force sailed. As a result, I believe the F6F was the most important Allied aircraft in the Pacific during 1943–44. After all, the B-29s flew from bases in the Marianas where the Hellcat's greatest victory took place.

Despite the passage of three decades, the F6F story may hold lessons for today. The argument is made that the aircraft carrier is obsolete, that no other major power builds fixed-wing aircraft carriers, and that the flattop is vulnerable to the cruise missile. This line of thought ignores the fact that the Soviet Navy has commissioned its own aircraft-carrying warships—the VTOL-equipped *Kiev* class. Nor does it consider the logic which insists that all surface vessels are potentially vulnerable to the new missile threat. And it completely overlooks an historical parallel from the Hellcat's career. The U.S. Navy has already dealt with the cruise missile in its most gruesome form—the Kamikaze suicide aircraft. Hellcats were instrumental in defeating this threat, the most serious ever directed against carriers. It is a fact which should not lead us into complacency, but neither should it warp our perspective or our confidence.

This volume makes wide use of nautical and aviation terminology. Distances are in nautical miles, though in most cases where airspeeds are given in knots, statute miles per hour are included. The jargon and acronymns of W. W. II naval aviation have hopefully been minimized, but to eliminate them entirely would detract both from the purpose and character of the story.

Each chapter has a list of Hellcat squadrons in combat for the particular period covered in that chapter. There are two exceptions, however. Since one chapter is devoted exclusively to night fighters, the F6F night fighter squadrons have been grouped at the end of Chapter 8. And the Hellcat squadrons which flew from escort carriers are listed in a separate compilation. Since space considerations precluded a full chapter on these unheralded but valuable support squadrons, I must invoke the charity and understanding of their former personnel.

In the course of researching *Hellcat*, I contacted dozens of naval aviators who flew the F6F in combat or who had other direct association with the type. They have been generous with their time and resources, enthusiastic in their assistance, and encouraging in their support. *Hellcat* is their story. It deals with the most memorable period of their lives, when they were part of the greatest armed conflict in all history. It was a time of youthful friendship and its attendant sorrow in loss, a time of fear in mortal danger and of exultation in victory. It was a time, now long gone, when wars were meant to be won, and the sooner the better.

Because I was born 25 years too late to live the F6F story, I must be content with merely writing it. But I will be happy if, after reading these pages, some former Hellcat pilot can lean back, close his eyes and say softly to himself, "Yes, that's the way it was."

Barrett Tillman
Athena, Oregon
July, 1978

Hellcat

1 Fox-Six-Fox

A wonderful weapon of war.

Captain David McCampbell, USN (Retired)

The early morning had seen heavy clouds and rain squalls along the Honshu coast, but by noon the weather had improved. From 50 to 100 miles offshore it was a bright, balmy summer afternoon.

It was now shortly past 1300, and in the previous 90 minutes a half-dozen Japanese aircraft had been shot down approaching the carrier fleet known as Task Force 38. Then, far to the west-southwest, a single Mitsubishi Zero carrying a 550-pound bomb flew boldly towards the armada, hoping to dive into the deck of an American ship. The "Zeke" reflected an electronic beam which illuminated a dot on a radarscope, and an anonymous fighter direction officer radioed short, precise instructions to a few of the many sentries orbiting high in the sky. With more than enough fighters available, the best-positioned flights were vectored to bracket the lone hostile. Within minutes, no matter which way the Zeke turned, it would be trapped.

The end came quickly. Four dark blue Grumman Hellcats sighted the intruder and pounced. No Zeke could outrun a Hellcat; the range decreased, the deflection angle narrowed, and at 300 yards the Zeke filled the ring of an illuminated gunsight. The Hellcat leader waited a few more seconds, just to be sure.

Six Browning M-2 machine guns fired at a combined rate of 4,000 rounds per minute. In a two-second burst, 130 of the 709-grain bullets were loosed, of which perhaps 35 struck the target. The effect was shattering. At a muzzle velocity of 2,840 feet per second, 4.3 pounds of metal impacted the Zero. The .50-caliber bullets tore out chunks of aluminum, severed a wing spar, penetrated fuel tanks, and ignited volatile gasoline. In seconds the delicately built Mitsubishi was falling towards the Pacific Ocean.

It was nothing new or unusual for the young men who flew the angular Grummans. The date was Wednesday, the 15th of August, 1945, and this same lethal sequence had occurred 5,000 times in the past 24 months. But the story had actually begun 15 years before.

The Grumman Aircraft Engineering Corporation opened for business at Baldwin, Long Island, in January of 1930. Following a series of moves elsewhere on Long Island, Leroy R. Grumman's firm settled at Bethpage in 1936, and there it would remain. When Pearl Harbor was attacked, the company was already well established as a leading manufacturer of carrier fighters and was working on a successor to its stubby little F4F Wildcat. For in June of 1941, the Navy had asked Grumman to work up an improved version of the Wildcat as insurance against the possibility that Vought's promising F4U Corsair might be delayed in reaching the fleet.

It proved a wise precaution. The Corsair had first flown in 1940, but due to the loss of the prototype in a crash and subsequent delays, the F4U would not reach combat until early 1943. Meanwhile, the Navy's concept of an improved F4F was abandoned when the Bureau of Aeronautics decided it wanted more range, firepower, and armor than the Wildcat allowed. The design philosophy was altered accordingly, and Grumman's chief engineer William T. Schwendler went to work. When war broke out, Grumman Design Number 50 was being built as the XF6F-1.

The new fighter was desperately needed, for the Wildcat, though holding the line, was incapable of reversing the situation in the air. One of its chief drawbacks was insufficient range, and the Pacific Theater was the largest of the war, covering one-quarter of the earth's surface.

Of more immediate concern to Navy and Marine fighter pilots was the exceptional performance of the main Japanese fighter being encountered. The Mitsubishi firm's little A6M "Type Zero" fighter, later code-named "Zeke" by U.S. intelligence, had come as a decidedly unpleasant surprise. With phenomenal range, superior maneuverability and climb rate, Zeros were totally unlike anything the Allies had put in the air. Following the carrier battles of Coral Sea and Midway in May and June of 1942, U.S. Navy pilots asked for more speed and better climb from Grumman.

An early production F6F-3 Hellcat, the premier U.S. Navy carrier fighter type from August 1943 to mid 1944. Photo: R. L. Lawson

The new fighter bore a distinct family resemblance to the Wildcat, but was bigger and beefier in every dimension. Lieutenant Commander A. M. Jackson of BuAer's fighter design desk had an important role in shaping the F6F. He knew the importance of visibility in a fighter, saying "You can't hit 'em if you can't see 'em."[1] As a result, he got the original F6F cowling design trimmed down for better aerial gunnery. This superior geometry would aid Hellcat pilots in combat with Zeros.

Two prototype Hellcats were built, BuAer numbers 02981 and 02982. The test pilot assigned to the project was Robert L. Hall. He had joined Grumman in 1936, and with nearly 1,300 hours logged, he had already made the first flights in three Grumman aircraft, including the XF4F-2 Wildcat.

Bob Hall lifted the Hellcat off the ground for the first time on 26 June 1942 when he took up the XF6F-1 for a 25-minute test. There was nothing unusual to report, but it seemed obvious that the Wright R-2600-16 engine, producing 1,600 horsepower, was inadequate. The Wright Cyclone could not deliver the desired speed and rate of climb, so Grumman suggested a change of engines to the Navy. The answer was Pratt and Whitney's R-2800-8 Double Wasp, with 18 cylinders in two rows producing 2,000 horsepower. It was the same engine that powered the Corsair, but the addition of water injection for limited use in combat boosted the rating to 2,200 horses in the R-2800-10. Widely considered the best reciprocating engine ever built, the R-2800 was characterized by incredible ruggedness and dependability, plus relative ease of maintenance.

When the XF6F-1 was fitted with a Pratt and Whitney, it was redesignated the XF6F-3. The lone XF6F-2 never entered production because its proposed turbo-supercharger proved unreliable.

Meanwhile, Bob Hall conducted more test flights. On 30 July he flew the "dash three" for the first time, a short 11-minute hop to check the P&W's performance. But the XF6F-3 came to an inglorious end on 17 August when the R-2800 quit in flight and Hall dead-sticked it into a bean patch, "banging it up real well."[2]

Nevertheless, the Navy was satisfied, and the new Grumman was ordered into production. It was easier said than done. Regardless of how important the F6F was to the war effort, Grumman had to stand in line with everyone else for priority material. Chief among these was steel for a new factory building; the airplanes could not be built until there was a plant in which to manufacture them.

Grumman's general manager, Leon "Jake" Swirbul, demonstrated an early example of the firm's resourcefulness when he purchased the needed steel from the scrap-pile remains of New York City's old Second Avenue elevated railway. A corrupted version of this story made the rounds in the

Grumman test pilots Bob Hall and Selden Converse who performed the earliest flight checks of the F6F. Hall flew the prototypes and Converse made the first flight in the production F6F-3. Photo: The Grumman Corporation

fleet, rumor having it that the F6Fs, not the factory building, were made of the old steel. Consequently, early Hellcats were sometimes greeted with the cry, "Here comes a piece of the Second Avenue El!"

Production began quickly in the new Plant Number 3. The first flight of a production F6F-3 was on 3 October with Grumman pilot Selden "Connie" Converse behind the stick. By the end of December a total of 12 airframes had been built. After that, production accelerated steadily. Grumman delivered a dozen F6Fs in January 1943, 35 in February, 81 in March, and 130 in April. The firm's productivity was such that in November 1943 Grumman built more airplanes in one week than it had in all of 1940. That same month saw F6F deliveries reach 400 units for the first time, in addition to 135 TBF torpedo bombers and 20 amphibians.

In all, over 12,200 Hellcats were built from 1942 to 1945. The peak month was March of 1945, when the Navy accepted 658 Grumman aircraft. Of these, 605 were Hellcats. The balance included 48 F7F Tigercats, 2 F8F Bearcats, and 3 JRF Goose utility amphibians.[3]

The primary reason for this exceptional success story was superb management. Equal credit goes to Roy Grumman and Jake Swirbul. They oversaw the efforts of some 20,000 employees working in a 2.5-million-square-foot complex, turning out an average of almost one million dollars' worth of aircraft and parts every day. Even more amazing is the fact that virtually none of the wartime workers had previous experience in building airplanes. A large percentage were women, but Grumman's turnover rate was less than 3 percent—half the rate for the rest of the industry. And there was never a strike or work stoppage; the employees saw no reason to unionize.

In short, Grumman was a happy place to work. Though the payroll expanded to more than ten times the prewar figure, the company still functioned like a small, close-knit family. Mr. Grumman (hardly anybody called him Roy) maintained the company tradition of giving a Christmas turkey to each employee. Asked why he didn't observe the more usual time of Thanksgiving, Grumman explained that it would have made things difficult for Long Island turkey growers.

There were other features: daycare centers for children of working mothers, noon softball games, periodic airshows, frequent dances, even counseling offices. But the best known, and probably the most appreciated, was Jake Swirbul's "Green Car Service." The object was to keep people on the job, relieving them of small distractions. A phone call or a word in the right place would send Jake's Green Car scurrying off to perform almost any kind of service: fix a flat tire, start a dead battery, make sure the oven was off at home, deliver a message. Anything to keep the employee on the job.

Grumman's production methods were equally imaginative. Probably the best example was demonstrated during an efficiency expert's tour of the factory. The visitor asked how a supply of hose clamps was maintained on the assembly line. His guide dug into a barrel of clamps and showed the expert with one glance. A quarter of the distance from the top, painted on the inside, was the notice, "See Joe."[4]

Eventually Grumman outpaced even the Navy's demand for Hellcats, and the factory was asked to cut back on production. Veteran Grummanites recall an incident in mid 1944 related to this request. Jake Swirbul decided that with over 20,000 employees, there must be at least 1,000 who weren't pulling their load. So he quietly told his foremen to arrange for the release of their less-productive workers. When the word got around,

The Hellcat production line at the Grumman factory in Bethpage, Long Island, where over 12,000 F6Fs were built from 1942 to 1945.

the remaining employees thought a general housecleaning was in progress. As a result, next month's production increased by 20 Hellcats.

Swirbul decided that if his people were working harder, he could let another thousand go. But again the plan backfired. After the second thousand were laid off, the other workers decided they might be next. So they worked even harder, and built a few more additional planes the following month! Asked if he wanted to try reducing the payroll by another thousand, Swirbul said no. He didn't think the Navy could absorb the additional production.

Because of Grumman's immense energy, the Hellcat went from first flight to combat in little over a year. And it was fortunate that the F6F progressed so well, for the Corsair, with its exceptional speed and combat potential, was considered unsafe for carrier landings. The F4U had four problems which were not solved until 1944, and after the remedies were implemented it was even longer until the Vought operated regularly from carriers. Inadequate visibility was solved in the F4U-1A, with its redesigned canopy, but the other problems took longer to correct. These were adverse stall characteristics, particularly dangerous when turning at low level, plus bounce on landing and frequent failure of the tail hook to engage a carrier's arresting wires. A wing spoiler solved the stall problem to a large degree, and modifications to the landing gear and arresting hook took care of the deck-landing problems. But aside from small night-fighter detachments in early 1944, Corsairs did not regularly operate from U.S. carriers until the end of that year.

As a result, the F6F's arrival in combat was doubly important, since it offered a much greater chance than the Wildcat of defeating the Zeke.

The big new Grumman would not only be able to engage the Japanese fighter on equal terms; it could dictate the rules of combat. And it had the range to seek out the enemy so he could be brought to battle.

There were differences in performance between the two production Hellcat variants, the F6F-3 and -5, and in the Zero series from A6M2 to A6M5. But general trends were widely applicable. The Hellcat was considerably faster in level flight than the Zero at all altitudes—on the average by 55 mph. Maximum speeds for the F6F-5 and A6M5 were 409 mph (355 knots) at 21,600 feet for the Grumman, and 335 mph (290 knots) at 18,000 feet for the Mitsubishi. Above 10,000 feet the F6 could nearly match or slightly exceed the Zeke's rate of climb, and in most performance categories was superior at higher altitudes. Because the Hellcat had twice the Zeke's power and weight, no A6M could hope to escape in any kind of prolonged dive.

However, the Zeke retained its fabled advantage in turning radius right up to the end of the war. At airspeeds below 230 mph (200 knots) the little Mitsubishi's much lighter wing loading easily enabled it to out-maneuver the Hellcat even though the Grumman airframe allowed more available Gs. But at higher airspeeds the aerodynamic forces upon the A6M's control surfaces—particularly the ailerons—caused considerably stiffer control responses, and Hellcats could then match turns with their opponents.

When fast, heavily armed Japanese fighters like the Kawanishi N1K George and the Mitsubishi J2M Jack were met in late 1944, Hellcats then fought aircraft similar in design to themselves. But numerically the Zeke remained the most important fighter the enemy had in the Pacific, all through the war.

Similarly, the Hellcat was modified remarkably little throughout its career. The F6F-3s were flown in combat almost until V-J Day. But by the fall of 1944 they represented only half of the Fast Carrier Force fighters, as -5s began reaching the squadrons that summer. Externally, there was little difference between the two models. Tri-color paint schemes on the -3s contrasted with an overall gloss blue on the -5s, but there were also differences in canopy design. The most important changes were internal; there was additional armor plate in the F6F-5, and a rein-forced empennage to prevent structural failures which bothered some -3s. And most -5s had R-2800-10 engines with water injection for a limited boost in combat power.

Following its first flight in April of 1944, the F6F-5 was shown to be 15 knots faster than the -3, though rate of climb was variously reported as marginally better or even slightly less. But with the addition of spring tabs on the ailerons, the -5 had greater maneuverability—a quality dear to the heart of any fighter pilot.

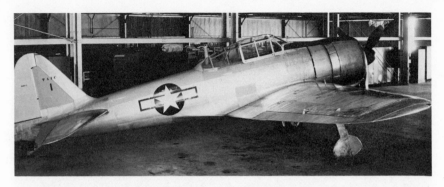

The Hellcat's arch enemy, the Mitsubishi Zero. This model A6M2 was found crashed on an Alaskan island in June 1942 and was restored to flying condition at NAS North Island, San Diego. Information learned from this and other captured Zeros greatly aided in F6F development and combat tactics. Photo: W. N. Leonard

Both models contained ample internal fuel, with 250 gallons, and could carry a 150-gallon belly drop tank. The jettisonable external tank provided an unintended benefit since its distinctive shape facilitated quick recognition in combat.

Perhaps the F6F-5's primary virtue was its versatility, with the emphasis on increased offensive capability. With more fighters required for fleet defense in late 1944, the Hellcat's strike potential was needed to offset the reduced number of bombers aboard fleet carriers. Like the -3, the -5 carried six Colt-Browning .50-caliber machine guns, with 400 rounds per gun. And both models could carry 1,000-pound bombs. But the F6F-5's heaviest punch was six high velocity aerial rockets (HVARs), the equal of a destroyer's broadside. From late 1944, F6Fs commonly carried bombs or rockets (or both) on all missions except combat air patrols and some fighter sweeps. Hellcats on search missions were usually fully armed.

Thus, originally intended primarily to defeat the Zero in air combat, the Hellcat eventually became the fleet's "do everything" aircraft, with the exception of carrying torpedoes. Even this specialized role was within the F6F's capability, as tests demonstrated, but it was never implemented. Otherwise, Hellcats filled in whole or in part every function required of carrier-based aircraft for the latter part of the Pacific War.

The pilots who flew Hellcats in combat were a typical mixture of young Americans. Largely reservists, they ranged in age from 19 to 35. It is probable that a majority of squadron commanders were Naval Academy graduates, but this was certainly not always the case. Nor could it be, with the vastly expanded aviation cadet program.

11

An early F6F-3 is catapulted from the hangar deck of the USS *Yorktown* during a shakedown cruise in 1943. In operations, this technique was seldom used.

A fighter squadron invariably had an intriguing assortment of personalities, and a sensitive leader knew which pilots had to be calmed down and which ones needed motivation. A delicate balance had to be maintained between individual initiative and the simultaneous need for mutual dependence and trust. It was not an easy task, but leadership in war never is. There was often little in a pilot's demeanor on the ground to indicate how he would perform in the air. Personality traits essential to survival and success in aerial combat sometimes lay concealed under disarming exteriors. But in each case, squadron commanders most valued those eager youngsters who understood the need for teamwork as well as the value of intelligent aggressiveness.

The physical skills necessary for success in fighter aviation are easier to define than the psychological. Learning to fly an airplane is a skill which can be learned with approximate uniformity by large numbers of individuals. Aerial gunnery is not so easily taught. Latent ability can be markedly improved with practice, but the inherent hand-to-eye coordination and judgment are in most cases instinctive. Technology, in the form of lead-computing gunsights late in the war, could significantly im-

An F6F-3 modified to carry eight High Velocity Aerial Rockets, dramatically increasing the Hellcat offensive potential. Rocket rails were standard on the F6F-5.

prove an average pilot's gunnery. The boy who had grown up hunting pheasant or quail would probably shoot well in nearly any situation. Thus, the top scorers were the best shooters with the most opportunity.

The U.S. Navy never consciously accepted the concept of the "ace" system, preferring with good reason to emphasize teamwork. But it is an historical fact that a tiny percentage of all fighter pilots accounted for a hugely disproportionate share of the victories. A case in point is VF-11, which was aboard the USS *Hornet* from October 1944 to January 1945. Of the 121 pilots attached to the squadron during its four-month tour, only 45 gained a confirmed victory, for a squadron total of 103. The five pilots who gained five or more victories during that period accounted for 33 kills. In other words, only 4 percent of VF-11's pilots were responsible for 30 percent of the total score. This does not imply that the aces were supermen, but in VF-11's case, those who experienced three to five firing encounters were all division or section leaders.

Shooting down enemy planes was only part of the F6F pilot's job. He was also responsible for defending the dive bombers and torpedo planes of his air group, and it was not necessary to destroy hostile aircraft to perform this vital role. Simply by maintaining formation, refusing to be drawn away from the bombers, fighters discouraged enemy interceptors from attacking. Air discipline was rigidly enforced; no kill was worth the loss of a bomber. Some F6F squadrons completing combat tours in the first half of 1944 boasted proudly—with justification—of never losing a bomber to Japanese aircraft. This achievement became a mark for other squadrons to strive for, as it denoted 100 percent efficiency in the escort role.

Hellcats performed numerous other duties, the most popular being fighter sweeps. Usually launched at dawn to catch enemy aircraft on the ground, the sweeps were the fighter pilots' favorite job because there were no bombers to protect, and purely fighter-versus-fighter combats frequently developed.

A good deal less exciting were the combat air patrols (CAPs) which flew almost constantly over each carrier task group, awaiting instructions from the fighter direction officer (FDO). Naval battles were no longer fought exclusively by big-gunned ships arranged in battle line, pounding each other at several thousand yards, and since May of 1942 the decisive fleet engagements had followed the pattern of the Coral Sea battle. The invisible, Argus-eyed sentry called radar saw what no lookout could ever see, and directed carrier fighters to investigate any suspicious intruder. This concept, known as forward interception, resulted in air battles being fought "below the horizon," beyond the line where the sea met the sky.

Unless unidentified aircraft, or "bogeys," were reported by the task group FDO, the patrolling Hellcats orbited until relieved, "bored stiff and stiff as a board," said one squadron commander.[5] A four-hour CAP could be dreadfully dull, for there was little to do except maintain formation, check the instruments periodically, and perhaps recall that last date at the "Top of the Mark" before deploying west. Sometimes it helped to sing, but it was surprising how quickly one could exhaust all the favorite tunes, even those of Miller, Dorsey, and Goodman.

But if radar established a set of blips as hostiles, the "bogeys" became "bandits" and the tedium was instantly gone. Long-range identification was possible by IFF transponders (Identification, Friend or Foe) in U.S. aircraft which "painted" a distinctive blip on a radarscope. If the blip did not paint properly, it was assumed hostile and at least one four-plane division of fighters was vectored out to investigate. Pilots could always tell how urgent the situation was by the command the FDO gave over the radio. If the order was "Saunter," there was no rush; the bogeys were still far distant. If he said "Liner" or "Buster" they were getting much closer. And if the FDO gave a "Gate" order, throttles were bent to the stops in order to intercept the hostiles before they reached the task force.

Hellcats also flew long-range searches for Japanese ships—sometimes in teams of one F6F and two Avenger torpedo bombers, sometimes in sections or divisions of fighters. The Hellcat's fuel capacity gave it a search radius of 500 nautical miles under favorable conditions, and in extreme cases search planes could be airborne for over six hours. Most aviators found that long experience tended to negate, or at least diminish, the airman's natural fear of flying single-engine aircraft over immense expanses of water. Confidence in one's navigational skill—fabled among carrier pilots, who relied upon their circular "ouija board" plotting charts—left engine failure as the main concern. It was the one factor over which fliers had virtually no control.

Hellcats were also involved in ground-support operations against invasion beaches, where they were called upon to deliver their considerable offensive payloads. Bombs, rockets, and napalm were all used to help soften the always tenacious Japanese defenses wherever Marines or GIs were making an amphibious landing. But this phase seldom developed until air superiority had been won.

Hellcats also performed two special-mission functions—night fighting and photo reconnaissance, as the Fast Carrier Force had to bring its own nocturnal protection and intelligence-gathering aircraft along with it. Radar-equipped F6F-3s and -5s flew from land bases as well, and were effectively used in the Philippines and Ryukyus by Marine night-fighter squadrons. A variety of internally mounted vertical and oblique cameras were installed in F6F-3P and -5P aircraft, with 6-, 12- or 24-inch lenses. A typical combination was a 12-inch vertical and 24-inch oblique K-17 for damage assessment and strip mapping.

There has always been a dash of glamor inherent in carrier operations, and World War II saw this at its peak. The big, handsome *Essex*-class ships, accompanied by their smaller *Independence*-class teammates, made an unforgettable sight steaming under the tropical sky as they prepared to launch full deckloads.

Gaily colored signal pennants snapped from their halyards below the Stars and Stripes as the diamond-design Fox flag was hoisted to signal commence flight operations. As the carriers turned smartly into the wind, trailing 30-knot wakes, aviators rushed from their ready rooms. Each was loaded down with Mae West, parachute harness, pistol and survival knife, goggles and helmet with oxygen mask, and the pilots' ever-present plotting boards. They trooped up steep companionways, emerging topside where the ship's island, offset to starboard and top-heavy with radar antennae, looked incongruously narrow in comparison to the width of the flight deck.

The Douglas fir decks became a pandemonium of organized confusion as khaki-suited fliers climbed into their aircraft while plane directors in yellow jerseys shouted orders to deck hands who pushed planes into position, unfolded and locked wings, or removed wheel chocks. Red-shirted ordnancemen removed safety wires from bomb and torpedo fuses; asbestos-suited fire fighters stood by while catapult crews in green jerseys waited to see if the wind would remain strong enough for an unassisted launch.

The aircraft themselves—with F6Fs in front, as they needed less deck room than the strike planes—were no less colorful. Three-tone or dark gloss-blue paint schemes vividly offset white geometric air group symbols bodily emblazoned on tail surfaces.

But it wasn't only color and salt spray. There was noise, too. The incomparable sound of perhaps 60 radial engines turning over, forming the bass chorus for the high-pitched whine of inertia starters, and the punctuation of shotgun-type cartridges kicking over pistons in Pratt and Whitneys or Wrights, was deafening. Three-bladed Hamilton-Standard propellers on blunt-nosed Hellcats and big-bellied Avengers, and four-bladed Curtiss Electrics on round-tailed Helldivers, jerked into motion by fits and starts then blurred into invisibility. The clouds of light blue smoke which seemed to hang over the flight decks never stayed long, for they were swept away in the relative wind and ever-increasing prop wash.

And then, in just a few minutes, nearly all the varicolored tunics were gone from the decks. Only the fire fighters and launch crews remained, for the squadrons were now ready to launch. Hellcats, Avengers, and Helldivers stood ready on the 800-foot flight decks of the CVs; the 600-foot CVL decks accommodated only F6Fs and TBMs. But regardless of the carrier's size, the scene was much the same. With crews looking on from galleys, gun sponsons, and islands, pilots taxied into position, their canopies locked open and shoulder harnesses as tight as they could stand. The most important man on each flattop was "Fly One," the launch officer who would send each plane on its way.

It took nearly a full minute, on the average, to taxi a plane into position, ready it for catapulting, and fling it off the deck. Only half that much time was required for a conventional takeoff. If the cats were not needed, Fly One stood at the starboard wingtip of each plane in its turn and whirled a small black and white checkered flag in circles over his head. When the ship's bow was just coming up in the swell, he slashed the flag down and forward. At this signal the pilot—with engine run up to maximum RPM, prop in flat pitch, and flaps lowered for more lift—kicked in right rudder to offset the powerful port torque, released his brakes, and was lunging down the deck.

Then the sky was filled with climbing, circling aircraft as sections and divisions and squadrons formed up to combine into air groups. The fighters were paired in sections which became four-plane divisions; dive bombers and torpedo planes flew either three- or four-plane divisions.

And before long, frequently less than 15 minutes after launch commenced, the formations headed out toward their targets. The mission lead was usually rotated among the four air group commanders (CAGs) of each carrier task group, the standard organization of which was two *Essex*- and two *Independence*-class carriers. From late 1943 more and more CAGs began flying F6Fs, so it wasn't long before most strike leaders and mission coordinators were Hellcat pilots.

16

Usually four hours or more passed before the planes would return to the position known as "Point Option," where the carriers would be waiting to receive them. In that time, almost anything could happen to a pilot. He might splash into the water off his carrier's bow with an engine failure on launch. He could collide with a friendly aircraft in the darkness of a predawn rendezvous or with an enemy aircraft in a dogfight. And though very few fighter pilots ever admitted they thought it could happen to *them*, they might be shot down by a Japanese pilot.

A more likely fate was enemy antiaircraft fire, which was the main reason most fliers hated strafing well-defended airfields and other protected installations. In aerial combat, his shooting and flying skill gave him at least an even chance against his opponent. Strafing at low level in the face of automatic weapons which were often unseen, a pilot took his shake of the dice like everyone else.

Given a choice of being captured by the Japanese or being forced down at sea, most fliers preferred the latter. At least then there was a reasonable chance of being rescued by a friendly vessel or floatplane. But though air-sea rescue received a high priority from task force and task group commanders, nothing was ever certain. Sometimes rescue might come in a few hours, sometimes only after several days. And sometimes, not at all. It was a very big ocean.

But it was a vastly bigger sky. All pilots, and particularly fighter pilots, were trained to keep their heads and eyes moving constantly. Doctrine varied among squadrons, but most of the better ones had a standing policy that any pilot who "eyeballed" a bogey immediately assumed the lead, regardless of his rank or position in formation. It was sound procedure. In aerial combat the victor is inevitably the one who sights his enemy first. "Eternal vigilance or eternal rest" was the way Commander Jimmy Flatley put it.[6]

But even if you were the most vigilant pilot, you could sometimes be caught unaware. You heard the sudden metallic plink of bullets hitting your airplane, the belated warning in your earphones of bandits overhead. Then came the wrapped-up, gut-wrenching sensation of high G-forces alternately trying to push you through the bottom of your seat or out through the canopy as you maneuvered to get out of the way or bring your guns to bear.

There were glimpses of blue Hellcats and camouflaged Japanese fighters, radio frequencies jammed with shouts, warnings, curses, or cries for help; the heavy pressure of gravity during a steep turn or dive recovery in the days before G-suits, and the attendant partial loss of vision or consciousness as the blood rushed from the brain.

17

There was also the shock of seeing a friend's plane tumbling out of control into the water, the knowledge that this wasn't the time to dwell on it. And there was the satisfying thrill which came as an enemy aircraft slipped into the illuminated reflector sight, and you knew you had a certain kill.

Then there was nothing. An empty sky, impossibly empty after so many planes had been engaged in combat only seconds before. But such is the nature of air battles. They never remain in one place, but cover miles of sky and thousands of feet of altitude in a few minutes.

Your engine had been running at maximum power for most of the engagement, and the task force could be 200 miles away. It was now necessary to reduce the throttle setting to the most economical cruising speed, lean out the fuel mixture as much as possible, hike up the manifold pressure while running at low RPM, and trim the plane for the most efficient flight attitude.

Now, which way is home? A grin at the pilot flying off your wing— perhaps a forced grin—suggests the old joke, "What do you mean, you're following me? I'm following you!" Tune the Hellcat's ZB receiver to the carrier's YE radio navigation transmitter, listening for the Morse Code letter in each 15-degree segment, and home in when within range.

More than an hour passes, and then up ahead are the wakes of the task force. Let down to approach altitude, picking out the appropriate task group and the flight deck which is home. Perform the day's recognition turns and hope none of the AA gunners is nervous or trigger happy.

Now comes the part of the mission which makes you proud to be a naval aviator. Anybody can take off from a carrier. But you are one of the few thousand men in the world who can land on one.

As the carriers steamed into the wind with plane-guard destroyers trailing in their wakes to pick up ditched fliers, the squadrons broke into divisions. Wheeling overhead in racetrack patterns with 40-second intervals between aircraft, the pilots executed their prelanding check lists: canopy back and locked, shoulder harness tight, mixture rich, fuel on fullest internal tank, cowl flaps partly open for engine cooling, and prop in low pitch at 2400 RPM.

Then the pilots reached over to their left and dropped their tail hooks. The Hellcats slowed to an indicated airspeed of 120 knots before lowering wheels and landing flaps, the latter marked by a slight downward pitching motion. Turning on final approach, the F6Fs made about 90 knots in a nose-high attitude above the wakes of the carriers. Stable and well behaved in this configuration, the Hellcat was one of the easiest-

to-land carrier planes ever built. It allowed the pilot to fly by feel while keeping his eyes on the most important man now aboard ship—not Fly One anymore, but the Landing Signal Officer.

Standing on a platform at the after port side of the flight deck, the LSO was protected by a canvas windscreen behind him. This made him easier to see from the air, but the pilots concentrated on the colored paddle he held in each hand. The LSO relayed vital information with his paddles to each pilot by a set of standardized signals. Some LSOs were stylish, waving the paddles with a flair not unlike a busy traffic cop who knows he is being watched by scores of spectators; some were professionally precise. But all used the 13 basic signals. Ten of these told a pilot of some error in technique or procedure, such as his height, wings not level, approach speed too fast or too slow—occasionally even flaps, hook, or wheels not down.

The other three signals were "roger," "cut," and "wave-off." Each pilot hoped for a "roger pass" in which the LSO held his paddles straight out from each shoulder, indicating a satisfactory approach. As the aircraft hung several feet over the flight deck, the LSO abruptly slashed his right arm across his body and dropped his left hand to his side—the "cut" signal which told the pilot to chop his throttle, pull the stick back, and stall the plane in. As the tail hooks engaged the arresting wires, the planes were brought to an abrupt but safe halt. But even a good landing could result in a blown tire or nicked prop blade.

A less than satisfactory approach ended as the LSO waved the paddles over his head, ordering the pilot to go around for another try. There were several reasons for a wave-off, which a pilot might not always know. Imminent enemy attack, a barrier crash farther up the deck—anything unexpected—could result in the abort of even a perfect approach. Regardless of the reason, a wave-off carried the force of law, and to ignore it was a sin.

Despite all the built-in dangers of carrier landings, the F6F maintained as good a safety record as any plane. And many Hellcat pilots would echo the sentiments of Chester Leo Smith, a Marine aviator who flew F6Fs off the escort carrier *Block Island* in 1945. Recalls Smith, "I was lucky to take my run of the percentages in such a common-sensibly designed aircraft."[7]

Pilots weren't the only ones who grew to appreciate the F6F. So did those men equally important to the war effort—the men who "kept 'em flying."

Aircraft maintenance has always been a major concern in carrier aviation. With a limited number of planes available, the "up" or "down" status of each individual aircraft assumes unusual importance. Unlike airports, carriers have precious little room for storing unflyable airplanes,

so heavily damaged planes were frequently pushed overboard to make room for replacements.

This is the reason that carrier aircraft have always maintained a higher in-commission rate than land-based planes. And few have ever proved as consistently "up" as the Hellcat. A cross section of Army, Navy, and Marine land-based aircraft during World War II typically showed an average of 75 to 80 percent operational at any one time. Some complex or sophisticated aircraft could run as low as 35 or 40 percent operational. Hellcats commonly maintained a 90 percent in-commission rate, and averages as high as 98 percent over a four- to six-month period were not unknown. But such exceptional maintenance was never achieved without the expenditure of considerable time, skill, and dedication.

Most carrier squadrons had their own maintenance crews aboard ship. For a typical F6F squadron in late 1944, this would involve perhaps 30 enlisted men—machinists, ordnancemen, and radio or electronics personnel. A senior pilot was designated as squadron engineering officer, and maintenance was his collateral duty. The materiel officer was not an aviator, but he frequently possessed an intimate knowledge of the airplane. But as usual, it was the chief petty officers who had the most experience and know-how. They directed the day-to-day maintenance work within their specialties, depending upon whether they were rated in engine, airframe, electronics, or ordnance.

In addition to the squadron mechanics, each fleet carrier had a larger maintenance staff permanently attached. These were Carrier Aircraft Support Detachments, shortened to CASD. They handled the major repairs which the squadrons were unequipped to perform: they manned machine shops, conducted engine overhauls, provided spare parts, and so on. Frequently, air group technicians were absorbed into a ship's CASD for the duration of a cruise, in order to consolidate all maintenance resources.

Life aboard a carrier is frequently portrayed as easy living. But that is often only in relation to some other methods of waging war. During World War II, few compartments of carriers were air conditioned— usually only ready rooms, radar rooms, and senior officers' quarters. Mechanics and ordnancemen frequently worked below decks as much as 16 hours a day in sweltering heat with little or no ventilation. Few of these men were professional aviation mechanics, but they learned fast. They had to.

Fortunately for everyone concerned, Grumman built considerable "maintainability" into the F6F. It was a concept which has also been described as the "shoe clerk approach" to aviation. One of Grumman's field service representatives was Ralph Clark, a young New Yorker who spent over two years in the Pacific helping the air groups get their TBFs

and F6Fs operational. "We had shoe clerks building Hellcats. We had shoe clerks working on Hellcats, and mainly we had shoe clerks flying them, too," Clark recalls. "Not that I have anything against shoe clerks, or any other nonprofessionals. But we had to remember that most of the people involved with the F6F had never met an airplane face to face before 1942."[8]

Between them, the Hellcats and the shoe clerks helped win the war.

The following is a guide to the drawings on page 22. Area 1: Radio mast shown in configuration for BuNo 65890 (910th F6F-3) and all subsequent. Mast canted forward on first 909 F6F-3s (BuNo 04775 through 26195). Mast located slightly to right of centerline on BuNo 04775 through 41294 (2,560th F6F-3); located slightly to left of centerline on BuNo 41295 (2,561st F6F-3) and all subsequent. Area 2: Approximately 909 F6F-3s (BuNo 04775 through 26195) delivered with fairing over two inboard gun-barrel extensions on each wing. Area 3: Landing light (underside of port wing) omitted on BuNo 08886 (273rd F6F-3) and all subsequent, except night fighters. Area 4: Lower cowl flap omitted on BuNo 39999 (1,265th F6F-3) and all subsequent. Area 5: Bulged fairing over lateral exhaust stacks omitted on BuNo 40235 (1,501st F6F-3) and all subsequent. Area 6: Access panel for ADI system fluid tank; installed on BuNo 40634 (1,900th F6F-3) and all subsequent (R-2800-10W). Area 7: BuNo 42185 (3,451st F6F-3) and all subsequent with provision for rocket projectiles. Area 8: All F6F-5 with provisions for three .50-Cal. MG, or two .50-Cal. MG and one 20 mm in each wing; all late model F6F-5Ns delivered with mixed battery. Area 9: Rear-vision window on all F6F-3s, and approximately the first 1,500 to 2,000 F6F-5s. Area 10: Dorsal recognition light between stations 112½ and 127 omitted on BuNo 70289 (1,298th F6F-5) and all subsequent. Area 11: All F6F-3s with one controllable trim tab on left aileron, and one fixed tab on right aileron. Area 12: All F6F-5s with one servo tab and one fixed tab on each aileron; left servo tab also controllable from cockpit. Area 13: F6F-3 windshield; the flat, bullet-resistant glass panel was mounted inside the laminated plate glass windshield with space between to allow for heated air to be blown for defrosting. Area 14: F6F-5 and F6F-3N windshield; the laminated plate glass windshield was eliminated, and the flat, bullet-resistant panel was incorporated as an integral part of the windshield.

Grumman maintained cordial relations with the other aviation companies in the area: Republic, Chance Vought, and Pratt and Whitney. The four firms discussed mutual problems and exchanged ideas which would aid in the war effort. It was not difficult, for Republic's plant at Farming-

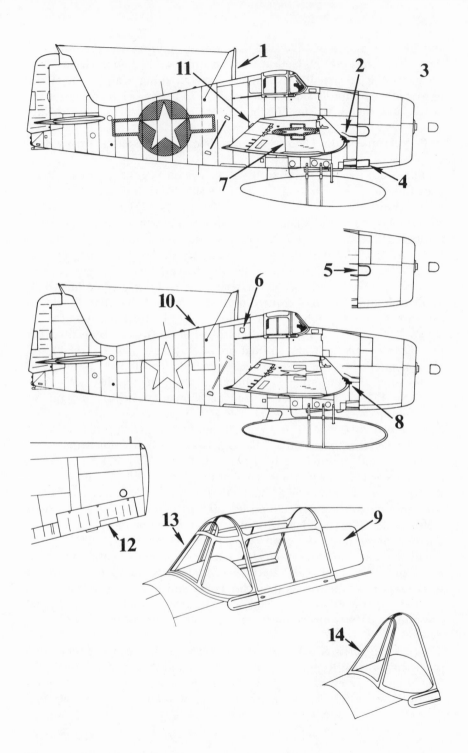

F6F BuNos in Fabrication Sequence

BuNo	Fabrication Sequence	Delivery Date Span
F6F-3		
04775–04958	1–184	9/42–4/43
08798–09047	185–434	4/43–6/43
25721–26195	435–909	6/43–8/43
65890–66244	910–1,264	7/43–9/43
39999–43137	1,265–4,403	9/43–4/44
F6F-5		
58000–58999	4,404–5,403	4/44–6/44
69992–72991	5,404–8,403	6/44–12/44
77259–80258	8,404–11,403	12/44–6/45
93652–94521	11,404–12,273	6/45–11/45

Reference sources: *Erection & Maintenance Manual*, F6F-3; *Pilot's Handbook*, F6F-3/5; various photographs from National Archives; tabulation, *Aircraft Produced under Navy Cognizance 1941–1945.*
Drawings by R. M. Hill.

dale was almost next door to Bethpage. Vought, at Stratford, Connecticut, was just across Long Island Sound, and Pratt and Whitney was slightly north at Hartford.

One of Republic's test pilots was Kenneth A. Jernstedt, a former Marine aviator who had gone to China with Colonel Claire Chennault's "Flying Tigers." Jernstedt came back with a bad case of malaria which prevented his return to military service, so he joined the P-47 flight test department.

Republic and Grumman test pilots were well acquainted with each other, and frequently swapped rides. Recalls Jernstedt, "We would exchange flights in different airplanes. When we developed a new model, Connie Converse and some of the boys from Grumman would come over and fly it. Then when they came out with something new, we would go over and fly theirs."

One afternoon, probably in early 1943, Jernstedt was at Bethpage awaiting his turn to fly an F6F. While in the men's room he met a tall, middle-aged Corsair pilot. Just then another Republic pilot rushed in, exclaiming, "Hey, Jerny, Lindy is around here someplace." Jernstedt pointed to the tall stranger and said, "Yes, I know."

Charles Lindbergh proudly showed off his borrowed F4U, as he was a consultant to both Vought and Pratt and Whitney. But this particular day he was at Bethpage for the same reason as Jernstedt and the others—to fly a Hellcat.

Though Jernstedt was ahead of Lindbergh on the flight list, the Republic pilot offered his boyhood hero the first chance. Lindbergh said it wasn't necessary, but Jernstedt insisted. "I'm going to drive home, but you're going to fly when you leave, and it's getting late so why don't you fly it first."

Lindbergh said, "Well, to tell you the truth, I really would appreciate it." After a thorough preflight check, Lindbergh climbed into the F6F, started the engine, and took off. He returned over the field about 25 minutes later, but did not land. Quickly the word passed that the Hellcat's wheels were jammed in the up position.

"If you've never seen a nervous airplane factory, you should have been at Grumman that day," says Jernstedt. "Here was Charles A. Lindbergh in one of their Hellcats, trying to land and he couldn't get the gear down. He had more radio help and advice than any pilot I ever saw. Engineers and mechanics flocked to the control tower. Finally, after three dives and sharp pull-outs, he was able to lock his wheels down and he landed safely."

As Lindbergh shut down the engine and started to climb out, Jernstedt walked up and said, "Thanks for checking out that F6 for me, Lindy."

Jernstedt finally got to fly a Hellcat. But he loyally maintained, "It wasn't as good as the P-47."[9]

Roy Grumman unquestionably would have disagreed. For though he never flew a Thunderbolt, he did fly a Hellcat. One day in the summer of 1944, Grumman told Connie Converse that he wanted to fly an F6F. Converse met the idea with less than unbridled enthusiasm, but the boss had already made up his mind. The fact that he hadn't flown in several years made no difference. Grumman had business problems on his mind, and he wanted to do what he used to do in the old days—take his troubles upstairs and leave them there.

According to legend, Converse gave Mr. Grumman a ten-minute cockpit check. Then the president shooed his test pilot away, started the engine, and took off. He made a smooth turn out of the traffic pattern and disappeared.

About 20 minutes later the lone Hellcat entered the pattern, turned on final approach, and settled toward the runway. Roy Grumman made a professionally smooth landing and taxied back to the flight line.

Rather than praise their employer for his skill, the factory pilots insisted that he pay a dollar to the party fund for taxiing with his flaps down. Grumman replied that it was unfair for him to pay the penalty after only one flight in an F6F, but dropped in a five dollar bill, "for things he'd done in the air that they hadn't seen!"[10]

When Roy Grumman flew that Hellcat, he was a 50-year-old executive who had not touched a throttle in a long time. It was a tribute to both the man and the machine.

2 Into Combat

To war and arms I fly.

Richard Lovelace, 1649

Fighting Squadron Nine was, in the words of one pilot, "a happy crew."[1] It had already been together through one short combat tour by the end of 1942, flying F4F-4s from the *Ranger* (CV-4) in support of the North African invasion in November. During that brief fling the VF-9 Wildcats had been credited with six Vichy French aircraft shot down in French Morocco. Now, a few days after New Year's Eve 1943, Commander Jack Raby and his pilots were preparing to take delivery of the first F6F-3s assigned to an operational squadron.

It had not been planned that way. Upon its return, Fighting Nine was to convert to F4U-1s, but in January 1943 Vought production was insufficient to allow all squadrons slated for the Corsair to receive it. As a result, Raby's squadron was in line for Hellcats and would take delivery of the first few airplanes in mid month.

Raby and two of his experienced pilots, Lieutenants (jg) Herbert N. Houck and Armistead B. "Chick" Smith, brought back the first Hellcats from the factory at Bethpage to Chambers Field near Norfolk on 16 January 1943. Deliveries continued three and four planes at a time for the next few weeks, weather allowing. As Grumman completed technical inspection and acceptance flight tests, Raby's pilots were sent up to Long Island to sign for the Hellcats and bring them to Chambers Field. One such expedition on 5 February again involved Chick Smith along with Lieutenant Keenan "Casey" Childers, Lieutenants (jg) Mayo "Mike" Hadden and Reuben H. Denoff.

Even under the press of wartime needs, the Hellcat program was not yet nearly as efficient as it would become. This early in the production program there were still no pilot handbooks available, so Grumman test pilots gave the four Navy fliers cockpit checks, helped them start the big Pratt and Whitneys, and sent them on their way. All four took off without difficulty.

About halfway home, Casey Childers was leading the flight when he suffered an engine failure. He was 30 miles north of Cape May, New Jersey, over a heavily wooded area sown with young pine trees. There was no choice but to make a wheels-up deadstick landing. He set up his glide path and plunked the heavy fighter down among the trees, sliding for what seemed an interminable distance. Looking down from their cockpits, Smith, Hadden, and Denoff watched Childers's Hellcat cut a swath through the pines, destroying itself as it went. When the F6F slid to a halt and the dust and debris settled, Childers was seen to climb out and wave to his friends. Thanks to the rugged Grumman airframe, he was unharmed.

Despite Childers's misadventure, Fighting Nine took to the big new fighter with enthusiasm. Unlike its little brother, the F4F, the F6 had a large roomy cockpit, was some 60 mph faster than the F4F-4, and had a one-third better climb rate. Pilots like Denoff, Smith, and Hadden who had flown against the Vichy French over Morocco also appreciated the Hellcat's greater ammunition capacity.

The squadron performed its F6F carrier qualification landings on the escort carrier *Long Island* (CVE-1). The pilots found that the Hellcat's large wing area gave it surprising stability on landing approaches for so heavy an aircraft, and that it came aboard about five mph less than the Wildcat. Some pilots had only 12 field landings in F6Fs before their first carrier landings in the type. When Air Group Nine departed the West Coast that summer, bound for Hawaii, most of the fighter pilots had over 50 hours in their new Grummans. Another 30 hours were flown before the squadron entered combat in August. Rube Denoff, for instance, had a total flight time of 680 hours before his first Pacific mission, including 85 in F6Fs. By later wartime standards this was unusually low; many fighter pilots would log 300 hours in Hellcats prior to their first missions. But in the summer and fall of 1943, when the offensive against Japan was building rapidly, planes and pilots were needed "the day before yesterday."

In mid-August, while still in Hawaii, Jack Raby became Commander Air Group Nine and VF-9 acquired a new skipper. He was Lieutenant Commander Philip H. Torrey, son of a Marine Corps general but Regular Navy. Fighting Nine was frankly disappointed to get a new and—to them, anyway—untried CO, especially after serving so long under Raby. But Torrey quickly proved himself a capable leader, an accomplished aviator, and he shared his pilots' enthusiasm for the Hellcat. "You wouldn't catch me flying around in anything else," he told a correspondent.[2]

Meanwhile, several other F6F squadrons were in Hawaii preparing for the start of the Central Pacific offensive. One was VF-6 under Lieutenant Commander Edward H. O'Hare, already famous for an exploit off Rabaul in February 1942. Flying an F4F-3 from the old *Lexington* (CV-2), O'Hare was credited with downing five Japanese bombers in one sortie, probably saving the ship from heavy damage or destruction. For this feat he became the second naval aviator to win the Medal of Honor in World War II. At 29 the dark, stocky O'Hare was highly esteemed by his men as both a leader and fighter pilot.

O'Hare preached the Bible According to Thach. He had flown in Commander John S. Thach's VF-3 early in the war, and his combat experience had intensified the principles learned there. Teamwork and marksmanship were the virtues O'Hare stressed, and the factors he looked for when selecting a wingman. He settled upon Lieutenant (jg) Alexander Vraciu, the 24-year-old son of Romanian immigrants who had grown up in the Chicago area. The two became close friends, but that didn't mean O'Hare was inclined to overlook anything. Quite the contrary.

29

"There were some Army P-40s near us in Hawaii," Vraciu would recall, "and several of us wanted to fly them." O'Hare was vocal in his disapproval. "Why do you want to fly a P-40?" he asked. "Just so you can say you've flown one and look like a hot pilot?" He told his fliers in no uncertain terms that it was much more important to gain as many hours as possible in F6Fs, the planes they would fly in combat. In retrospect Vraciu said, "Butch was right, of course. But we flew the P-40s anyway."[3]

Marcus Island lies about 2,700 miles west of Pearl Harbor. Since the early days of the war, it had been one of the larger Japanese bases in the Central Pacific, and as such it was selected as the first target in a series of training raids by the new generation of aircraft carriers. Rear Admiral Charles A. Pownall took two CVs and a CVL—the *Essex* (CV-9), *Yorktown* (CV-10) and *Independence* CVL-22—to Marcus at the end of August and thereby initiated the F6F into combat.

In order to achieve tactical surprise, a predawn launch was called for. First in the air were 45 aircraft of the *Yorktown*'s Air Group Five, including 16 Hellcats of VF-5 under Commander Charles L. Crommelin, a ten-year veteran naval aviator who had already flown in two fighter squadrons and an observation unit. It was 0422 when the first F6Fs rolled down the *Yorktown*'s deck, guiding only on the shrouded stern lights of leading destroyers. Appropriately, the brightest light shining in the inky tropical sky was Mars, visible in the direction of the target.

The *Essex* strike included VF-9 Hellcats led by the skipper, Phil Torrey, who insisted he was afraid of the dark and would rather go home. It was fortunate that stars were visible for some sort of reference, as none of Torrey's Hellcats had operable gyro horizons. The rush of training and transport had been such—and would remain so—that Fighting Nine flew all through its North African and first Pacific tour with the gyros in "caged" position.

In a minor way, the launch sequence was to have repercussions in F6F history. Since the *Yorktown* launched first, VF-5 could claim the honor of being the first to fly the Hellcat in combat. On the other hand, two VF-9 aircraft strafed Japanese picket boats on the way in—the first shots fired by the new fighter.

The last F6F to leave the *Yorktown* was piloted by the CAG, Commander James H. Flatley. One of the oldest hands around the Pacific, Flatley had earned a formidable reputation in F4Fs dating from Coral Sea and then as CO of Fighting 10 during the Solomons actions, where he brought his personal victory score to six and one-half kills. Now he had a larger responsibility, directing the air strikes on Marcus from his Hellcat with two under-wing tanks added to prolong its endurance.

The strike planes were led to Marcus by navigation TBFs, which broke off when the attack began. Surprise was achieved in the early dawn light; very little return fire was experienced during the first strafing runs as the Hellcats slanted down on Marcus's airfield. Eight twin-engine planes were destroyed on the ground, after which the bombers went to work on runways and facilities while F6Fs engaged in flak suppression.

No Japanese planes got into the air, and Butch O'Hare's VF-6 detachment, flying CAP from the *Independence,* had little to do. Orbiting high above it all, taking stock, was Jimmy Flatley who by 0700 estimated the island's facilities were one-third destroyed or damaged. By the middle of the afternoon even the AA guns had ceased firing, though not without first taking a toll. Fighting Five lost two Hellcats to antiaircraft fire and the *Yorktown* also lost an Avenger. These were the only combat casualties, though Lieutenant Mike Hadden of VF-9 had to put his F6 in the water with engine trouble. Fortunately he splashed down near a U.S. destroyer.

Hadden bobbed in the swell, supported by his Mae West, anxiously awaiting rescue as he repeatedly thought of the last words spoken during briefing: "The waters around Marcus are infested with sharks."[4] Abruptly his thoughts were interrupted by a splash next to him, and he glimpsed a round dark form in the water. Hadden grabbed his knife from its sheath and desperately swam away, only to find two more threatening shapes around him. He seemed in the midst of a school of sharks. At that moment the destroyer let down a cargo net and the fighter pilot scrambled up, immensely thankful to escape a horrible death.

Once on deck, Hadden heard a sailor remark, "That's the first time I've ever seen anyone swim *away* from a life preserver."[5]

Far to the southeast the next day, 1 September, more Hellcat history was made. Light carriers *Princeton* (CVL-23) and *Belleau Wood* (CVL-24) provided a continuous CAP over Howland and Baker Islands where a landing force was going ashore. The *Princeton* embarked VF-23 and a detachment of VF-6 while the *Belleau Wood* operated Fighting 22 and 24, all equipped with F6Fs.

A VF-6 division under Lieutenant (jg) Richard L. Loesch had launched at noon and was assigned a CAP station over the landing force at Baker. Loesch had first entered combat a year before when Fighting Six was engaged in the Battle of the Eastern Solomons, and had scored his first victory in that engagement. Now his division received a vector from the fighter director, ordering the four Hellcats at 10,000 feet onto a bogey heading east towards the task group at 7,000 feet.

The intruder was a Kawanishi H8K flying boat, called "Emily" by the Americans, and apparently it never saw the four fighters coming. Loesch and his wingman, Ensign A. W. Nyquist, made a high nose-to-nose gunnery run, opening fire at 500 yards and pressing the attack down to 100 yards. They both fired about 300 rounds, getting a good concentration of hits on the cockpit and inboard engines. The Emily fell away in an easy right-hand dive, completing a 180° turn as it exploded on the water.

The Hellcat had made its first kill, and Dick Loesch became the first pilot to score in both Grumman "cats."

Two days later it was VF-22's turn as an Emily fell to the *Belleau Wood*'s fighters. Then on 8 September the *Princeton* FDO vectored two VF-6 Hellcats onto a third Emily. The tail gunner opened fire but scored no hits as the Grummans sent the big flying boat down from 8,000 feet. None of these snoopers had been able to get off a radio report to their base in the Gilberts, so quickly had they been dispatched.

The new fleet carrier *Lexington* (CV-16), with Air Group 16 aboard, led the *Princeton* and the *Belleau Wood* into a two-day strike on Tarawa Atoll in the Gilberts during mid-September, but no aerial opposition developed. The Hellcats would have to wait till six fast carriers merged to form Task Force 14 for their first crack at real aerial combat. That opportunity developed during the strike at Wake Island on 5 and 6 October.

It was the first time in the war the U.S. Navy had been able to put a half-dozen carriers on the line, though they operated in two-ship groups. The *Independence* and the *Belleau Wood* were assigned "shortstop" position northeast of Wake to intercept Japanese reinforcements flying up from the Marshalls. The *Essex* and *Yorktown*, along with the *Lexington* and *Cowpens* (CVL-25), were responsible for reducing Japanese strength on Wake Island as much as possible during the two days allotted for the operation.

Commander Charlie Crommelin, newly promoted to CAG-5, added a bit of personal incentive to the Wake raid. The night before launch he gathered Fighting Five in its ready room and made an announcement: he had a bottle of Old Crow which he would personally present to the first pilot to shoot down a Japanese airplane. The pilots needed no such stimulus, but it did add a bit of spice to the whole affair. Fighting Five had been Crommelin's squadron, and the pilots knew and respected him. He hailed from a well-known Alabama family which made a significant contribution to the war effort. He had four brothers in the Navy, all Annapolis graduates, including three like himself who were aviators. They were all known as pilots' pilots.

Each of the four strike carriers launched three fighter divisions, beginning 30 minutes before sunrise on 5 October. As if darkness weren't enough to contend with, a strong squall blew up. Several planes got lost in the predawn gloom and missed rendezvous with their squadrons. One VF-5 pilot spun in, probably from vertigo. It was hardly an encouraging way to start the day, catapulting off a pitching deck into a black void.

Things got more unpleasant even before the sun was fully up. Wake's radar detected the 47 Hellcats about 50 miles out and the Japanese got 27 Zero fighters into the air, plus five Betty bombers. What resulted was the first in thousands of individual confrontations between Hellcats and Zekes.

Lieutenant M. C. Hoffman and Ensign Robert W. Duncan of VF-5 were the first to engage the Zekes. Duncan spotted several bandits initiating an attack and turned into them, drawing a bead on the nearest. He put a full deflection burst into the Zeke's cockpit and saw it flame brightly in the dark sky. Duncan then engaged the next Zero, forcing it off a Hellcat's tail, but he took hits in his own fuselage just aft of the cockpit. The Zeke pulled out of its gunnery pass and hauled up into a loop with Duncan close behind. As both fighters hung seemingly motionless for a second as they went over the top, Duncan fired and scored. Like the first one, this Zeke also burned and spun into the water.

During the same short dogfight, two other *Yorktown* pilots claimed a third Zeke and a Betty. Fighting Five then devoted its attention to strafing parked aircraft, destroying at least four Bettys. Hoffman and Duncan were regaining altitude when yet another Zeke appeared overhead. They both fired but Duncan spent the last of his ammunition and Hoffman completed the kill. A highly experienced flier, "Boogie" Hoffman had come up as an enlisted pilot and had test-flown the A6M2 Zero which had been made airworthy at NAS North Island after force-landing in the Aleutians in June 1942. Consequently, he was knowledgable about the Zeke, and proved it by chasing another and shooting it down.

It wasn't all one-sided. Heavy and accurate flak came up from Wake, knocking down two VF-5 Hellcats, but one pilot was rescued by a U.S. submarine.

Back aboard the *Yorktown*, Commander Crommelin kept his word by presenting the fifth of Old Crow to young Bob Duncan. With two kills in his first fighter combat, Duncan was bound to admit the CAG's offer worked powerful medicine.

Meanwhile, the *Essex* Hellcats also found action. Fighting Nine skipper Phil Torrey tangled with three Zekes over Wake, shooting down the first in a one-on-one fight and evading the second two by dodging in and out of clouds. Upstairs at 16,000, Lieutenants Mayo Hadden and J. S. Kitchen turned into a pair of Zeros which jumped the formation, then were pounced upon by two more. All four bandits muffed their gunnery passes, failing to score any hits. The last Zeke was overhauled by the two Hellcats, who shared him for breakfast. But while tall, youthful Mike Hadden watched his victim fall into the ocean, he was bounced by

Lieutenant (jg) Robert W. Duncan of VF-5, the first Hellcat pilot to shoot down a Zero. He was credited with two of the Mitsubishi fighters during the first Wake Island raid of October 1943. Photo: R. W. Duncan

an unseen Zeke which shot him up pretty badly. Like Torrey, he ducked into some convenient clouds and got back to the *Essex* with his engine oil almost completely siphoned out through several 20-mm holes.

Lieutenant (jg) Hamilton McWhorter III had his Zeke virtually served up on the proverbial platter. He estimated there were nearly 20 bandits all around him when one unexpectedly appeared in his gunsight. The Georgia pilot triggered one burst and the Zeke exploded. They didn't all come that easily, however, as "One Slug" McWhorter would later testify.

The *Cowpens*'s VF-25 found out that very day. Two Hellcats failed to return from the dawn mission, presumed lost to AA fire. A third was so badly shot up that its pilot made an emergency landing aboard the *Lexington*.

The two detached CVLs also saw combat. Butch O'Hare was leading his VF-6 division south of Wake when he spotted three Zekes and gave chase. The outnumbered enemy dove for the safety of their airfield but O'Hare downed one before they got there, his first since his only previous combat a year and a half before. O'Hare's section leader was Alex Vraciu who, despite an inoperative radio, sensed what the skipper was up to and closed on the second Zeke. He was almost mesmerized by the enemy fighter, so close did he attack, before he shot it down. The third Zeke hastened to a landing, lurched to a stop, and the pilot jumped out just in time. The *Independence* pilots were right behind, burning the Zeke and two bombers despite the thick AA. On the way home Ensign Hank Landry got a Zeke while flying O'Hare's wing, and then O'Hare picked up an airborne Betty below the cloud layer. With Landry covering him, O'Hare pressed a close attack which left the bomber in the sea. It was his seventh confirmed victory, and it would be his last.

Aerial opposition was considerably reduced by 6 October, and when the carriers retired they left 22 of Wake's 34 aircraft destroyed. The Zekes had shot down six Task Force 14 planes, but enemy AA gunners proved just as dangerous—raising total carrier aircraft combat losses to 12.

The Wake Island raid inflicted considerable damage upon an important Japanese base, but for the Hellcat pilots it had more significance. For the first time the F6F had met the Zeke, and had more than held its own. It wouldn't have been safe to draw too many conclusions from this first, brief encounter, but the dogfights did indicate that the tactical doctrine was correct: maintain a high airspeed, fight in the vertical when possible to negate the Zeke's low-speed turning advantage, and stick together. Teamwork got results.

While the first F6F carrier squadrons were acquiring their sea legs, a few other Hellcat units were flying from advanced airfields in the Solomons. The first of these was VF-33 under Lieutenant Commander Hawley Russell, with 24 Hellcats and 36 pilots based first at Guadalcanal and then at Munda. The squadron entered combat on 28 August and in the next three weeks flew ten bomber escorts against such notorious Japanese air bases as Kahili, Ballale, and Morgusai. In the course of this first tour, Russell's pilots claimed 21 victories, all Zekes, against four F6Fs and two pilots lost.

Fighting 33 returned to the Solomons in October and was joined by two additional Hellcat units, VF-38 and VF-40, the latter having become operational there in September. They were just in time, as November would be an exceptionally active month, the F6F's busiest to date.

Much of the work load fell upon the venerable 33,000-ton *Saratoga* (CV-3) and her new teammate, the light carrier *Princeton*. "Sara" operated Air Group 12, which had been in training in the Southwest Pacific since June. The fighter squadron was led by colorful Commander Joseph

C. Clifton, the energetic Paducah, Kentucky, aviator who had been universally known as "Jumpin' Joe" since his Annapolis days.

Fighting 12 had collected its Hellcats at Nandi in the Fiji Islands, but almost had them "borrowed" before it could start flying them. In July, VF-11 staged south from a successful tour at Guadalcanal as the last squadron to employ the F4F in prolonged combat. Some of the senior VF-11 pilots, including the operations officer, Lieutenant William N. Leonard, took advantage of the opportunity to fly some of the F6F-3s being held for Clifton. Immensely pleased with the Hellcat's potential, Leonard and a few other enthusiastic Fighting 11 troops requested to return to Guadalcanal and initiate the new Grumman into combat. Clifton got wind of the scheme and quickly made his views known—he wasn't about to have his airplanes taken away, even "on loan."

Clifton's concern was in one way well founded, because in late 1942 VF-12 had received the Navy's first F4Us, but the Corsair had flunked its carrier qualifications and Clifton's embryo unit was rescheduled for Hellcats. In the end, Jumpin' Joe got his way because, as Bill Leonard recounted, "He yelled louder than we did."[6]

The *Saratoga* and *Princeton* began November by supporting the landings at Torokina on Bougainville, but were quickly directed to strike well-defended Rabaul Harbor at New Britain after intelligence learned of a heavy Japanese shipping concentration. There was no time for planning, as the orders were received on 4 November and called for an attack on the fifth. Only one launch was planned—a hit-and-run raid to get in fast, do the job, and get out of shore-based air range as quickly as possible.

Shortly before 0900 on 5 November, big old *Saratoga* and new little *Princeton* began launching all their 97 operational planes into rainy overcast skies some 230 miles southeast of Rabaul. Between them, VF-12 and VF-23 put up 52 Hellcats to cover the 45 SBDs and TBFs, leaving only a few fighters with the ships. The strike coordinator was Commander Henry H. Caldwell in his CAG-12 Avenger, but both Clifton, with 33 *Saratoga* Hellcats and Commander Henry L. Miller leading 19 of the *Princeton*'s VF-23, had big jobs. Their duty was to keep the Hellcat escort intact and properly positioned to ward off the heavy fighter interception that was sure to develop. The 52 F6Fs flew a stepped-up formation above the bombers with Miller's four divisions providing top cover.

The poor weather improved considerably en route, and the fliers picked up Rabaul visually from 50 miles out. Simpson Harbor was crammed with Japanese ships—about 40 merchantmen plus 8 heavy cruisers and perhaps 20 light cruisers and destroyers. There had been little hope of achieving complete surprise, and this proved to be the case. Nearly 60 Zekes were up and waiting when the carrier planes swung over St. George Channel two hours after launch.

Keeping their air groups together, Caldwell and Miller denied the Japanese a chance to strike two unsupported formations until the last moment. By then the F6Fs, SBDs, and TBFs were into the thick, well-directed flak and the Zekes demonstrated no interest in pursuing the Americans into the AA fire. Instead, enemy fighters stooged around just out of range, stunting and playing with one another in hopes of sucking the Hellcats away from the bombers. Though they were sorely tempted, Clifton's and Miller's pilots refused the bait. One fighter division remained with each bomber flight all the way to the target.

Only a few Zekes intercepted until the Dauntlesses and Avengers had attacked, and by then, of course, the damage had been done: bomb or torpedo hits on six cruisers, including three badly damaged.

Once the SBDs and TBFs were strung out during retirement, they were more vulnerable to interception. Between the AA and the Zekes, five bombers went down and a pair of Hellcats fell to the flak gunners. But the F6s covered the strike planes most of the way, and Joe Clifton showed Fighting 12 how it was done by smoking one Zeke with his wingman and bagging a second as his number two lured it into the skipper's sights. The *Saratoga*'s Hellcats thought they'd downed at least 11 Zekes and probably 14 more at a cost of four F6Fs, but this was clearly on the optimistic side. Total Japanese losses were about a dozen.

The VF-23 fighters that remained topside were persistently picked at by large numbers of Zekes, but with little result. Miller's Hellcats returned with a claim similar to Clifton's, though Lieutenant H. M. Crockett and Ensign Carlton Roberts, escorting Commander Caldwell's Avenger, had more business than they could easily handle. Bounced by eight Zekes, the three Grummans were all badly shot up but fought their way clear, claiming three kills. Wounded and without the use of his flaps, Crockett put his fighter down on the *Princeton* with 200 bullet holes in the Hellcat's tough hide. Roberts diverted to the uncompleted field at Vella Lavella.

Ten carrier planes were lost in this important strike which deprived the Japanese Navy of the bulk of its surface warships in the Solomons. Five Hellcats had been shot down, but Fighting 12 and 23 had stuck with the bombers and earned the appreciation of their crews. Clifton's pilots were now convinced that the Hellcat was "far and away the best fighter in the air."[7]

A follow-up strike was quickly planned to finish the shipping at Rabaul, and appropriately—or ironically—it came less than a week later, on Armistice Day.

The plan called for Rear Admiral Frederick C. Sherman's *Saratoga* and *Princeton* to put their planes over the target 30 minutes before the main strike by Alfred Montgomery's Task Group 50.3 arrived from the

Essex, Bunker Hill (CV-17), and *Independence*. Hopefully the timing would catch Japanese fighters refueling on the ground. Sherman approached from the north and launched 225 miles east of the target on 11 November. But unlike before, this time the weather was in the enemy's favor. The 55 Hellcats, 25 Avengers, and 21 Dauntlesses had to contend with clouds and squalls most of the way to Rabaul, then at 0830 found Simpson Harbor almost completely hidden beneath an overcast. The bombers concentrated on the three visible cruisers in the big harbor—the others were hidden by clouds or rain—and hit one of them. Nearly 70 Zekes were up, chasing the raiders in and out of the weather, but they intercepted only seven. Five of these returned with battle damage, and VF-12 claimed a solitary kill. The main blow was still on the way.

Montgomery had launched 160 miles southeast of Rabaul, and Air Group Nine's formation barged straight into five dozen Zekes in limited visibility over Cape St. George at 0900. Lieutenant (jg) Ham McWhorter was one of VF-9's 12 pilots who tangled with about half the bandits over the harbor mouth. In a short, confusing dogfight McWhorter claimed three Zekes but didn't have things entirely his own way. He headed back to the *Essex* with 11 nonregulation holes in his airplane. Chick Smith, leading the second section of Phil Torrey's division, got a pair of Zekes.

Lieutenant Casey Childers, who had mowed a swath through the pine trees back at Cape May, New Jersey, was escorting SBDs when several Zekes bounced his division from above. He never saw how many there were, except for the one which got on his wingman's tail and opened fire. Childers saw the Hellcat pull up, trailing flames from its drop tank, and then plop down to a water landing. Fighting Nine then took the strike planes home, minus two bombers. The *Essex* Hellcats claimed 14 enemy aircraft shot down.

The brand-new *Bunker Hill* put the next formation over Rabaul giving Air Group 17 its combat initiation. Her fighter squadron was VF-18 under Lieutenant Commander Sam L. Silber, a husky former Maryland football star. Lieutenant Commander John Blackburn's Fighting 17 had been orphaned from both ship and air group when the Navy decided the Corsairs were unsafe for carrier operations. The VF-17 pilots would see action that day, however. They were based at Ondonga, New Georgia, and were scheduled to provide CAP over the task group, as they had during the raid on the fifth. So were seven VF-33 Hellcats under Lieutenant John C. Kelley, which landed aboard the *Independence* and took up CAP again.

"Sambo" Silber's pilots tangled with several Zekes over Rabaul but, like VF-9, they stayed close to the bombers. Lieutenant (jg) James D.

Billo did get involved with a pair of Japanese and returned to *Bunker Hill* to report both went down. Air Group 17 lost six planes to Zekes and flak, then withdrew as the *Independence* planes went in. Her Air Group 22 was augmented by a 12-plane detachment from VF-6, and four *Independence* fighter divisions claimed four for three.

Within some 30 minutes of the *Essex* planes' arrival, the cloudy sky above Rabaul was clear of American aircraft. A Japanese destroyer had been sunk and four other warships damaged, but only six Zekes had gone down—half the U.S. losses. In the hectic, confused dogfights amid heavy cloud cover, the four Hellcat squadrons thought they had shot down 30 enemy aircraft over Rabaul.

Both carrier groups planned to launch second strikes, but increasingly poor weather forced Sherman to cancel his follow-up blow. Little more than an hour after Montgomery's planes returned, search radar picked up a large bogey 120 miles out, approaching the task group. Hellcats were scrambled to investigate, and refueling and rearming for a second strike continued. Under the circumstances, it was the only thing Montgomery could do. By 1330 the bombers were again being launched, but only to clear the flight decks.

About 20 minutes later some VF-33 Hellcats spotted the bogey only 40 miles from the task group. A fighter controller asked for an estimate and was informed "There are millions of them!"[8] Actually, there were 69 Zekes, Vals, and Kates from carrier squadrons temporarily based ashore at Rabaul. An undetermined number of Bettys were also seen.

The next three-quarters of an hour was absolute mayhem. Hellcats and Corsairs hammered away at the determined enemy squadrons flying in beautiful formation under a three-tenths cloud cover. The Val dive bombers attacked first, concentrating on the *Bunker Hill*, though the *Essex* and *Independence* also received unwelcome attention. All three carriers had near-misses, but no direct hits were scored.

The *Essex* and *Independence* handled the fighter direction, but there were mistakes both in the radar rooms and fighter cockpits. The earliest interceptions were made against Zekes instead of the Vals and Kates, and four divisions of fighters were vectored far from the battle to investigate another bogey—12 Hellcats from the second strike which unaccountably were not recalled to help repel the attack.

As a result, the Corsairs of VF-17 had much of the early combat to themselves until the rearming Hellcats could be launched. Four VF-33 Hellcats made the first interception, chasing some Zekes and two Bettys back towards Rabaul.

By now there was no further thought of continuing with the second strike. The hard-pressed carriers were relying on their AA guns as their primary defense. Confused fighter pilots, either hearing no vector instructions or being confused by what they did hear, simply headed for the bursting flak over the task force. Many others lifted off their decks and were instantly engaged. One was Ensign C. T. Watts of VF-18, who was the last off the *Bunker Hill* and was raising his landing gear as the dive-bombing attack began. Watts sighted a Val, quickly armed his guns, and shot the Aichi down in flames.

Lieutenant (jg) Rube Denoff of Fighting Nine had a similar experience. He had no sooner cleared the *Essex*'s deck when a Val crossed his sights. "I didn't even have time to retract my wheels," he would recall,[9] but he shot it down. Moments later, joined by his wingman, Denoff latched on to one of the few Kates to survive VF-17's initial pass and splashed it for his second kill. Then he was hit in the port wing by "friendly" five-inch shrapnel and returned to the *Essex*. As Denoff's Hellcat dropped onto the deck with the customary jolt, his guns fired several accidental rounds over the heads of the plane handlers. Investigation showed that the flak splinters had cut the charging wires to the Brownings, leaving them armed even though Denoff had turned the switches to "Off."

Exaggerated combat estimates put enemy losses at 90 in the attack on the carriers, plus nearly 30 claimed over Rabaul. But it was a fact that the Japanese had taken a beating. Over 40 of the enemy strike planes were actually shot down—17 of the Vals, all 14 Kates, two Zekes, two Judy recon planes, and several Bettys. Thus, true enemy losses for Armistice Day 1943 were on the order of 50. Fighting Nine alone claimed 55, including 41 over the carriers; this figure demonstrates how heavily engaged were Torrey's pilots. They carried the main burden of the day's fighter combat, and at one time *Essex* sailors counted 11 Japanese planes burning. Sam Silber's VF-18 claimed 20 kills, and John Blackburn's F4Us of VF-17 reported 18½. The fraction was a Kate shared with VF-33, which also claimed five other kills. But the land-based Hellcats lost their leader, Lieutenant John Kelley, who was last seen chasing a Betty into the task force AA fire. Another three Hellcats fell to the strong Zeke escort, raising the carrier-plane loss to 18 in all.

The Rabaul raids were successful in their immediate objective in that they sank or crippled numerous Japanese warships, relieving the surface threat to future operations in the Solomons. But enemy air power was also crippled, and had been unable to defeat carriers operating well within range of land-based bombers. Three Japanese air groups totaling 173 aircraft had been operational at Rabaul on 1 November. Two weeks later only 52 were available for return to Truk, and nearly all of them were Zekes.

The way was now clear to the Gilberts.

After Rabaul, the Fifth Fleet carriers were reorganized as Task Force 50. The six fleet carriers and five light carriers were assigned to four task groups, with Montgomery's 50.3 keeping its designation. Pownall had 50.1, Arthur Radford had 50.2, and Sherman's Task Force 38 became TG-50.4. For the first Central Pacific operation—the invasion and occupation of the Gilbert Islands—these task groups were deployed over a wide area in order to provide protection to the landing forces and to prevent enemy air reinforcement from getting through.

D-Day for Tarawa Atoll was 20 November. In addition to eight escort carriers which would provide tactical air power to the Marines, TG-50.3, still composed of the *Essex*, *Bunker Hill*, and *Independence*, would also be on hand. The choice position, as far as the Hellcat pilots were concerned, was Pownall's 50.1 location between the Gilberts and Marshalls. From there, the *Yorktown*, *Lexington*, and *Cowpens* fighters would be almost certain to contact Japanese aircraft shuttling between the island groups.

An F6F squadron brand-new to the carrier force was not destined to remain with it very long. This was VF-1 under Commander Bernard M. Strean, a career professional from the Annapolis Class of '33. A naval aviator since 1936, "Smoke" Strean was a highly experienced fighter pilot with 4,000 hours' flight time. His 44 Hellcats were equally divided between the escort carriers *Nassau* (CVE-16) and *Barnes* (CVE-20), and began ground-support missions against Tarawa on the 21st. Fighting One was to be the atoll's garrison air force and would remain there after the invasion.

Japanese air strength in the area was considerably reduced by D-Day, largely due to transfers earlier in the month to Rabaul. At dusk on the 20th, 16 Bettys from the Marshalls were belatedly sighted in the failing light, deploying against TG-50.3 which was then landing the day's last strike. The *Bunker Hill* CAP dropped on the intruders, but too late to prevent them from launching their torpedoes. One struck the *Independence* in the stern, forcing her out of the campaign, and she shaped course for Funafuti in the Ellice Islands to the south. Fighting 18 and the antiaircraft gunners shot down nine Bettys, but this and other nocturnal attacks clearly indicated the need for full-time night fighters in the task force. Butch O'Hare, newly promoted to CAG of the *Enterprise*'s Air Group Six, was lost the night of 26 November in an early night-flying experiment.

Until now, the *Lexington*'s air group had seen relatively little action, but Lieutenant Commander Paul Buie's VF-16 was rewarded by being in the right place at the right time—not just once, but twice in a row.

Patrolling with the *Yorktown* and *Cowpens* in the waters between Makin in the Gilberts and Mili in the Marshalls, the *Lexington* fighter

Hellcats of VF-1 on Betio Island, Tarawa Atoll, 25 November 1943. Fighting One flew ashore from escort carriers on D-Plus Three, 23 November, and remained until January 1944.

pilots made their first significant contact on D-Plus Three. Buie was up with 11 of his "Pistol Packin' Airdales" at midday when the *Lexington*'s controller called that he had a contact. The dozen Hellcats were directed to what Buie called "a fighter pilot's dream position,"[10] 4,000 feet above and upsun of 21 Zekes. The Japanese were flying their usual exemplary formation, evidently unaware of the Hellcats overhead.

Buie led his pilots down in a coordinated side and overhead attack at 23,000 feet. Buie himself splashed two Zekes, and by the time the first few passes had been made, only a few stragglers remained. Most of these were pursued to low level. The 12 Hellcats returned to the *Lexington* where the score was tallied: 17 confirmed and 4 probables. Even more impressive was the bag of Ensign Ralph Hanks, a young Philadelphian. In his first combat he had scored five confirmed victories—the first Hellcat pilot to achieve ace status, and the first to become an "ace in a day." Over 40 more F6F pilots would equal or exceed Hanks's one-day score in the next two years.

About noon on the 24th, Buie was again leading three divisions on CAP at almost the same location as the day before. The FDO directed VF-16 to 20 Zekes and 2 Bettys, again at 23,000 feet, but this time the Zekes held the altitude advantage. Buie turned his formation to meet the first attack, and though one Hellcat went down, the enemy "never got another chance," Buie recalled.[11] The scrap developed into a vertical combat which topped out at 28,000 feet and worked down to 5,000. Buie got another kill, and Lieutenant (jg) Francis M. Fleming also scored again. The day before he had bagged a pair of Zekes and split a third, then scored another double in the second dogfight. In all, VF-16 claimed 13 confirmed and 6 probables on the 24th. Their two days ended with a total of 30 enemy aircraft destroyed and 11 probables, against the loss of one Hellcat.

That constituted the major portion of aerial combat in the Tarawa operation. Commander Strean took his Fighting One Hellcats ashore to tiny Betio Island on D-Plus-Three, before the last of the Japanese defenders were rooted out. The airfield had a 3,000-foot runway which was more or less operational, but was hard-pressed to handle nearly four dozen aircraft. Staff planners estimated the island could support 100 fighters, but on 30 November when Joe Clifton brought 36 *Saratoga* Hellcats ashore, both squadrons became almost immobile. "Neither of us could move after Clifton arrived," recalled Strean, "so his squadron stayed only one night, during which we had one of our biggest night attacks."[12]

High-flying Japanese bombers appeared virtually every night, and were opposed only by searchlight-directed AA guns. No night fighters were available, so Strean and Lieutenant Paul M. Henderson took turns flying night patrols at over 30,000 feet, hoping to catch one of the night riders in the glare of a searchlight. They had no such luck, for no bomber was ever illuminated for more than 90 seconds.

In December, VF-1 moved to nearby Mullinex Field on Buota, which had a longer runway. Living conditions were little improved from Betio, however. There were numerous false-alarm scrambles and missions escorting Army Air Force bombers, but no Japanese aircraft were engaged. Strean summarized his squadron's stint in the Gilberts: "We slept with our aircraft, flew a lot, but did little damage. There were no combat or operational losses. We always had 44 aircraft up and in the air at appropriate times."[13]

Half the squadron was returned to Hawaii in mid-January while the other half remained at Tarawa for another six weeks. Fighting One was eventually reunited for a two-month deployment aboard *Yorktown* in June and July of 1944, at which time the lack of combat at Tarawa would be more than offset.

Meanwhile, the war continued at sea, and it didn't go entirely in the U.S. Navy's favor. Early in the morning of 24 November, a Japanese submarine torpedoed the escort carrier *Liscome Bay* (CVE-56) and she sank in 22 minutes. One of the survivors was Captain John Crommelin, a senior staff officer whose younger brother Charles was the *Yorktown*

A Hellcat landing at the newly won Tarawa airfield in late November 1943. Two F6F squadrons, VF-1 and VF-12, both operated from this crowded field shortly after it was captured from the Japanese.

CAG. John had a formidable reputation as a pilot—he was capable of putting a TBF into an inverted spin at 1,500 feet and recovering at sea level.

But Charlie was also a skilled aviator, as he demonstrated under extremely adverse circumstances. Leading an Air Group Five strike against Mili the same morning that his brother swam away from the sinking CVE, Charlie Crommelin's Hellcat took a direct hit while strafing a grounded bomber. A 40-mm shell exploded against his cockpit, smashing most of the instruments and fracturing the windscreen with thousands of hairline cracks which destroyed forward visibility. His own injuries were serious: no vision in the left eye, broken right wrist, a bad chest wound, and numerous minor cuts.

It was 120 miles back to the *Yorktown*, but Crommelin ignored the pain enough to maintain formation with VF-5 Hellcats all the way back to the ship. Then he showed why he was CAG. Looking into a 100-knot slipstream through one eye, he made a perfectly normal carrier landing. As if that weren't enough, he taxied forward, parked his shot-up Hellcat, and started to climb out. But that proved too much. He collapsed in his cockpit and was rushed to sick bay. After three months in the hospital, he returned to command another air group and lead it into combat. They grow tough airmen in Wetumpka, Alabama.

Lieutenant Commander Edgar Stebbins replaced Crommelin as CAG-5. Stebbins was a 3,600-hour SBD and TBF pilot, previously CO of VB-5, but he chose to fly an F6F as air group commander. More CAGs were selecting the Hellcat at this time, as it afforded the defensive merits of a fighter, but also had sufficient range and endurance for a command aircraft. Stebbins's pet Hellcat was fitted with an oblique-angle K-28 camera that he used to obtain strike photos.

Two carrier groups were assigned to the Marshalls strikes which began on 4 December. These were Pownall's 50.1 (*Yorktown, Lexington,* and *Cowpens*) and Montgomery's 50.3 (*Essex, Enterprise,* and *Belleau Wood.*) The *Lexington*'s air group commander, Ernest M. Snowden, pressed for a fighter sweep before the first strikes went in, but was turned down by Rear Admiral Pownall. Ever cautious, Pownall assumed that the carriers would be seen on the way in, and as a result all of the fighters would be needed for CAP and escort. It was one of a series of defensive-minded decisions which would cost him his job.

Launch commenced at dawn 150 miles north of the target area. The carriers put up an unusually strong strike force—nearly 250 planes—which included 91 Hellcats. Pownall's pessimistic assessment that surprise could not be achieved during the approach proved inaccurate, for the Japanese only learned of the Americans' presence by radar when the strike was 40 miles away.

The *Essex* and *Lexington* formations went to Roi, where about 50 Zekes had scrambled into the air. This was one of the first missions for Commander William A. Dean, Jr.'s, VF-2, temporarily attached to the "Big E's" Air Group Six. The 22 "Rippers" were stacked up as top cover above 20,000 feet and consequently missed the aerial combat which occurred mostly at low altitude. But 12 of Dean's Hellcats were called down by the *Enterprise* strike leader to work over numerous moored floatplanes at Ebeye Island, which they did, leaving 11 burning ashore or on the water. Only one flight of Fighting Two tangled with any Zekes. That was Lieutenant R. J. Griffin's division, covering a photo TBF over Roi. The Hellcats saw four Zekes climbing up from takeoff and, leaving one F6 upstairs with the Avenger, three Rippers caught the bandits at 2,000 feet. Nose-high at low airspeed, the Zekes turned to get out from under, but it was too late. Three went down burning and the fourth barely got away with a whole skin.

The *Yorktown* fighters found more of a contest. "Boogie" Hoffman's division was homeward bound after shooting down a lone Dave scout biplane northeast of Kwajalein. Climbing through 4,000 feet, Bob Duncan saw 18 Zekes coming down and shouted a warning into his microphone, but his radio was out. The bandits hit the four F6Fs unexpectedly, making expert use of sun and clouds. Hoffman quickly recognized the Japanese pilots as "a first-line team."[14] They put six Zekes on each two-plane section with the remainder keeping above. Caught at low level, almost out of ammunition from strafing, the Hellcats were in serious trouble.

All they could do was weave, turning into each attack. But the Zekes' numerical advantage allowed them to make high side runs in pairs regardless of which way the Grummans broke. With detached professionalism the *Yorktown* pilots considered the enemy tactic "a pure and simple, graceful and beautiful aerial display of the best in fighter attacks."[15]

Though Duncan's plane was holed from the port wingtip clear back to the cockpit aft of the armor plate, it kept flying. But Lieutenant K. B. Satterfield's Hellcat was hit on the outside of a weave. Streaming flames from both wings, the F6F hit flat in the water and then was gone.

After several interminable minutes, the other three Hellcats got away. The action report summarized, "Why they didn't shoot us all down is a mystery. We would have destroyed them if the situation had been reversed. The one thing we did learn was that they weren't as good gunners as we are."[16] Sy Satterfield would remain the only VF-5 pilot lost to enemy aircraft.

It was a day of mixed fortunes for Fighting Five. The skipper, Ed Owen, was alone when he picked one of two Zekes off the tail of another Hellcat, and was then surrounded by four or five more. By the time he disengaged, his plane was a flying wreck—one aileron shot off, most of the instruments out, a wheel dangling down, and his engine rapidly losing oil. En route home another pilot formed up and asked, "You don't expect to land that crate, do you?"[17] Owen didn't have to, for his engine packed up and he bailed out. A destroyer returned him home to the *Yorktown*.

The *Lexington*'s fighters had things more their own way. Twelve of VF-16's planes locked horns with an estimated 30 Zekes and gunned down 19, with a Betty for good measure. In dogfights over the atoll, Hellcats claimed a total of 28 Zekes for three F6Fs. But returning pilots reported "a field full of torpedo planes"[18] which hadn't been dealt with. Though the Kates and Jills attacked in small groups beginning at noon and were consistently beaten off or shot down by AA gunners, still they came. Rather than remain longer in reach of land-based planes, the carriers pulled out, launching preemptive strikes against Wotje on the way. Fighting Five got a Betty taking off and claimed four planes destroyed on the ground, but the main threat would come from Bettys on Roi and Maleolap after dark.

Though the two task groups bent on 24 knots to the northeast, they could not outdistance the long-range bombers. From 1850 until 0130, when the moon finally set, attacks were made by as many as 37 Bettys. Only one of them got a hit, but it was enough to send the *Lexington* limping home with torpedo damage.

The only other noteworthy carrier operations of the year involved the *Bunker Hill* and *Monterey* (CVL-26). They convoyed five battleships

A Hellcat of VF-16 comes to an ungraceful but successful landing aboard the USS *Lexington* after sustaining a 3-inch antiaircraft shell which knocked out its radio and injured its arresting gear.

from the Gilberts to the Solomons, striking Nauru on 8 December and Kavieng Harbor, New Ireland, on Christmas Day. There was poor hunting for the Hellcats; they had only a brief scuffle with some torpedo bombers.

Land-based F6F squadrons were still active in the Solomons at this time, and one of the pleasant surprises associated with them was an unusually high in-commission rate. On 17 December, for instance, the Solomons Fighter Command possessed 268 Army, Navy, Marine, and New Zealand aircraft, of which 199 were operational. Fifty-three of the 58 Hellcats were in commission—more than any other type, even though Corsairs and P-39s outnumbered the F6Fs. Therefore, Hellcats represented 21 percent of all fighters, but 26 percent of those available for missions. There were 71 F4Us, of which 47 were operational. This meant that two-thirds of the Corsairs were in commission, compared to 91 percent of the

Hellcats. It was this comparison of the two Navy fighters which prompted Grumman partisans to observe that the F4U was faster than the F6F three days a week. The rest of the time, they said, the Corsair was down for maintenance.

So ended 1943. In the Solomons and Gilberts raids, nearly 230 Japanese aircraft were thought shot down by Hellcats, against a combat loss of fewer than 30. Tactical doctrine and refinements in equipment, both of which had been tested in late 1943, would be all but perfected in early 1944. A substantial shakeup was in store for the fast carriers, which in the new year would embark upon the most successful campaign in the history of modern naval warfare.

And the Hellcats would be right up front.

Hellcat Squadrons in Combat: August to December 1943

VF-1	Tarawa	Commander Bernard M. Strean
VF-2	*Enterprise*	Commander William A. Dean, Jr.
VF-5	*Yorktown*	Commander C. L. Crommelin, Lieutenant Commander E. M. Owen
VF-6	*Independence*	Commander Edward H. O'Hare
VF-6	*Princeton*	detachment
VF-6	*Belleau Wood*	detachment
VF-6	*Cowpens*	detachment
VF-9	*Essex*	Lieutenant Commander Philip H. Torrey
VF-12	*Saratoga*	Commander Joseph C. Clifton
VF-16	*Lexington*	Lieutenant Commander Paul D. Buie
VF-18	*Bunker Hill*	Lieutenant Commander Sam L. Silber
VF-22	*Belleau Wood*	Lieutenant L. L. Johnson
VF-22	*Independence*	Lieutenant L. L. Johnson
VF-23	*Princeton*	Commander Henry L. Miller
VF-24	*Belleau Wood*	Lieutenant Commander John O. Curtis (KIA), Lieutenant R. P. Ross, Commander R. H. Dale
VF-25	*Cowpens*	Lieutenant Commander Mark A. Grant
VF-30	*Monterey*	Lieutenant Commander J. G. Sliney
VF-33	Solomons	Lieutenant Commander Hawley A. Russell
VF-38	Solomons	
VF-40	Solomons	Commander John P. Rembert, Jr.

3 With the Fast Carriers

We will go up and fight.
Deuteronomy 1:41

On 6 January 1944 the Fast Carrier Task Force came into its own. It had a new designation, TF-58, and a new commander, Rear Admiral Marc A. Mitscher. And it had a big job. Kwajalein Atoll in the Marshall Islands, just north of the now-conquered Gilberts, was the next target for amphibious invasion.

Organized into four task groups, the task force now consisted of six fleet carriers including the *Saratoga* and *Enterprise* (CV-6), and six light carriers. The aircraft complements of these 12 flattops included over 350 Hellcats, plus another 36 F6F-3s on three of the escort carriers which would lend tactical support to the infantry.

As usual, a dawn fighter sweep was planned to open the campaign. On 29 January, TG-58.2 was responsible for putting 30 Hellcats over Roi and Namur, and they were all in the air before 0600. Lieutenant Commander Herb Houck led 18 other planes of VF-9 from the *Essex*, and the light carrier *Cabot* (CVL-28) put up 11 under the leadership of Lieutenant Commander Robert A. Winston, a fighter pilot for eight years. Kwajalein was the first operation for Winston's VF-31, which on this deployment would set the record for the most kills by a CVL squadron in one tour.

In the dark predawn sky three of the *Cabot* pilots failed to rendezvous with Winston, but rather than wait he proceeded towards Roi's airfield. The *Essex* fighters were to strafe parked planes there, and would need top cover. The VF-31 skipper didn't know that his missing trio had joined forces with VF-9.

Climbing to 20,000 feet on instruments, Winston unexpectedly received a radio call from Houck. Approaching the target, the Fighting Nine CO had found a 6,000-foot overcast above the island. He decided to break radio silence in order to provide Winston with this information, and he was right. Japanese radar had picked up the incoming Hellcats, and over 20 Zekes were upstairs waiting. The *Cabot* fighters followed Houck's advice without question, Winston placing his division below the cloud cover and sending the other division well above it.

Fighting 31's top cover could see target markers being dropped over the airfield by TBFs, then the tracers of Houck's low-flying Hellcats as they began to shoot up visible enemy aircraft in the still-dim sunlight. Then the Zekes appeared, dropping onto the strafers with a height advantage. One VF-9 plane went down early in the battle, but whether to Zekes or flak was difficult to say. The *Essex* fighters had orders to refuse combat if possible and to concentrate on destroying grounded planes, but several pilots were forced to engage.

Meanwhile, at 5,000 feet Bob Winston caught sight of a column of aircraft and led his wingman, Ensign Cornelius Nooy, over to join up. But the darkness had played a trick on him; the planes were Zekes. Fortunately, the two Hellcats had approached from behind and Winston fired at the last plane in line. He missed, and the Zekes broke formation like a flushed covey of quail. Then they turned back.

The two Hellcats immediately initiated a defensive weave, pulling high-G turns to force the bandits off their tails. There were at least seven Zekes, however, and they persisted in their attacks. One pressed too close to Nooy's tail and Winston had enough time to pull deflection and fire a burst which dropped the Zeke into the lagoon. After more weaving and snap-shooting, both Grummans disengaged and outran their assailants, heading for the rendezvous point.

Another *Cabot* pilot got distracted on his way to regroup. Lieutenant Douglas Mulcahy and his wingman, separated from Winston under the clouds, were jumped by several Zekes and had to dive away to evade them. Now alone, Mulcahy found five Zekes heading towards him but as they passed, one latched onto his tail and hit his F6 with a burst of machine-gun fire. Again Mulcahy evaded by diving, but then climbed up to 20,000 feet in search of his assailants. Remarkably, he found them. Diving from six o'clock high, the New Yorker drew a bead on the rearmost Zeke and shot off its port wing. Evidently the other Japanese never saw their friend's demise, as they maintained formation. Thus encouraged, Mulcahy climbed for another crack at them but the four broke when he opened fire and he wisely decided against pursuing the matter.

By singles, sections, and divisions 26 Hellcats returned to the task group and landed. One of *Cabot*'s damaged fighters ditched near a destroyer and the pilot was rescued, but three *Essex* planes were missing. Houck's pilots, forced to defend themselves, claimed eight victims and Winston's crew turned in their first five tallies. *Essex* dive bombers which struck the field shortly after the fighter sweep saw only a few Zekes, and by mid morning there were no more enemy planes over Roi-Namur. Over 100 had been destroyed on their airfields.

But the atoll was not yet entirely free of Japanese aircraft. During the afternoon CAP, ten VF-6 Hellcats found seven airborne targets. Six were Bettys, apparently based on Burlesque Island. Lieutenant (jg) Alex Vraciu and his wingman ran across four of them.

Vraciu noticed the first emerge from a pall of smoke on the south end of the island and quickly caught up, diving from 7,000 feet. He made a high side run from starboard, fired one long burst, and the Betty went down in flames from 400 feet. The pair from *Intrepid* (CV-11) had hardly pulled up when another Betty was seen about 300 feet over the lagoon. As Vraciu and Ensign T. A. Hall closed from astern, the Betty descended to within 100 feet of the water but Vraciu's first burst exploded the fuel in one wing.

Yet another pair of bombers was sighted as the Hellcats climbed to about 3,500 feet. The section dived to engage, and the Bettys split up.

Lieutenant (jg) Alexander Vraciu of VF-6 aboard the USS *Intrepid* after the first carrier strike on Truk. In that raid, 16 February 1944, Vraciu shot down four Japanese fighters, raising his confirmed victories to nine. He made two subsequent deployments to the Western Pacific, ending the war with a total of 19 victories. Photo: R. M. Hill

Hall took the leader, which was bagged by other VF-6 planes, and Vraciu went after the Betty which turned west. Vraciu's first pass had no visible effect, and he found on the next run that only one gun was firing. With the Betty ducking and turning below 100 feet, Vraciu had all he could do to keep his one gun functioning and line up the target. He pursued the bomber for 25 miles, making eight or nine passes, before it nosed into the water. These three kills made Alex Vraciu an ace, but it would take more than five enemy planes to compensate him for the loss of Butch O'Hare.

The other three task groups were unable to scare up much opposition at Taroa, Wotje, or even Kwajalein Island itself. Only 14 Japanese aircraft were encountered in the air, and all were shot down or wrecked on landing. Another 45 bombers, fighters, and floatplanes were destroyed on the ground or in the water. It was a rather disappointing operation to the pilots in some respects, as heavier opposition had been anticipated, but the invasion of Kwajalein proceeded without interference from Japanese aircraft.

Mitscher's keen young fighter pilots may not have felt that way, had they known that in another two weeks they would fly into the teeth of the most formidable enemy naval base in the Central Pacific.

Truk Atoll in the middle of the Carolines was known as "The Gibralter of the Pacific." It was the main Japanese fleet anchorage beyond the home islands, yet the U.S. Navy knew almost nothing about its facilities or base forces. Because of its foreboding reputation—founded more on rumor than on evidence—Truk was widely considered to be the toughest objective the carrier pilots would encounter. Beyond that, little was known—not even its pronunciation, which is actually "Trook," not "Truck" as the fliers called it.

In mid-February, Japanese air strength at Truk was twice that calculated by U.S. intelligence. The estimated strength was 185 aircraft, but in reality Truk's three island airfields held 365 planes, including transients bound for the Solomons.

Task Force 58 was well on its way before the senior officers let the destination be known. All air group commanders flew to the *Yorktown* for a conference and returned to their respective ships to pass the word. When Commander Phil Torrey, newly promoted to CAG-9, heard the task force's destination, he confessed his first instinct was to jump overboard.

Admiral Raymond A. Spruance, flying his flag in the battleship *New Jersey*, planned a two-day raid on Truk. If things went well, the Hellcats would gain air superiority the first day. Then dive bombers and torpedo planes would deal with Japanese warships found in the vicinity. Submarines stood by to provide rescue services for downed fliers—now a standard practice. The nine carriers deployed in Task Groups 58.1, 58.2, and 58.3 contained over 250 Hellcats for fighter sweeps, strikes, and CAPs.

The force arrived at the launch point, 90 miles east of Truk Atoll, nearly two hours before dawn on 16 February. Five carriers prepared to launch 70 Hellcats on the fighter sweep, and by then the pilots knew they would find combat that day.

The first F6Fs lifted off their flight decks well before dawn, which came at 0640 local time, and began joining formation. The *Bunker Hill*'s VF-18 contributed the most planes to the day's first fighter sweep, with 22 Hellcats led by the CO, "Sambo" Silber. His five divisions were assigned "what we considered the choice role of top cover"[1] at 20,000 feet. The *Bunker Hill* CAG, Commander Roland H. Dale, also launched in a

Hellcat to coordinate the sweep and subsequent strike. Twelve Hellcats were put up by VF-10 from the *Enterprise* and *Intrepid*'s VF-6, while the *Yorktown* also contributed 12 and Fighting Nine launched 11 from the *Essex*.

Leading the sweep was Lieutenant Commander William R. "Killer" Kane of the *Enterprise*, whose dozen fighters joined the 12 from the *Intrepid*. These six divisions were in the vanguard and, completing rendezvous at 1,500 feet, swung around on a course which would take them north of the atoll for the final approach. The 24 Grummans maintained an altitude of about 1,000 feet halfway to the target before they began climbing. Once the 30-mile-wide lagoon was visible in the early light, Kane led his force into a climbing spiral to gain more altitude before proceeding. At this same time VF-5 approached below while the 22 *Bunker Hill* fighters were almost out of sight overhead. There was no sign of enemy activity, though radio monitors back in the task force heard Truk go off the air at 0714.

The sun wasn't quite above the horizon when Kane's formation arrived over the target at 0805, heading southwest at 13,000 feet. The Hellcats circled Moen Island before attacking, drawing some AA fire which was mostly wide. Fighting Six pilots sighted two Bettys taking off just as Kane led his "Grim Reapers" down to strafe the field.

Ten *Intrepid* Hellcats had followed VF-10 and the last section was about to peel off when the section leader, Alex Vraciu, called out bandits about 2,500 feet above and to port. But his tally-ho went unheeded by the rest of Fighting Six. They were following Kane in a steep spiral to get at the planes parked on the field.

Al Vraciu identified the bandits as Zekes and led Ensign Lou Little in a break into the Japanese attack. The enemy leader was forced to abandon his run and dive below the two Hellcats. But Vraciu and Little were quickly surrounded by more Zekes and the hassle was on.

Vraciu led Little into a steep chandelle and came down on a Zeke which had been on their tails. The Zeke stalled out of its climbing turn and found a pair of Hellcats rolling hard behind it. When cornered in this manner the Japanese inevitably rolled over and dived for the water or attempted to dodge into the clouds. It was a fatal error, for the big Hellcats easily reeled in the Zekes during a dive. Vraciu gunned down two Zekes and a Rufe floatplane this way, all within the confines of Truk lagoon. Lou Little also got a Zeke.

Climbing back to altitude, Vraciu spotted another Zeke near a cloud and turned towards him. The Mitsubishi ducked into a cumulus cloud bank and Vraciu gave chase, occasionally catching glimpses of his quarry. After several inconclusive moments he climbed upsun and waited for the Zeke to reappear. When it did, Vraciu dropped down into the four o'clock position and closed the range before firing. Vraciu was sure the Japanese pilot never knew the Hellcat was there.

Meanwhile, VF-6 was downing a dozen more hostiles as the dawn fighter sweep erupted into the largest dogfight most of the Americans had been in. With the sun tinting the clouds reddish-white and scores of planes suddenly engaged in combat, the air over Truk reminded Fighting Five skipper Ed Owen of "a Hollywood war." As he later recalled it, "Jap airplanes were burning and falling from every quarter, and many were crashing on takeoff as a result of being strafed on the ground. Ground installations were exploding and burning, and all this in the early golden glow of dawn. At times it might have been staged for the movies."[2] Owen had more than a bit part, with two kills.

It was beautiful, it was fascinating, and it was deadly. Killer Kane and his wingman Lieutenant (jg) Vern Ude splashed five planes in five minutes before they could devote their attention to strafing.

The Japanese had barely scrambled an estimated 40 to 50 interceptors when Kane led his two squadrons in a dive towards Moen Field. The 47 low-altitude Hellcats were all engaged, with more enemy planes taking off all the time. For the next several minutes it was estimated that not 30 seconds ticked away without at least one aircraft falling somewhere over the atoll. Some F6F pilots swore they saw Japanese pilots parachuting in colorful pajamas—evidence that surprise had been achieved. But the enemy fliers were both aggressive and competent, and in the heat of combat the wrong targets sometimes got hit. Alex Vraciu saw one Hellcat shoot down another. It wasn't entirely unheard of—he'd seen similar things before—but the "victim" quickly bailed out.

Fighting Ten found the Rufes surprisingly tough opponents, despite the unwieldy floats mated to the Zero airframes. Lieutenant J. E. "Frenchy" Reulet flamed a Zeke after a short fight and then followed a Rufe into a loop and burned it at the top. He then shot a Hamp off an F6's tail and shortly thereafter was gratified to see his wingman perform a similar service by knocking a Rufe off his own tail.

Lieutenant Jack Farley, another Grim Reaper, shot one of the float fighters out of a tight turn seconds before a 20-mm shell exploded in his own cockpit, shattering the instruments and wounding Farley. He got away with a damaged Hellcat, but evidently the same unseen Rufe had shot down Ensign Linton Cox, his wingman.

The *Enterprise* Hellcats finally got through the fighters and flak to work over their target, and burned 17 planes on the ground to go with the 14 they shot out of the sky. But not everyone did so well. Sambo Silber's VF-18 saw only 16 enemy planes during the three-hour mission and could engage only half of them for one destroyed and one probable. Silber had decidedly mixed emotions about the combat: "Our fellow squadron commanders did a fantastic job of clearing the sky of the Japanese before they got over 15,000 feet. So there were almost none left for us at 20,000!"[3]

Lieutenant Commander Harry W. Harrison, an old friend and flying buddy of Silber, considered it more than equitable. As instructors the two had often argued about which one was the better fighter pilot. Silber had seven kills to his credit, including three in the course of one 360° turn during a January strike against Kavieng, and contended that this proved his superiority. But Harrison returned from Truk with his first and only victory, a Zeke, which was one of two enemy aircraft he saw during the whole war. With a batting average of .500, the VF-6 CO now claimed he was the better.

Fighting Nine also had good hunting, as the *Essex* Hellcats engaged large numbers of bandits. Eight VF-9 pilots claimed 19 enemy planes between them. Two of the pilots were Lieutenant (jg) Gene Valencia and his friend Lieutenant Bill Bonneau. Separated from one another, Valencia was set upon by half a dozen Zekes. They chased him miles out to sea, firing continually, without results. The 22-year-old Californian finally decided "they couldn't hit an elephant if it was tied down for them"[4] and racked his Hellcat around to challenge the enemy head-on. He gunned down three in short order and the others disappeared towards the horizon, making knots. Valencia returned to the *Essex* and found that Bill Bonneau had claimed four victories during their separation.

Exultant after the mission which made him an ace, Gene Valencia bubbled over with praise for the Hellcat. His remarks, widely reported in the U.S., pretty much summed up what most Navy fighter pilots felt towards the F6F: "I love this airplane so much that if it could cook I'd marry it."[5]

By the time the smoke had subsided and no more airplanes fell into the lagoon, over 30 Japanese had gone down and as many as 40 more were shot up on Moen, Eten, and Param Islands. The most spectacular fighter battle of the Pacific War to date had ended in an overwhelming American victory, with the loss of but four F6Fs. However, there were still plenty of targets left for the Hellcats escorting the incoming strikes.

During the early afternoon, Admiral Mitscher decided to eliminate enemy access to undamaged runways. Consequently, Fighting Ten launched five F6Fs, each armed with a delayed-action bomb. Their target was Moen's bomber field; other air groups struck remaining airdromes that also posed a threat. All five Hellcats put their bombs on Moen's single runway and were followed by 14 bombers. Additional Hellcats conducted a free-wheeling strafing party which left 11 single-engine planes burning in addition to the 12 bombers destroyed by dive-bombing Dauntlesses.

Most pilots flew two or even three sorties during the day. But Lieutenant (jg) Walter Harman of VF-10 was one of the few to score on two different missions. In the morning he claimed two Zekes and a Rufe. During the *Enterprise*'s afternoon strike against Moen, an odds-even dogfight developed when four Zekes jumped Harman's division as it completed a strafing run. For the next quarter-hour, Harman and a Zeke engaged in a rare one-on-one combat in which both pilots were so evenly matched that neither could gain the upper hand. At last Harman got off a burst which connected, and the Zeke crashed into a mountain.

Harman barely jumped back into the dogfight before it was too late, for Lieutenant (jg) Larry Richardson found his plane falling apart around him. Part of his windscreen was shot away, his engine had been hit, there were two large holes in one wing and another in the fuselage. A portion of his rudder was gone and the hydraulic system was out. The rugged Grumman stayed in the air long enough for Richardson to find a destroyer and splash down alongside.

Though it hardly seemed possible, Lieutenant W. M. Hampton of Harman's division had bigger trouble than Richardson. Hit during the scuffle with the Zekes, Hampton started back towards the *Enterprise* but encountered three Japanese fighters evidently on the prowl for lone stragglers or cripples. Woody Hampton definitely fit that description. With no other F6Fs around, the Mitsubishi trio—composed of a Zeke, a Hamp, and a Rufe—went after the damaged Grumman.

The Hamp got careless and passed close to port and a little above, climbing for another try. Hampton pulled up, boresighted his target, and fired. The Hamp expelled a large cloud of smoke and disappeared towards the water. Then the Zeke elected an overhead pass, but it was a fatal mistake. Hampton met him nose-to-nose and set him on fire with only three guns still firing. The Rufe gave up and left.

The dauntless Hampton finally located a destroyer and ditched nearby, but banged his head on the gunsight. Momentarily stunned, he was pulled out of the sinking Hellcat by swimmers from the ship.

The top VF-5 score was turned in by Lieutenant (jg) Bob Duncan, who got the first two Zeke kills of any F6F pilot back in October during the Wake Island raid. Escorting the *Yorktown*'s 1300 bomber strike, Duncan's division was flying rear side cover when he sighted 10 to 15 Zekes diving out of the sun from 20,000 feet. The *Yorktown*'s planes were caught at a 6,000-foot altitude disadvantage, and the Hellcats began a defensive weave.

Duncan and his wingman turned into one Zeke attacking from port. The Japanese pilot opened fire, hitting the second F6F in the fuselage, but Duncan flamed the Zeke as it passed his nose. Almost immediately he set another afire when it tried a head-on pass.

Engaging a third Zeke, the Illinois pilot scissored violently on his opponent, who then attempted to disengage by diving. Duncan caught up at 8,000 feet and this victim, too, fell in flames. While he was climbing back through 8,000 feet another Zeke attacked from 300 feet above, then rolled inverted and bored in. It looked like a suicide attempt. Duncan pulled up sharply after firing head-on, though all three port guns were inoperative. He banked around hard for another shot but the Zeke was falling in a slow graveyard spiral toward the hills of Dublon. Bob Duncan thus became the fifth pilot to score a quadruple victory over Truk.

Fighting Nine was also escorting bombers, and Commander Phil Torrey's division was the *Essex* strike's first flight over the target. As usual, his section leader was Chick Smith, the amiable North Carolinian who had brought one of the first three Hellcats to Ream Field 13 months previously. In a fierce, hard-fought dogfight, Smith claimed three victories and emerged with his Hellcat badly damaged. He tried to nurse the shot-up fighter back to the task force but couldn't quite make it. Like several other F6F pilots that day, he plunked down to a water landing and was rescued by a destroyer.

Escorting the same strike was Ham McWhorter, who spotted three bogeys in the distance. From three miles away they looked friendly, but as the SBDs dived and the strangers turned towards him, McWhorter led his wingman in for closer examination. Not until the bogeys were 3,000 feet away were they recognizable as three bizarre orange and black Zekes. The enemy leader had proper deflection on the F6s but unaccountably held his fire.

McWhorter and his number two, Lieutenant (jg) Bud Gehoe, turned in behind the Zekes. Each shot one into the water, then McWhorter wrote off the third with a single burst. All three Japanese went down inside ten seconds. Less than a mile away another Zeke was fast approaching but, like the first, inexplicably passed up a shot. Another of "One Slug" McWhorter's economical bursts set the Zeke afire and the pilot bailed out. From this brief scrap, Ham McWhorter, with ten victories, temporarily emerged as the top scorer among carrier fighter pilots. Alex Vraciu of VF-6 was right behind with nine.

Fighting Nine claimed top honors during this spectacular day of combat, with a total bag of 36 planes. Twelve of Herb Houck's pilots were now aces, not to mention Houck himself who had brought his own score to five.

At dawn there had been 365 Japanese aircraft at Truk. By 1400 the Hellcats had made a considerable dent in that number, claiming 204

Fighting Squadron Nine was the first F6F unit to complete a combat tour, leaving the USS *Essex* (CV-9) in March of 1944. Here, VF-9 pilots pose with their scoreboard, showing six Vichy French planes shot down while flying F4Fs over North Africa in 1942, as well as Japanese aircraft destroyed in the Pacific.

destroyed in the air and on the ground. Nearly 130 had been claimed on the wing, and though Japanese records only showed little over half that number downed in air combat, it was a fact that Hellcats owned the sky over Truk from early afternoon onward.

It was now becoming evident that greater destruction was done to grounded aircraft than to those that were airborne. But regardless of the relative claims, the Japanese lost some 270 aircraft, including at least 200 on the ground during the 17th and 18th. About 110 transient aircraft were destroyed at Eten Island's field alone; nearly 70 of 150 planes were destroyed at Moen.

Task Force 58's dominance was such that no Japanese aircraft were seen in the sky during the second day of the raid. In fact, by evening of the 18th there were only six operational planes left at Truk. The SBDs and TBFs went about their business, sinking 47 Japanese merchantmen, warships, and auxiliaries, completely unhindered from the air. The only enemy success came the night of the 17th when the *Intrepid* was torpedoed by a nocturnal raider, but she returned safely to Eniwetok.

U.S. aircraft losses were much lighter than had been anticipated; eight F6Fs were lost to enemy action during the two days, mostly to AA fire.

One was flown by the VF-6 exec, big, red-headed Lieutenant George C. Bullard. He already had four air and five ground kills to his credit, but outdid himself over Moen's bomber strip. In a dozen passes Bullard left six Bettys and four Zekes burning where they sat. Then he went after a light cruiser. But return fire damaged his engine, and he made a water landing too close to shore for rescue aircraft to retrieve him. When the Japanese came out and took "Bull" Bullard, they saved themselves much future grief. He remained a POW until 1945.

There were other raids on Truk in coming months, but none exceeded the first for prolonged intensity of aerial combat. As Ed Owen summarized: "Up till that time the Truk raid was the greatest show in town, and I wouldn't have missed it for anything."[6]

After Truk, the fast carriers briefly dispersed to handle various assignments in the mid Pacific. Task Groups 58.2 and 58.3 swung immediately north to take a look at the Marianas. In four months these strategically located islands would become the focal point of the Pacific war, and more intelligence was required about them.

Early in the morning of 22 February, some 40 Japanese bombers assaulted the force, losing over half their number to radar-directed AA fire and operational accidents. No ships had been hit, but the Betty attack forced an hour's delay in launching the 48-plane fighter sweep.

It was probably a blessing, as the weather proved deplorable—a 300-foot low, drizzly overcast with few breaks. Saipan, Tinian, and Rota were all scouted by Hellcat pilots who had very little reliable information about them, so they simply looked for something promising and acted accordingly. Numerous Zekes were up but the weather tended to disperse them, and in scattered dogfights during the day, 20 were shot down for the loss of five F6Fs—including those downed by flak.

Lieutenant Commander Edgar Stebbins led the *Yorktown* strikes on Saipan and Tinian, and Phil Torrey took the *Essex* squadrons into a cloud-shrouded area which his plotting board told him should include Saipan. "All of a sudden God opened a hole in the soup," he said. "I looked down, and so help me, there was the Jap airfield."[7] He called his dive bombers, informing them of the providential break over the target, but he had to persuade them to come down and take a look. Twenty planes were thought destroyed on Saipan, 70 on Tinian.

A VF-18 flight off the *Bunker Hill* took advantage of a navigational error which put the Hellcats over Guam. They fortuitously ran across a large airfield and wrecked 11 planes on the ground, then shot 4 more out of the leaden clouds.

But most of the combat occurred over the water, where a large number of Bettys and Judys threatened the task force. Nearly 40 of these bombers were shot down by the F6F CAP, but several came perilously close to some ships. One Betty passed the *Essex* 50 feet away, without a shot being fired.

Fighting Nine was experimenting with a new close-defense tactic which seemed ideally suited for such a situation. It was called "Vector Base Pronto," and was intended to simplify many last-minute interceptions by routing fighters directly to their ship in order to cut off hostiles that had penetrated the CAP.

Chick Smith had splashed a Betty within easy sight of the *Essex* when he was ordered "Vector Base Pronto, 270."[8] The troublesome Betty escaped, but task group AA gunners kept their fingers depressed on their triggers. Smith's wingman was shot down by the "friendly" gunfire. Vector Base Pronto was subsequently abandoned.

With their recon photos filed for future reference, the fast carriers made another safe getaway. Nearly 170 Japanese aircraft had been destroyed—almost 50 more than claimed. Sixty-seven of the 74 hostiles that got in the air were shot down.

The operation also marked an end to Air Group Nine's tour, making VF-9 the first Hellcat squadron to complete a combat deployment with the task force. But it would return to the Western Pacific in less than a year.

And the fast carriers would return to the Marianas.

March and April found TF-58 heavily engaged in a series of three raids in the Western Pacific. For the Hellcat these operations offered relatively little in the way of tactical innovation, but did reinforce the lessons of previous combats.

A two-day strike on the Palaus began at the end of March. The main objective was Japanese shipping, of which there was plenty. This was the farthest westward penetration the task force had yet made; the Palaus are on the same longitude as Osaka, only about 500 miles east of the Philippines. Another big dogfight along the lines of the Truk battle was widely expected.

But it didn't develop. At least not on the first day. Though the force was snooped on the way in, and a few shadowers were shot down by the CAP, only about 30 enemy fighters were met by the 72-Hellcat dawn sweep of 30 March. These included several planes of a type not previously encountered by F6Fs—Japanese Army Air Force "Oscars." The Nakajima-built fighters were similar in appearance to the Zeke but were a good 20 knots slower than the Zero at altitude. Fighting Five had little trouble with any of them and claimed ten kills upon returning to the *Yorktown*. The rest of the first day, the Hellcats devoted most of their efforts toward suppressing AA fire for the dive bombers and Avengers.

The next day air combat picked up dramatically. Over 40 enemy fighters had flown from the Philippines into the island group during the night. Hellcat pilots reported that most of the enemy planes looked factory-new, but so, apparently, were most of the Japanese pilots. Lieutenant John Gray of VF-5 declared that the most frustrating part of the hour-long combat over Palau was beating some other F6F to a bandit. Nevertheless, Gray and his wingman dropped all four of a Zeke flight between them.

Palau was the first combat for the *Bunker Hill*'s new Air Group Eight. And it was the first combat test of an amazing new device which Lieutenant Commander W. M. Collins's VF-8 employed. This was the brand-new zero-gravity, or Z-, suit. In early 1943 VF-8's tactical officer, Lieutenant E. Scott McCuskey, had been one of three instructors at Cecil Field, Florida, who tested the "zoot suit." A veteran of VF-42 at Coral Sea and Midway with six and one-half kills, McCuskey immediately recognized the value of the suit, which allowed him to pull about one and a half more Gs than he normally could without graying out. The result, of course, was improved maneuverability for almost no weight increase. The suits, with air-activated bladders over the pilot's calves, thighs, and abdomen, weighed about five pounds, and required only minor modifications to the F6Fs to install the air system.

When McCuskey reported to VF-8 in June 1943 at NAAS Pungo, Virginia, he inquired about the Z-suits and was told they were unavailable. The west coast evaluation team had recommended against their use. But McCuskey remembered meeting the manufacturers of the experimental suits he had tested, and wasted no time. "I called the Berger Brothers in Hartford, Connecticut, whom I had met at Cecil Field, and they personally provided the suits," he recalls. "Permission was granted by the Navy to equip the F6Fs in VF-8 with the anti-blackout equipment."[9] Thus did Fighting Eight become the only Hellcat squadron to receive semiofficial sanction for G-suits.

But acceptance was slow in coming. Some of the young VF-8 pilots were uncertain about using such a strange new piece of equipment. McCuskey figured the best way to get a vegetarian to eat a steak is to give him a taste. So he challenged every pilot in the squadron to a mock dogfight, he wearing his zoot suit, they without one. None could stay on his tail through mind-blurring three-to-five-G maneuvers. Scotty McCuskey made his point. All but three of VF-8's 49 pilots elected to wear the suit by the end of training.

After the first few days of combat, even the three holdouts changed their minds. And small wonder. In the squadron's initial dogfight over Palau, the *Bunker Hill* fighters racked up a score of 11 kills and 3 probables without a loss. McCuskey got two of the victories.

That evening, Lieutenant Commander Bob Winston of VF-31 was on CAP when his division was vectored 75 miles west of the task force to investigate a bogey. The four Hellcats found nine bandits inbound, flying in three "V of Vs." Winston identified them as Zekes and immediately attacked. He shot down the Japanese leader and his two wingmen in about ten seconds before he realized they were not Zekes, but Judy dive bombers. Lieutenant (jg) Conny Nooy also splashed three, and the other two *Cabot* pilots finished the remaining four as the sun set. This combat brought the raid's two-day total to 93 claimed aerial victories, including 29 by Fighting Five and 25 by VF-30 off the *Monterey* in the last operation of its tour.

The next day was the third in a row of sweeps, strikes, and patrols as Mitscher turned directly east to hit the nearby Western Carolines. In missions over Yap, Ulithi, and Woleai, Hellcats gunned down 18 more Japanese planes. The final official count—probably not much exaggerated —was 111 aerial victories and 46 planes destroyed on the ground. Only three U.S. planes were lost in air combat, though antiaircraft fire raised Hellcat losses to eleven.

After only a week for rest and refit at Majuro, the fast carriers again sortied for the Southwest Pacific. Their task was to neutralize Japanese air power on New Guinea's north coast around Tanahmerah Bay. Army troops were due to wade ashore at Hollandia on 22 April, so the carrier air groups began working over the area on D-Day Minus One. Aerial opposition was scanty—only 30 kills were claimed in the next four days, and the major F6F activity was ground support.

Flying on the inland side of the coastal mountain range on D-Day was a formation of *Lexington* and *Enterprise* fighters, searching for apparently nonexistent Japanese aircraft. One of the VF-16 division leaders was Lieutenant Francis M. Fleming, the *Lexington* pilot who had been sweating out his ace rating for the past five months. Since the two-day back-to-back dogfights near the Gilberts in November, Fleming's score had remained at four and one-half victories. Today didn't look at all promising.

But luck was where one found it, and Fleming noticed a Japanese twin-engine bomber being harried at treetop level by two F6Fs. He tally-hoed the hostile and dived to the attack from 12,000 feet. His approach gave him a perfect quartering run from starboard as he opened fire at maximum range. "I made a slight correction after observing my tracers going over the plane, then I hit the Sally in the mid-fuselage and wing-root area. The plane immediately caught fire in the right wing tank and engine nacelle."[10]

Fleming pulled out below and behind the Sally, which then dived into the ground and exploded on impact. He was now an ace—with half a victory to spare.

Only two Hellcats were lost to enemy action during the Hollandia operation, both to AA fire. Though air combat remained sparse, 103 enemy aircraft were thought destroyed on the ground by carrier planes. The actual tally was uncertain because a great many had obviously been shot up or bombed earlier by U.S. Army aircraft.

If the Hollandia operation was something of a disappointment to the Hellcat squadrons, they could have cheered up. The fast carriers were going back to Truk.

More than two months had passed since the first Truk raid, and in the interim Japanese air strength had been partially rebuilt. By 29 April, slightly over 100 aircraft were operational on the atoll's airfields—far short of the number which had been mauled during mid-February, but respectable nonetheless. As a result, 62 Zekes were airborne when two divisions of VF-32 off the *Langley* (CVL-27) arrived in the early morning light of the 29th, well in advance of the main sweep of 24 bomb-toting fighters from the *Enterprise* and *Lexington*.

Fortunately for Lieutenant Commander Eddie Outlaw's *Langley* pilots, low thick clouds prevented the Japanese from organizing properly, and his formation had to deal directly with "only" 30 or so Zekes.

Approaching the lagoon at 10,000 feet, Outlaw orbited his eight planes for ten minutes to size up the situation. Then his second division leader, Lieutenant Hollis Hills, sighted a strange formation eight miles to the west at about 6,000 feet, heading toward the Hellcats. Hills's flight remained as top cover while Outlaw went down to investigate with his own division.

The 25 to 30 Zekes were flying three-plane vees, but the formation abruptly scattered when enemy pilots at the rear opened fire, warning the others. Outlaw's Hellcats waded into the Japanese from starboard with a 2,000-foot altitude advantage, and all four F6Fs scored in the first pass.

The Japanese showed no air discipline or planned tactics other than two Lufbery circles, one above the other. Outlaw dropped on to the tails of three Zekes in succession and burned them from almost dead astern. Lieutenant (jg) Donald Reeves also bagged three more Zekes, two of which exploded or flamed. Then Hills came down from above, lined up a Zeke and fired into the cockpit. He passed by close enough to see "the pilot's head practically shot off."[11] While Outlaw was engaged in his own shooting, Hills knocked two more off his skipper's tail and also claimed one probable. Outlaw then shot down another Zeke, his fifth of the battle.

The two divisions were able to remain in range of one another for mutual support all through the combat, depriving the Zekes of any chance to destroy the Hellcats piecemeal. Outlaw's element leader was tall, lanky Lieutenant (jg) Richard H. May, a debonair Oregonian who burned or exploded three bandits. May also hit three others which fell into the overcast and went unclaimed. His wingman, Ensign John Pond, claimed a pair.

Fighting 32 had recorded a lopsided victory, with 20 destroyed and two probables for one F6F damaged. Eddie Outlaw became an ace in this one combat, and Dick May ran his own score to five, counting two snoopers he had dispatched off Eniwetok and Woleai. But in one respect the most remarkable performance was that of Hills. The dark-haired

This VF-16 pilot flew his shot-up Hellcat back to the *Lexington* after the second Truk raid, 29 April 1944. Note the large shell holes and smoke stains on the port wing.

Californian may have been the only American pilot of the war to gain confirmed victories against both major Axis powers while in the service of two countries. His first combat had come nearly two years before when, flying with an RCAF squadron in the Dieppe Raid of August 1942, he shot down a Focke-Wulf 190. It was the first victory scored by North American's famous P-51 series, as Hills had then flown the Allison-powered Mustang I built for the Royal Air Force.

Another noteworthy event of the day was two Zekes shot down by Alex Vraciu. He had scored four kills over Truk in the first raid, but when VF-6 rotated home Vraciu transferred to VF-16 for more combat. When he had landed aboard the *Lexington* for the first time, his Hellcat sported an "A" gasoline ration sticker on the canopy. The "A" coupon allowed wartime motorists four gallons of gasoline per week. It took 400 gallons to fill a Hellcat with drop tank attached!

The second Truk raid lasted into the next day, but with little more air combat. The final claim was 65 aerial victories and 85 bombed or strafed to destruction on the ground. The aerial claim was quite accurate, as Japanese records showed 59 of their planes shot down, but they admitted to only 34 destroyed on the airfields. Five carrier planes were lost in the air and 21 fell to the always-dangerous flak. But by now it was apparent that Truk was mastered. No important ships were found, and when the carriers departed only a dozen or so enemy aircraft were left operational at Japan's once-proud Gibralter of the Pacific.

Now the path was clear to the Marianas.

Hellcat Squadrons in Combat: January to April 1944

VF-2	*Hornet*	Commander William A. Dean, Jr.
VF-5	*Yorktown*	Lieutenant Commander Edward M. Owen
VF-6	*Intrepid*	Lieutenant Commander Harry W. Harrison, Jr.
VF-8	*Bunker Hill*	Lieutenant Commander William M. Collins, Jr.
VF-9	*Essex*	Lieutenant Commander Herbert N. Houck
VF-10	*Enterprise*	Lieutenant Commander William R. Kane, Lieutenant R.W. Schumann
VF-12	*Saratoga*	Lieutenant Commander Robert G. Dose
VF-18	*Bunker Hill*	Lieutenant Commander Sam L. Silber
VF-23	*Princeton*	Commander Henry L. Miller
VF-24	*Belleau Wood*	Lieutenant Commander Edward M. Link
VF-25	*Cowpens*	Lieutenant Robert H. Price
VF-30	*Monterey*	Lieutenant Commander J.G. Sliney
VF-31	*Cabot*	Lieutenant Commander Robert A. Winston
VF-32	*Langley*	Lieutenant Commander Edward C. Outlaw

4 The Marianas Campaign

O suns and skies and clouds of June,
Helen Hunt Jackson

The 15 fast carriers of Task Force 58 brought some 475 Hellcats to the Marianas in the second week of June 1944. Another 66 F6Fs were aboard three of the five escort carriers assigned to support the invasion beachheads in Operation Forager. It was by far the largest Hellcat gathering to date; nearly 550 of them embarked in 18 CVs, CVLs, and CVEs. To naval historians the forthcoming confrontation would be the First Battle of the Philippine Sea. To Hellcat pilots and nearly everyone else, it would always be the "Great Marianas Turkey Shoot."

D-Day in Normandy had come and gone by the time Admiral Mitscher's seven CVs and eight CVLs were in position to open Forager. But D-Day for Saipan wasn't until the 15th, allowing the Hellcats four days to gain air supremacy over the Marianas, the last of the major Central Pacific island groups to be captured before the Philippines. As it turned out, two days would be sufficient.

Mitscher's staff was aware that by now the Japanese were accustomed to dawn fighter sweeps as the forerunner to amphibious invasion, and they devised a new schedule to throw the enemy off guard. Ordinarily the first sweep would have been launched on the morning of 12 June, but instead it was advanced to early afternoon of the 11th. And it was none too soon, for a Japanese snooper spotted the task force that morning. Four intruders were downed during the noon hour by the CAP.

Then at 1300 the fast carriers, steaming into a 14-knot wind, began launching 208 Hellcats. The large flattops each sent off four divisions; the *Independence*-class ships sent three divisions each, in a fairly complex plan. The *Hornet, Yorktown, Belleau Wood,* and *Bataan* of Rear Admiral Jocko Clark's TG-58.1 were assigned targets at Guam. Rear Admiral Alfred Montgomery's 58.2 and Rear Admiral J. W. Reeves's 58.3 took Saipan and Tinian, while the smallest task group, Rear Admiral W. K. Harrill's 58.4, with the *Essex, Langley,* and *Cowpens,* shared Tinian and had Pagan to themselves. The Marianas lie nearly north-south, and the distance from Saipan to Guam is almost 150 miles. Pagan to Guam is even farther. It meant the Hellcats were launched 180 to 240 miles from their targets.

In the widespread dogfights that resulted, claims were made for over 70 aerial victories. About half the day's total was contributed by the *Hornet's* VF-2, reunited with its air group since March. The skipper, Commander Bill Dean, led his troops over Guam and attacked airfields there, but his attention was diverted when Lieutenant (jg) Howard B. Duff was shot down by AA fire. Cruising at about 1,000 feet, attempting to guide SB2Cs to Duff so they could drop life rafts, Dean was alerted by Lieutenant (jg) J. T. Wolf's "Heads up."[1]

Nearly 30 bandits jumped VF-2 below the 2,000-foot overcast. A pair of Zekes came down behind the lead division, but Dean and his wingman

Lieutenant (jg) Davy Park did simultaneous right and left chandelles into the attack and set both assailants on fire. Dean also chased a Tojo in a climb, catching up by using water injection, and burned it. He then bagged another Zeke for a total of five and one-half kills since November. Wolf claimed three Zekes, and the squadron tally for this battle was 21 Zekes and two Tojos.

But VF-2 wasn't finished for the day. The *Hornet*'s CAP picked off three Bettys above a picket destroyer, and a second sweep-strike to Guam netted seven Zekes, two Tojos, and an Irving without a loss. Another Irving late that afternoon boosted Fighting Two's total claims for the 11th to 37, the only loss being Duff's Hellcat.

Three VF-31 divisions flew top cover under Lieutenant Doug Mulcahy, the only *Cabot* pilot on the sweep with a previous score. The 12 Hellcats claimed 13 and two probables destroyed in the air—with three pilots scoring doubles—and four wrecked on the ground. The only loss was Ensign R. G. Whitworth's plane. The young flier was fished out of the ocean three days later.

The *Belleau Wood*'s VF-24 made only one kill near Guam, but it was encouraging anyway. A four-plane division sighted a lone Zeke north of the island and gave chase, spotting the bandit a three-mile head start. The F6 pilots poured on 55 inches of manifold pressure and 2,700 RPM, indicating 240 knots. After an eight-mile low-level tailchase, the Hellcats hauled into gun range, even though three kept their drop tanks and the Zeke jettisoned its own. The Zeke outmaneuvered individual Hellcats at 200 knots airspeed, but was boxed in and Lieutenant (jg) R. H. Thelen made the kill. It was further proof that the F6F was considerably faster than its primary opponent.

Another single victory during the day was notable, but for a different reason. Farther north, near Saipan, the CAG of the *Essex*'s new Air Group 15 saw a lone Zeke drop out of the cloud cover. Commander David Mc-Campbell, a former intercollegiate diving champion from the Annapolis class of '33, instantly turned towards the Mitsubishi and fired three bursts. The Zeke went down streaming smoke, the first in what would become a long, long string for the CAG.

McCampbell's initial success in aerial combat was met with a professional's cool detachment: "I knew I could shoot him down, and I did. That's all there was to it."[2] It was something of an understatement, for like all squadron commanders and CAGs, Dave McCampbell had had extensive practice. A naval aviator since 1938, he had assumed command of VF-15 in September 1943 and moved up to air group commander while in training aboard the new *Hornet* in February. McCampbell had some 2,000 hours of total flight time, including 800 in F6Fs, when he led Air Group 15 on its first combat mission against Marcus Island on 19 May.

During that strike his Hellcat was so badly shot up it was pushed overboard upon landing.

Eleven F6Fs were lost on 11 June, though three pilots were recovered. Lieutenant Commander Robert H. Price suffered two weeks of drifting, scorching tedium in a raft before he was finally rescued. His F6F had gone down while leading a *Cowpens* attack upon a Japanese convoy northwest of Saipan. But enemy air power in the Marianas was so depleted that Mitscher's fighters claimed only a dozen victories the next day. By the 13th, D-Minus Two, the Hellcats owned the sky over the islands. The Japanese had no recourse but to attempt funneling aircraft into the Marianas via Iwo Jima to the north and the Carolines to the south.

The former possibility had been anticipated, as Iwo Jima and the Bonins were almost exactly halfway between the Marianas and Japan—an excellent staging area. Task Groups 58.1 and 58.4 were ordered northward to strike these bases on the 15th and 16th, despite the forecast of poor weather over the targets.

The meteorological pessimists proved accurate. When launch position was reached in the early afternoon of the 15th, low ceilings and limited visibility greeted the fliers, who also had to contend with a fairly rough sea. But launch commenced 135 miles east of Iwo Jima, and 44 Hellcats in three formations set out to bomb and strafe Iwo's two fields before the SB2Cs and TBMs arrived.

About 100 Japanese aircraft were based on Iwo, but only 38 were scrambled in time to intercept the unexpected Hellcats, so the odds were nearly even. The combat wasn't. Fighting One, newly arrived aboard the *Yorktown*, and Fighting Two from the *Hornet* had things almost entirely to themselves, destroying nearly all the airborne Zekes.

First over the target was VF-1, in its first large combat. The CO, "Smoke" Strean, led his division down from 10,000 feet in a 50° dive, dropping fragmentation bombs and strafing revetted fighters. Strean himself caught a Zeke taking off and dropped it from 300 feet, then two of his four divisions tangled with the late-reacting enemy fighters.

Lieutenant Paul M. Henderson's three-plane division claimed half of VF-1's total of 20 kills. Henderson and Lieutenant (jg) J. R. Meharg were both credited with four Zekes, but Henderson was lost from sight after shooting the last one off the tail of his number three, Ensign A. P. Morner. Morner claimed a double and returned to the *Yorktown* with Meharg but Pablo Henderson never showed up. Another Fighting One Hellcat was lost to antiaircraft fire.

Seven *Hornet* F6Fs were next on the scene, led by Lieutenant Lloyd G. Barnard. Commander Bill Dean had democratically sent only pilots without victories to Iwo for a chance to catch up. They made the most of the opportunity. In the next 25 minutes, Barnard exploded three Zekes and shot two more into the water. Lieutenant (jg) Myrvin E. Noble and Lieutenant (jg) Charles H. Carroll both claimed three apiece, and the other four pilots accounted for six more. Barnard remembered Zeros "blowing up all over the place,"[3] but only two of his F6Fs received minor battle damage. The one loss was Noble's Hellcat, irreparably damaged in landing aboard in heavy seas.

By the time Fighting 15 arrived, there were only three Zekes available and the *Essex* pilots got them all. Thus, the claims were 40 "confirmed" kills—an obvious exaggeration—but even so the Japanese recorded the loss of nearly all their airborne fighters. During the rest of the day Hellcats, Avengers, and Helldivers concentrated on destroying parked aircraft.

Poor weather prevented air operations all morning of the 16th. Shortly after noon, however, strikes were resumed on facilities at Iwo and Chichi Jima. Flak brought total U.S. aircraft losses to 12, but Japanese air strength in the Bonins-Jimas was annihilated. The bomb-cratered runways would be quickly repaired, but no aircraft from Iwo would get to the Marianas in time to contest the invasion. Rear Admirals Clark and Harrill took their task groups back south for the main event.

Things had been relatively quiet in their absence. One of the few squadrons to find combat over the Marianas on the 15th was VF-51 off the *San Jacinto*, "Flagship of the Texas Navy." Commander Charles L. Moore's pilots accounted for seven confirmed and a probable. Three were Tonys downed by the unit's top scorer, Lieutenant W. R. Maxwell, whose division had splashed a pair of snoopers on the 11th. It was a welcome change of fortune for Bob Maxwell, whose first combat tour had been cut short on his fifth mission from Guadalcanal one year earlier. His VF-11 Wildcat lost its tail in a mid-air collision, and he spent two weeks making his way to safety from Japanese-controlled waters. The Marianas campaign was to be equally significant to the *San Jacinto* fighters, for during June VF-51 would gain 21 of its total 29 victories.

Aerial opposition remained skimpy even after D-Day, but that didn't lessen the risk. The *Enterprise* CAG, W. R. "Killer" Kane, discovered that the hard way on the 16th. As the day's first target coordinator, Kane arrived over the landing force west of Saipan with a wingman at 0540, before daylight. Suddenly Kane's F6F was jarred violently by an AA shell which exploded just under his port wing. Gasoline and smoke spewed from the Hellcat as more shells burst all around. The two fighters were 25 miles offshore, under fire from American ships.

Kane's first instinct was to bail out. But when he determined his engine was still running, he decided to dive out of range. Too late. Another AA barrage cut him off, and with zero oil pressure he plunked his riddled Hellcat down into the waves with a jarring deceleration which knocked his head forward into the gunsight.

Despite a nasty gash on the forehead, Kane scrambled into his rubber raft and watched his F6 sink as the sun rose. He was rescued 30 minutes later, unmollified by the knowledge that American gunners could knock down a plane with their first round. What was worse, Kane would be off flight status for three days, recovering from his injury. It had been a full three months since his first three kills as CO of VF-10 at Truk, and now with a fleet engagement in sight, he was grounded.

Admiral Spruance, in overall command of Forager, knew from submarine reports that a large Japanese task force was approaching the Marianas to contest the landings. There was little activity on Sunday the 18th, except that eight *Belleau Wood* Hellcats over Guam were bounced by about 15 Zekes, seven of which were downed by VF-24, including three to Lieutenant (jg) Bob Thelen. But it seemed fairly certain that the next day would see the war's fifth carrier battle, and Mitscher's people fumed at the orders which kept the task force tied down within 100 miles of the islands, guarding the beaches.

The Imperial Japanese Navy mustered nine flattops—five CVs and four CVLs—in three carrier divisions under Vice Admiral Jisaburo Ozawa. They embarked nearly 450 aircraft, of which half were Zekes: 145 fighters and 80 modified for dive-bombing. Thus, except for some Japanese Army Air Force planes which flew up to Guam from the Carolines, it would be a classic Zero-versus-Hellcat fighter battle. The Japanese 601st, 652nd, and 653rd Air Groups also included 99 Judy dive bombers, 87 Jill torpedo planes, and 39 of the familiar Vals and Kates.

No Hellcats or Helldivers had ever flown against enemy carriers, but almost 60 percent of the Japanese formations were composed of the same aircraft types which had begun the war at Pearl Harbor. Though large numbers of Japanese land-based aircraft brought the total air strength on both sides to about parity, Japanese coordination was poor; the Americans would deal with the seaborne and land-based threats separately. And at sea, the fast carriers stocked fully as many Hellcats as Ozawa's total strength.

In addition to these advantages, the F6F pilots possessed a less tangible but even more crucial edge. Though six fighter squadrons (VF-1, VF-14, VF-15, VF-27, VF-28, and VF-51) were relatively new to combat, the Hellcat pilots had had extensive, thorough training. Not so their adversaries. Excluding a smattering of veteran fliers, the Japanese squadrons were composed of aviators who could take off and land aboard carriers and fly formation. The tactical aspects of their training had been necessarily brief, and this would show up in the results they obtained. In the

Marianas the Imperial Navy would pay for its catastrophic personnel losses at Midway and the Solomons.

Still, the enemy air groups were to be reckoned with. Launched in sufficient strength, large formations stood a chance of penetrating the American CAP by sheer force of numbers. The full force of Hellcats could never be committed at any one time, nor even a majority of them. Ample reserves waiting on deck and those being refueled and rearmed would necessarily amount to at least two-thirds of the available F6Fs. As things developed, intercepting Hellcats would invariably be outnumbered. The equalizing factors were advance radar warning, superior pilot and aircraft performance, and carefully cultivated air discipline.

Daylight on the 19th brought beautiful flying weather. It was a bright, warm morning with a 10-knot easterly breeze. Ceiling and visibility were unlimited—perfect conditions for defending fighter pilots who, even with radar guidance, had to eyeball their targets as soon as possible. The few scattered low clouds would be no help to large formations seeking cover in them, and telltale contrails would form as low as 20,000 feet.

In so complex a military art as carrier warfare, the importance of communications was impossible to overestimate, and the upcoming battle had caught the U.S. carriers at an inopportune time. Only two fighter-direction channels were common to all four task groups, because radio equipment was being updated in the task force. The situation would demand that pilots suppress their radio chatter if tactical information were to be relayed.

Even more responsibility was borne by the four junior officers who were responsible for fighter direction of each task group. The force FDO was Lieutenant Joseph R. Eggert aboard the *Lexington*. A young reservist like the other FDOs, Eggert had been a New York stockbroker in civilian life. On this day his management skills would be fully tested. The experience, skill, and judgment of these young men was all-important, for they would actually be in tactical control of the largest carrier duel in history.

While Avenger search planes were out hunting the Japanese carriers, the day's first contact occurred. At about 0530 the task force radar picked up a blip west of the southernmost group, Montgomery's 58.2. A division of VF-28 from the light carrier *Monterey* was already airborne on Vector CAP and was sent out to have a look. The division leader, Lieutenant (jg) W. T. Fitzpatrick, sighted two Judys in tight step-down echelon only 30 miles west of the *Monterey*, probably land-based recon planes from Guam. Fitzpatrick and his wingman attacked from a 500-foot altitude advantage, diving from starboard in a 30° high side run.

Fitzpatrick fired and hit the lead Judy forward of the cockpit, continuing his dive below and to port. The second section of Hellcats saw the Judy pull up, roll inverted, and spin into the water. Immediately, the second Judy split-essed into some convenient clouds at 4,000 feet and was lost from sight, and after having drawn first blood the F6Fs were recalled to base.

Less than an hour later, a VF-24 division was dispatched to Orote airfield to investigate a suspicious radar contact. The four Hellcats encountered numerous airborne Zekes—evidence that the Japanese were sending aircraft north from Truk and Yap. The *Belleau Wood* pilots hollered for help and attacked, claiming ten shot down for one F6F damaged. This combat began a series of strung-out scraps which involved 33 more Hellcats until 0930. During the hour or so of on-again, off-again dogfights over and around Guam, these fighters claimed 30 Zekes and five bombers. But the F6 pilots reported more bandits taking off and many more still on the ground. Mitscher concluded that his force was "probably due for a working over by both land-based and carrier-based planes,"[4] and shortly before 1000 the fighters over Guam were recalled to the task force by the radioed phrase, "Hey Rube," first used by the old *Lexington* in early 1942.

At almost the same time, radar picked up enemy aircraft orbiting at 20,000 feet about 100 miles to the west. The general alarm was sounded at 1004, and 140 additional Hellcats were scrambled in 15 minutes to join the nearly 60 on CAP.

The battleship *Alabama*'s radar had estimated the strength of this first strike at about 50 aircraft, bearing 265° True. Actually, there were over 60: 14 Zeke fighters escorting 43 Zeke fighter-bombers and seven speedy Jill torpedo planes. Commander Charles W. Brewer, skipper of VF-15, was first on the spot, about 55 miles out. He called the tally-ho at 1035. The hostiles were flying at 18,000 feet, and from 6,000 feet above them Brewer maneuvered his two divisions for the attack. Three minutes after the tally-ho, Brewer rolled into a dive and in a few short minutes shot down three Zekes and a "Judy." His wingman Ensign Richard E. Fowler got separated while meeting an attack from port but shifted for himself, claiming four Zekes. Five of VF-15's other 12 kills were made by Lieutenant (jg) George R. Carr, who, like Brewer, identified the Jills as Judy dive bombers.

In the next 25 minutes, 54 more Hellcats from seven squadrons piled in. To say the affair was one-sided is to understate the matter considerably. Only three minutes after VF-15 struck, Commander Bill Dean and seven other VF-2 pilots dropped down from 27,000 feet. They picked off nine Zekes and three of the Jills which split away from the main formation. The surviving Jills poked their round noses down and outdistanced the F6F-3s, though eight *Cowpens* fighters chased after them.

The "Rippers" of VF-2 frankly considered this batch of Zekes "the best we've met." Back aboard the *Hornet,* Dean told his air intelligence officer, "I was fighting for my life for almost an hour out there."[5]

The larger formation was harried and chopped to pieces by F6Fs from VF-25, VF-27, VF-28, and VF-31 for about 20 miles. Aboard the *Cabot,* Lieutenant Commander Bob Winston won a footrace with two of his ensigns for the last available Hellcat and was nearly hit by two falling Japanese planes as he launched. He had not scored since the end of March and was nearly wild with frustration, intensified when he was only able to find a formation of SBDs circling clear of the fight.

The remnants were picked over by VF-8, VF-10, and VF-51. Only a few Japanese pressed on, and even then their efforts were wasted on the battleship task group. The *South Dakota* took a hit which did little harm. Twenty Zekes and two Jills survived.

In exchange for 42 enemy aircraft destroyed, three Hellcats and their pilots were lost, one from VF-25 and two from the *Princeton*'s VF-27. The latter formation was led by the CAG, Lieutenant Commander Ernest W. Wood, a gifted pianist fond of playing "Claire de Lune." Wood went into a vertical dive on an enemy formation and began a rolling pullout when his horizontal stabilizers sheared off under the exceptional stress. His Annapolis classmate, Fred Bardshar, exec of VF-27, took over.

Raid Two got considerably closer before it was intercepted. But again it was VF-15, this time led by CAG Dave McCampbell, that made first contact. At 1140 McCampbell's 11 Hellcats bounced 109 Zekes, Jills, and shark-mouthed Judys only 40 miles west of Task Group 58.7, the battle-wagons. The *Essex* fighters mauled the big formation for six minutes before 43 more Hellcats arrived.

McCampbell took the Judys which were stacked above the Jills, and his other eight planes handled the Zeke top cover. Actually, the CAG never did see the enemy fighters; he was too busy shooting down five Judys. The first one "exploded practically in my face," he reported.[6] The force of the *Essex* fighters' attack was spectacular. When he had time to look around, McCampbell saw the unforgettable sight of a line of splashes in the water where Japanese airplanes had crashed, and vari-colored parachutes floating on the surface.

Then the reinforcements arrived. The largest contingent was 23 of the *Lexington*'s VF-16, backed up by three divisions of VF-14 off the *Wasp* and two divisions of VF-27 from the *Princeton.* Lieutenant Commander Paul Buie led most of his Airdales in a high-power cruise which left five of his pilots in its wake with various mechanical difficulties.

One was Alex Vraciu, who found his supercharger would not shift into high blower. He reported to the FDO and was vectored onto a strung-out line of Judy dive bombers. In a fast eight minutes the Indiana ace caught up with and shot down six, chasing the last two right into task force AA fire. Vraciu's squadron mates splashed 16 more in the 25 minutes before noon.

Fred Bardshar had been sunbathing after an uneventful CAP when another scramble was ordered aboard the *Princeton*. He launched with two divisions in such a hurry that he was climbing through 10,000 feet before he got around to fastening his parachute pack to his harness. When a head-on interception occurred at 14,000 feet, the *Princeton* pilots noted that the top-cover Zekes were strangely inactive. Bardshar quickly shot down one bomber, then was drawn out of the fight by a diving bandit which he flamed at about 7,000 feet. By the time he regrouped, it was all over. The running battle had progressed farther east. Fighting 27's current top scorer, Lieutenant Dick Stambook, had downed two Zekes and a pair of Judys.

Again the enemy's remnants split their forces, attempting a forked attack on the battleships and two of the carrier groups. This phase of Raid Two was dominated by 21 *Yorktown* Hellcats in three formations. CAG-1, Commander J. M. Peters, took six F6Fs with him, while the fighter skipper, Smoke Strean, sailed in with ten more. A five-plane division rounded things out for VF-1. In an up-and-down combat, Peters's and Strean's pilots chased vectors from 30,000 feet down to 5,000 and back up again, claiming 32 of the 35 Zekes encountered. Lieutenant R. T. Eastmond splashed four Zekes and four other VF-1 pilots claimed three apiece. Strean got a double.

Though small attacks were made on four individual carriers, no significant damage was done. Again, barely 20 enemy aircraft returned to their ships in exchange for four Hellcats shot down and three pilots killed. Fighting 1, 14, and 15 all lost a plane and pilot while a VF-8 pilot bailed out. Additionally, VF-1 had to jettison a second Hellcat with extensive battle damage and another F6 ditched but the pilot was rescued. Ninety-four Japanese planes were claimed from Raid Two.

At 1230 the radarscopes were clear and most airborne fighters were instructed to land and refuel. But 12 minutes later a bogey showed up, and some VF-10 fighters were given a vector less than 40 miles out. First on the scene, however, was Lieutenant William B. Lamb, the new VF-27 exec, flying by himself after bagging two torpedo planes early in the raid. The Californian paced the 12 Jills, keeping out of gun range while reporting their position and asking for help. Then, often with only one gun firing, he made repeated runs on the formation and sent three spinning towards the ocean. To Fred Bardshar it was "a bit like Sergeant

York's shooting up the WW I German patrol—one at a time, like turkeys, from the rear!"[7] The rest of the Judys, which had been behind and below the main enemy formation, were broken up by other Hellcats.

Raid Three actually failed to develop as such. The strike's 27 bombers failed to find the U.S. carriers, but its 20 escorting Zekes were reported by *Yorktown* radar at about 1245. As the VF-1 CAP was now patrolling well to the west, the *Hornet*'s controller took over and vectored three divisions to intercept. The 17 Hellcats claimed 14 kills, and though Japanese records indicated the actual loss was half as many, the enemy were dispersed. The only harm suffered by the F6Fs was slight 20-mm damage to a VF-2 plane.

Admiral Ozawa's fourth and last raid was deployed in three parts, and nearly all its 82 aircraft were destroyed. Eighteen enemy planes aborted after searching in vain 100 miles southwest of Guam. An erroneous contact report had led them astray. While returning to their carriers, the ten Zekes and eight Jills came across a *Lexington* search team of two TBMs and a Hellcat. The Air Group 16 pilots turned into the attack, calling for assistance from the team in the next sector. By the time help arrived, at least three Zekes had already gone down, and the fight ended with another three claimed destroyed.

The balance of the Japanese 652nd Air Group turned for Guam and Rota in two formations. Fifteen of them hove into sight of TG-58.2 and made ineffective glide-bombing runs on the *Wasp* and *Bunker Hill*. Both carriers were recovering aircraft—an unenviable time to be attacked—but the enemy pilots failed to score. Though this formation escaped the attention of any Hellcats, five planes fell to shipboard gunfire.

Forty-nine planes of the third portion of Raid Four arrived over Orote on Guam, but 30 were spared the trouble of landing. The 27 Vals, 20 Zekes, and two Kates were met by a delegation of 41 Hellcats representing four carriers. It was all over in a few minutes.

Eight *Hornet* Hellcats, including three night fighters of VFN-76, had the best of the shooting. Ensign Wilbur W. Webb of VF-2 was circling a downed flier in the water west of Orote when he looked up and saw a large formation inbound. He was low over the water, and "all I could do was to enter the traffic circle at Orote Field and slip in behind."[8] Quickly he shot down one flight of three Vals and then two of the next three. He picked off one of the following division in a head-on run at 1,500 feet. That made six kills, but Webb lost two others he had smoking when other Hellcats cut in, forcing him to break off.

Lieutenant Russell L. Reiserer, a *Hornet* night fighter pilot, had much the same experience. Joining the landing pattern, he dropped wheels and flaps to stay with the fixed-gear Vals and methodically shot down five. Two other *Hornet* pilots accounted for a Zeke, a Kate, and a Val.

Dave McCampbell was back in the air, leading seven other *Essex* fighters into the milling, confused enemy air group after detouring to Rota where nothing was doing. Back over Guam he found "all the action we could safely handle."[9] The two VF-15 divisions were jumped by several Zekes and McCampbell bagged one; then he went after another by himself, intentionally violating his own tactical doctrine in the interest of operational research, as it were. Ever curious and willing to experiment, the CAG wanted to find out if an F6F with its drop tank attached could catch a Zeke on the deck—he'd been told that it couldn't.

As VF-24 could have attested from a few days before, the F6F-3 carrying a drop tank could in fact overhaul a Zeke down low. But as soon as McCampbell drew a bead on his quarry the Japanese pulled up, did a left wingover, and quickly reversed the situation. "I was unable to turn with him, so I dropped my belly tank, lowered my seat to get behind the armor plate and headed back for Orote, where hopefully I could find some friends," McCampbell remembered. "I called out that I would be passing Orote in about four minutes at 1,000 feet and that anyone not occupied, please come down and knock the Jap off my tail! Three Hellcats did."[10]

Heading for rendezvous, the CAG came across one of his planes with a Zeke on its tail. McCampbell shot the bandit out of its beautifully executed slow roll. At dawn he'd had two victories to his credit. Now he had nine.

The *Cowpens*, *San Jacinto*, and *Enterprise* fighters also got in some shooting before the air cleared. Of the 19 Japanese planes which succeeded in landing at Orote, nearly all were damaged beyond repair or were wrecked on the ground. Nine returned to their ships. Raid Four had been massacred at a cost of two Hellcats—one each from VF-10 and VF-51.

Fighter sweeps continued over the islands until dark. Fighting 15 was responsible for part of the island CAP, and on arriving back at the *Essex* McCampbell found Commander Brewer just launching with two divisions for Guam. The VF-15 CO called the ship, asking if that were all the fighters the task group could provide. The reply was affirmative. Hearing this, McCampbell contacted Brewer and advised him that the air over Guam was full of bandits, and that he "had better go in with plenty of altitude and be extra cautious."[11]

Brewer was over Orote at 1825 and attacked some Judys trying to land. He got one, but in doing so he lost his altitude advantage and was bounced by several Zekes. Brewer and his wingman were both killed, two of the three VF-15 pilots lost during the 19th.

Earlier in the day, Paul Buie had been listening to *Lexington* intelligence officers debriefing some of his VF-16 pilots. One exultant youngster compared the lopsided air battle to "an old-time turkey shoot."[12] Buie repeated the remark to Mitscher, and the phrase immediately caught on.

Thirteen hours after it began, the Great Marianas Turkey Shoot was over.

What was the score?

The single best-known and possibly best-documented air battle in history remains difficult to pin down. Japanese aircraft losses on 19 June are known to have totaled about 325 from all causes. This includes 22 that sank with the carriers *Taiho* and *Shokaku*, torpedoed by U.S. submarines. Hellcat losses amounted to 16 in combat, of which 9 were downed over Guam. Another six were lost in operational accidents, including one shot down by U. S. antiaircraft fire. Thirteen F6F pilots were killed in action.

Unfortunately, no two sources agree on the total claims made by Hellcats. The squadron histories and action reports amount to 354 kills, which include a few by Avenger search planes. Fighting 15 off the *Essex* was heavily engaged in Raids One, Two, and Four and consequently led the task force with claims for 68½ destroyed in the air. Next came the *Hornet*'s Hellcats with 52 and the *Lexington* with 46. The *Yorktown* claimed 33 and the *Princeton* was tops among the CVLs, her VF-27 claiming 30. Two-thirds of the kills were claimed by the CV squadrons, which were more heavily engaged than the CVL units.

Preliminary action reports showed 365 air and 15 strafing credits. In his report, Mitscher credited the F6Fs with enemy losses of 210 fighters, 93 dive bombers, 43 torpedo planes, and ten assorted types—a total of 356. Another 19 were believed downed by ships' gunfire and 13 destroyed on the ground, 388 in all. CinCPac figures showed 366 enemy aircraft shot down by Hellcats, 19 by AA fire, and 17 on the ground for a grand total of 402.

These figures were clearly overoptimistic. Ozawa's ships launched 354 carrier sorties, including 24 on searches, and 19 floatplanes. From these 373 sorties, 243 failed to return. Nearly 60 land-based aircraft were also lost in combat, accidents, or strafing attacks.

Therefore, taking the known Japanese loss of some 325 aircraft and subtracting the 22 that went down with the two carriers, and granting maximum claims of 19 destroyed on the ground and 17 by AA fire, we arrive at a combat and operational loss of some 275. This does not include numerous aircraft damaged beyond repair, never to fly again. Thus, it appears the F6F squadrons overclaimed by about 90, a factor of one-third. Claiming three victories for two actual kills has been a fairly consistent factor of large-scale air combat.

But a wise air commander does not let himself become engrossed in a "numbers game" or in "keeping score." The only thing that really mattered was whether or not air supremacy had been achieved, and most certainly it had. Admiral Ozawa's carriers had barely 100 operational aircraft on board at the end of the day; Mitscher had four times that many Hellcats alone.

From just over 400 fighter sorties, some 290 Hellcats contacted the enemy formations and inflicted losses of nearly 70 percent. Fighting Squadrons 1, 2, 15, 16, and 27 all claimed more kills than sorties, and seven F6F pilots were credited with five or more victories each. Three were from the *Essex*. McCampbell got seven in two sorties, Brewer claimed five in two sorties, and Lieutenant (jg) Carr downed his five in one flight. McCampbell's tally of five Judys and two Zekes was the highest of the day. It was also a record matched by only four other American fighter pilots, and exceeded by none—except McCampbell himself.

Lieutenant Bill Lamb's five Jills paced Fighting 27 while Webb and Reiserer, the two *Hornet* pilots, may have had the easiest pickings of all. They dumped 11 Vals between them, the Japanese employing virtually no evasive action. Alex Vraciu's bag of six Judys raised his tally to 18, tops not only among carrier pilots but for the entire Navy at the time.

Of the 39 planes credited to these seven men, only five were Zekes. The proportion reflected the nature of the combats, as once the Hellcats were among the Vals, Jills, and Judys there was virtually no chance of escape. A Jill could be difficult to catch in an F6F-3, spotted much of a lead, but was incapable of an effective defense.

The Japanese airmen displayed considerable courage in pursuing their attacks despite dreadful losses. About 50 penetrated the CAP during the day, but target selection was poor—they often went for battleships instead of carriers—and their aim was worse. No flattop was hit by a bomb or torpedo. The First Battle of the Philippine Sea was already a strategic defeat for Japan. Her seven remaining carriers withdrew westward, and by nightfall the U.S. search planes still had not found them. If Ozawa could elude detection for another full day, he would escape with his surviving carriers intact.

At dawn on the 20th, the *Essex*, *Langley*, and *Cowpens* sweeps began over Guam but netted only 18 kills. Throughout the day air opposition was negligible, and the carrier pilots claimed 52 more planes destroyed on the bomb-pitted, wreckage-strewn airfields. By mid-morning it was clear the islands would pose no serious threat to the invasion fleet, but by noon there was still no further word of the retiring Japanese carriers. They were just beyond American air-search range.

As nothing had been sighted to the west, search efforts were shifted to the northwest. At 1220 the *Lexington* CAG, Commander Ernie Snowden, led a dozen VF-16 Hellcats out on what was the longest U.S. Navy carrier-launched search to date; 475 miles. Fanning out over a 20° sector based on 340° True, the 12 F6Fs were each armed with a 500-pound GP and orders to attack any carriers they might find. There were also eight *San Jacinto* fighters flying top cover.

By 1500 the 20 Hellcats had reached the limit of their very long hunt. The VF-16 pilots jettisoned their external stores and turned back. It was a six-hour mission well beyond the range of easy rescue in the event of a forced landing. No wonder Snowden called for volunteers only.

About this same time the *Hornet* had launched eight fighters and four dive bombers on a 325-mile search. They found no ships, but Fighting Two bagged a pair of Jake floatplanes and a Kate. These planes were clearly from Ozawa's Mobile Fleet, hoping to find out how closely the Americans were pursuing.

While the search pilots were numbly boring their way home, things had perked up considerably. An Avenger had found Ozawa only about half an hour after Snowden's formation turned back, and Mitscher was quickly preparing to empty his flight decks before the quarry slipped farther out of range. Even so, it was a dicey proposition. The original contact placed the Mobile Fleet 220 miles from the task force, bearing west-northwest.

At 1624 the first of 85 Hellcats began launch into the southeasterly wind—almost exactly the opposite direction from the target. They would escort 77 dive bombers and 54 Avengers. Twelve minutes later all 216 aircraft were flying 290° True, climbing slowly to conserve fuel. The contact was at near-maximum range for armed strike planes, but shortly the situation was seriously compounded. A TBF search pilot caught a one-degree error in his navigation, which placed the Mobile Fleet 60 miles farther west. Combined with the carriers' easterly launch heading, it put the target very nearly 300 nautical miles away. Clearly, a night recovery would be necessary when the strike returned. Equally clearly, a lot of planes would go into the water. Mitscher canceled plans for a second strike. He wanted something left on deck next morning.

Task Groups 58.1, 58.2, and 58.3 launched the strike, each carrier but the *Princeton* putting up something. However, the *Cabot*, *Monterey*, and *San Jacinto* launched no fighters, so only 8 of the 12 flattops in these three groups contributed any Hellcats. Fighting Squadrons 1, 2, 8, 10, 14, 16, 24, and 50 sent off two to four divisions each, many armed with 500-pounders to gain more effect from the attack. A typical mix was Fighting Two's 14 Hellcats—ten with 500-pound semi-armor-piercing and four with 500-pound GPs. Ensign W. H. Vaughn, Jr., noticed his artificial horizon was not working, but he launched from the *Hornet* anyway—risky business on a mission which would require instrument flight on the return leg.

The three Japanese carrier divisions were found shortly past 1800, heading northwest roughly in line abreast over a 40-mile front. Their oilers and auxiliaries trailed some 50 miles behind, but were passed up by all but *Wasp*'s Air Group 14. Commander Ralph L. Shifley, leading the *Bunker Hill*'s strike, orbited the southern carrier group in his photo Hellcat, watching Bombing Eight's SB2Cs deploy for attack. Antiaircraft fire was intense but caused no serious damage, and as Shifley's planes pulled off the target—probably the light carrier *Chiyoda*—the *Cabot* and *Monterey* strikes went in.

The only serious air opposition met by Air Group Eight was handled by the CAG and his wingman, who fought a half-dozen Zekes near the rendezvous. The two F6s fired at several Zeros; Shifley claimed two splashed, then firewalled everything to outrun three bandits on his tail.

Enemy aircraft intercepted every formation but the *Hornet*'s, though only in small groups of six or seven each. It was poor coordination by the 75 or so that Ozawa put in the air. The Grim Reapers of VF-10 got in the most air combat, claiming seven certain kills while losing one of their own. Leading the *Enterprise* strike against the middle Japanese group, Killer Kane made up for the heavy action he had missed the day before, though his head was still bandaged under his flying helmet from the knock he took on the 16th. During a five-hour search earlier in the day, he'd shot down a floatplane and a Jill. Now, over the Mobile Fleet, he and his wingman splashed one of Fighting Ten's Zeke victims.

Air Group 16 also hit the center group. Nine Hellcats were deployed as top cover in twos and threes, and most climbed away to investigate reported bogeys at their seven o'clock. Alex Vraciu was leading two wingmen on the *Lexington* group's starboard beam when several Zekes hit the formation from behind and below. They set a TBM afire, and then eight of them hemmed in Vraciu and Ensign H. W. Brockmeyer.

One Zeke got behind Brockmeyer and began firing. Vraciu dropped his nose to get the bandit in his sights and exploded it with two bursts. But Brockmeyer's Hellcat fell towards the water streaming a plume of smoke. It went in without any visible attempt to pull out. With two Zekes on his own tail, Vraciu stomped the rudder pedal, jerked the stick into his belly, and snap-rolled his F6 in a speed-killing maneuver. He recovered with another Zeke coming head-on, and fired. His target smoked and rolled inverted, then was lost from sight. When Vraciu looked around he was completely alone.

The northern carrier group had only the *Shokaku* left, but air combat was fairly heavy. Two CVL fighter squadrons, VF-24 and VF-50, claimed three and four victories respectively in exchange for three F6Fs shot down. The eight *Belleau Wood* fighters would have had a rougher time, outnumbered as they were, if not for poor Japanese gunnery.

Both VF-1 and VF-2 went after carriers. Eight Rippers dived on a CVL but made no hits with their bombs. The four which attacked another carrier reported a "certain" hit, and the last two *Hornet* Hellcats went after a cruiser, with undetermined results. Lieutenant (jg) "Butch" Voris made VF-2's only kill over the Mobile Fleet.

Smoke Strean led his 12 bomb-laden fighters on a short sweep of the area, hunting for airborne hostiles, then returned to the center group and initiated a dive-bombing attack on one of the three flattops. Fighting One claimed three direct hits on the target, with five more bombs laid close aboard. But in the thick flak and confusion, actual results were hard to discern. It is possible Strean's pilots scored, however, as the *Junyo* and *Hiyo* both received damage during the 20 minutes the U. S. planes were over the enemy fleet.

Despite the efforts of 200 aircraft, the *Hiyo* was the only Japanese carrier sunk. *Wasp's* planes dealt with the oiler group, sinking two AOs, but Fighting 14 found itself in a hassle with several Zekes immediately afterward. The result was five to one, as Lieutenant E. E. Cotton, one of the best photo pilots in the fleet, smashed head-on into a Zeke when neither would break off.

Twenty-six Japanese planes were claimed shot down, including 22 by Hellcats. Though the actual figure may have been closer to 40, the aspect of the dusk attack which stuck most in the fliers' minds was the AA fire. It was intense, occasionally accurate, and wildly spectacular in its multi-hued colors. The *Yorktown's* CAG, Commander James M. Peters, summed up most of the pilots' feelings when he said the whole affair was like "watching a ten-ring circus with a sniper shooting at you from behind the lion's cage."[13] No Hellcats were lost to flak, but six bombers were known shot down by AA fire.

Six Hellcats had been shot down over the Japanese force in dogfights. The remaining fighters, with their strung-out Helldivers, Avengers, and Dauntlesses, set course into the blackening eastern sky. The F6Fs had launched with a maximum capacity 400 gallons of fuel, so the fighters were in better shape than most bombers. Even so, the pilots leaned their fuel mixtures and trimmed their aircraft for best cruise configuration. Their bunks were over 250 salt-water miles away.

At 2030 the first returning aircraft were in sight of the task force, and were overhead about 15 minutes later. The carriers immediately made 22 knots into the easterly wind, with 15 miles between task groups. Admiral Mitscher pondered the risks involved in lighting up his ships to enable the anxious fliers to get on board, then gave his famous order to turn on the lights. Nearly every ship in the force did so—an heroically well-intentioned move which was to cause problems.

Numerous SB2Cs and TBMs had splashed down short of the task force, but nearly all the Hellcats arrived overhead with fuel enough to get on board if there weren't too many delays. Some pilots couldn't believe the brightly lit ships when they hove into view. Alex Vraciu called the *Lexington* to ask if she were burning her lights. "Affirmative," came the reply. "Land on nearest base."[14] Vraciu was waved off his first approach on an *Essex*-class ship but got aboard the *Enterprise* on his next try.

Others weren't so lucky. Killer Kane went straight back to the *Enterprise*, took a wave-off, and flew into the water. He'd flown ten hours during the day's two sorties and was exhausted. He injured his head again and didn't return to the "Big E" till the 22nd. According to custom, the destroyer which delivered him received several gallons of ice cream in exchange.

Even returning to one's own flight deck could not ensure safety. Lieutenant M. M. Tomme of VF-1 landed on the *Yorktown* and was still in his cockpit when another plane hit hard, bounced, and crashed down on the F6, killing Tomme where he sat.

In all, at least 14 Hellcats were lost near the task force, either in deck crashes or ditchings. All eight fighter squadrons involved lost at least one airplane, but Bill Dean's Rippers had the worst of it. Seven of the *Hornet*'s F6Fs—half those launched—were lost to operational causes unrelated to combat. Five VF-2 planes were wrecked in barrier crashes—three aboard the *Yorktown*—and two more went in the water. One of the latter was Ensign Vaughn, who had flown the mission without an artificial horizon. But all of Dean's pilots returned unharmed to the *Hornet*.

The *Bataan*'s VF-50 suffered the next heaviest aircraft losses among the F6Fs, with two in combat and one operational. Even those squadrons with small losses were widely dispersed. Only five of VF-14's pilots got aboard the *Wasp*; ten others were scattered among five other carriers.

Still, Hellcat casualties were the lightest of all except for the SBDs. One-fifth of the F6Fs on the dusk strike were lost, compared with over half the Avengers and nearly all the Helldivers. The Hellcat's large fuel capacity was mainly responsible for the high survival rate, though the F6Fs which found a carrier deck that night had only about 40 gallons remaining. It wasn't much—well under an hour in landing configuration and power setting—but was four times the average fuel found in returning Avengers.

In analyzing the catastrophe in which 100 airplanes were lost, staff officers determined that lack of experience was the main cause of ditchings. Valuable time and fuel were wasted when relatively inexperienced pilots made nocturnal landing approaches on cruisers or destroyers which had their truck lights burning. It took a practiced eye to distinguish ship types solely by their running lights, and in many cases only an old hand could tell the difference before he was almost on top of the vessel.

"Pete" Mitscher has received high praise for his decision to expose the task force by turning on the lights. His personal regard for his aviators was almost paternal in nature, and anyone who knew the man was aware he could not act otherwise. Perhaps the best example of what his decision meant to the fliers trying to get down from a crowded, dangerous sky came from one of the admiral's favorite pilots. Years later, Al Vraciu would name his youngest son after Marc Mitscher.

Hellcats now had control of the air over the Marianas. Not until the 23rd did appreciable opposition arise once more, when VF-15 ran into 18 Zekes over Orote. The *Essex* fighters gunned down 14, claiming three probables, for the loss of two F6Fs and pilots. Ensign J. L. Bruce bailed out of his plane but could not be found again.

Later that day three of the task groups headed for Eniwetok to rest and resupply, but 58.1 took up a familiar northerly heading, returning to Iwo Jima. Rear Admiral Jocko Clark's four carriers—the *Hornet*, *Yorktown*, *Bataan*, and *Belleau Wood*—were to beat up the island again and disrupt its use as a staging base to the Marianas, just as they had on the 15th and 16th.

The weather had been unfavorable on the first Iwo strike, but on the morning of the 24th it was just plain bad. The *Belleau Wood*'s fighters remained as ForceCap while 51 Hellcats of VF-1, 2, and 50 launched 230 miles out, each carrying a 500-pound bomb.

The formation penetrated a thick front on the way in, weaving around the very worst of the weather, following radar-equipped TBFs. Near the target, 60-plus Zekes and perhaps 20 Judys were met; a snooper had spotted the task group and flashed the word to Iwo. There were 122 Japanese aircraft on the island, over half of them from carriers, as the Yokosuka Air Group had arrived only four days before.

Most Hellcats jettisoned their bombs and immediately engaged. For the hot pilots of Fighting Two it was almost—but not quite—a cake walk. Lieutenant (jg) M. W. Vineyard spotted a large bogey near Iwo and another farther west. The *Hornet*'s 15 Hellcats climbed to 9,000 feet, turned into the hostiles and began scoring almost immediately. Vineyard gunned down four Zekes while Lieutenant (jg) Everett C. Hargreaves claimed four kills and a probable. Lieutenant (jg) Carroll Carlson put one Zeke in flames from five o'clock and did some snap-shooting at others before he latched onto still another's tail. At that moment his guns jammed, and he was sure he'd have to let a certain kill off the hook. But the Zeke, attempting to evade its pursuer, dived into the water without firing a round. Fighting Two lost one plane and pilot, with another F6F badly damaged, but returned to the *Hornet* with claims of 25 Zekes and 8 Judys downed.

The *Yorktown's* VF-1 put up four divisions which ran into about 35 enemy planes five miles south of Iwo beneath a solid 15,000-foot overcast. Commander Strean's unit lost one plane and pilot for 18 kills and 5 probables. Top scorer was Lieutenant (jg) "Tank" Schroeder, a slim dark-haired pilot who splashed three Zekes in five minutes. He burned the first from astern and exploded another crossing his nose while it pursued a Hellcat. Schroeder noticed his third victim low on the water and made a side run. It went in without burning.

Four F6Fs got through to drop their bombs on the runways, but they were far too few to prevent two strike groups from taking off and heading for the carriers. The first was composed of some 20 Kate torpedo planes, and none of them returned to Iwo. The *Hornet* CAP got 17, including three by Lieutenant John Dear of VF(N)-76, and the ships' guns splashed the rest.

The next group was composed of nine Judys, nine Jills, and 23 Zekes, none of which could find the American ships in the poor weather. But the Hellcat CAP found the Japanese formation, and 14 of Fighting Two waded in, backed up by some VF-50 Hellcats. Seven of the torpedo planes went down quickly, then ten Zekes.

Total Hellcat claims for the day amounted to over 100. By their own admission the Japanese lost at least 34 fighters, 27 torpedo planes, and five dive bombers. Nearly half the 80 Zekes on Iwo Jima had been destroyed, while Clark's group lost six Hellcats. Fighting Two claimed 67 kills—the admitted total enemy loss—but if it was too high, it certainly demonstrated the squadron's role in the day's combats. The Rippers had claimed 117 victories in the two weeks since 11 June.

Jocko Clark wasn't finished with battered little Iwo Jima. Not quite yet. He returned to the area on 3 and 4 July, bringing Rear Admiral Ralph Davison's TG-58.2 with him. This raid would introduce the F6F-5 to combat, as Davison's task group included the new *Essex*-class carrier *Franklin*. "Big Ben" operated Air Group 13, and Commander W. M. Coleman's VF-13 was completely equipped with the new model Hellcat.

Some other squadrons received -5s as replacement aircraft while still at sea. This was made possible by the various service squadrons which ran fleet bases, conducted overhaul and repair or supply and logistics work. The seagoing service squadron was Servron 10, historically one of

This VF-1 F6F returned to the *Yorktown* despite damage to oil and hydraulic systems and slight wounds to the pilot. Plane handlers rush to help the "Top Hat" flier from his aircraft.

the most neglected organizations in the U.S. Navy. Though mostly composed of fleet oilers, supply ships, and other auxiliaries, Servron 10 also had a number of escort carriers attached. These CVEs did double duty: providing air protection for the auxiliaries, and supplying replacement aircraft to the CVs and CVLs while still at sea. In this manner the fast carriers could remain in action for longer periods without returning to a fleet base such as Majuro or Ulithi.

The sailors of the service squadrons—both afloat and ashore—won few decorations and even fewer headlines. But the Japanese knew of their worth. After the war, former premier and warlord Hideki Tojo identified the ability of the United States to keep task forces at sea for long periods as one of the major factors in Japan's defeat.

But to Clark and Davison's fighter pilots, the big news was the F6F-5's zero-length rocket rails. These allowed the use of 5-inch HVAR projectiles, and the *Franklin* Hellcats particularly would make effective use of them.

Raiding Iwo Jima was now a familiar routine to VF-1 and VF-2, and the pilots knew what to expect. "We got a hot reception every time we went to Iwo," recalled Smoke Strean.[15] This time was no different.

The fighter sweep of 3 July pitted 43 Hellcats from the *Hornet* and *Yorktown* against 40-odd Zekes which barely got off the ground in time. Seventeen VF-1 aircraft made contact under a 3,000- to 5,000-foot cloud layer as Strean's outfit claimed 11 confirmed and 5 probables for the loss of a plane and pilot plus 3 F6Fs damaged. Eleven of VF-2's 26 sweep Hellcats put their bombs on their airfield targets when the Zekes appeared overhead. Many of the Japanese were skillful and aggressive, maintaining their altitude advantage, but making poor use of it. Bill Dean and four other Rippers each scored triples as Fighting Two ran up a 33 to 3 claim.

Next morning the severely depleted Japanese air group could only put up eight torpedo planes and nine Zekes, all with orders to dive deliberately into the American carriers. This was four months prior to formation of the Kamikaze "special attack corps," but the enemy fliers had no opportunity to commit suicide. Instead, *Cabot* Hellcats celebrated the Fourth of July by dropping onto the Japanese from 10,000 feet. Lieutenant (jg) Conny Nooy paced Fighting 31 with three kills and a probable as the enemy formation was annihilated. Of the 17 hostiles, only four Zekes returned to Iwo in the thick weather. During three, sharp, hard-fought raids the F6Fs had destroyed over 70 of the 80 Zeros on Iwo Jima.

Fighting 13 had notched its first four victories during the operation, but of far greater interest was the first fighter use of High Velocity Aerial Rockets in Pacific combat. The *Franklin* Hellcats sent their big, 60-pound rockets smoking into a variety of Japanese ships in the Bonins and returned exultant. They claimed the destruction by rocketing and strafing of an escort and four small merchantmen.

Air Group One had 16 planes probing for Japanese shipping, too. The *Yorktown* fliers went after three vessels identified as two destroyer escorts and a medium cargo ship. Smoke Strean's Hellcats plunged through surprisingly thick AA fire, continuously strafing the two DEs, and began exploding depth charges which "went off like popcorn"[16] on the stern of one ship. The first escort shuddered from a large explosion and the second was wracked by fire when the *Yorktown* planes pulled off. The cargo vessel was last seen smoking. But VF-1's newest ace, Lieutenant Bill

Moseley, never turned up. He had shot down his fifth and sixth planes the day before and was awarded a posthumous Air Medal to go with his two DFCs.

So ended the unrelenting pace of midsummer in the Pacific. The month of June had seen Hellcats prowling over most of Micronesia, and the early July aftermath found Japanese air power in the region virtually nonexistent. The Marianas Campaign, which officially lasted until 8 August with more strikes on the Palaus, Carolines, and the Bonins, netted claims of 917 enemy planes destroyed in air combat. Against this, 65 U.S. carrier planes—mostly Hellcats—had been shot down by Japanese aircraft. It was an exchange ratio of 14 to 1, and even if it suffered from honest exaggeration, it was still impressive. And it did not include 306 planes thought destroyed on the ground by U.S. carrier aircraft.

With the arrival of the F6F-5 in the Fast Carrier Task Force, the Hellcat was entering its most successful period—the last 12 months of the war. For though Japanese naval aviation was no longer in serious contention at sea, momentous events were set in motion once the U.S. Navy went to the Philippines and beyond.

Hellcat Squadrons in Combat: May to August 1944

VF-1	*Yorktown*	Commander Bernard M. Strean
VF-2	*Hornet*	Commander William A. Dean, Jr.
VF-8	*Bunker Hill*	Commander William M. Collins, Jr.
VF-10	*Enterprise*	Lieutenant R.W. Schumann
VF-13	*Franklin*	Commander Wilson M. Coleman
VF-14	*Wasp*	Lieutenant Commander Edmund W. Biros (KIA), Lieutenant W. Q. Punnell (KIA)
VF-15	*Essex*	Commander Charles W. Brewer (KIA), Lieutenant Commander James F. Rigg
VF-16	*Lexington*	Commander Paul D. Buie
VF-19	*Lexington*	Lieutenant Commander Franklin E. Cook
VF-20	*Enterprise*	Commander Fred E. Bakutis
VF-21	*Belleau Wood*	Lieutenant Commander V. F. Casey
VF-24	*Belleau Wood*	Lieutenant Commander Edward M. Link
VF-25	*Cowpens*	Lieutenant Commander Robert H. Price
VF-27	*Princeton*	Lieutenant Commander Ernest W. Wood (KIA), Lieutenant Commander Fred A. Bardshar
VF-28	*Monterey*	Lieutenant Commander Roger W. Mehle
VF-31	*Cabot*	Lieutenant Commander Robert A. Winston
VF-32	*Langley*	Commander Edward C. Outlaw
VF-50	*Bataan*	Lieutenant Commander John C. Strange
VF-51	*San Jacinto*	Commander Charles L. Moore

5 Hellcats over Europe

. . . a two-ocean war for the Navy.
Samuel Eliot Morison

The F6F was built with the specific purpose of meeting the challenge of the Pacific war. Its range, endurance, and performance were intended to defeat the Japanese in an arena which covered nearly one quarter of the earth's surface.

Though the distances and logistics of the Pacific war dwarfed those of the Atlantic war, the European theater also saw Hellcats engaged in combat against the Axis. The requirements for fighting Germany, however, were often quite different from those of fighting Japan. Hellcats operating in the North Sea and the Mediterranean never had to establish aerial supremacy or defend a task force from air attack, and F6Fs supported only one major amphibious operation in European waters. The irony of the situation is that F6Fs might never have flown in Europe had it not been for the prewar short-sightedness of the British military aviation establishment.

Between the wars, the Royal Navy's Fleet Air Arm was largely dependent upon the Royal Air Force for aircraft and flight crews. Many British carrier planes were merely RAF types modified for naval use. Because of administrative and financial restrictions, the Fleet Air Arm failed to gain anything like the semiautonomy which American and Japanese carrier airmen enjoyed. As a result, observed one British pilot, "Between the first day of war and the last, the Fleet Air Arm received not one single British aircraft which wasn't either inherently unsuited for carrier work or was obsolete before it came into service."[1]

Nowhere was this more obvious than in fighters. The FAA concept of the carrier fighter's mission was one of implied rather than actual threat to enemy aircraft. If an interception resulted in destruction of a hostile plane, well and good. But the mere presence of a carrier-based fighter was deemed sufficient to ward off snoopers or occasional bombers, for carriers were not supposed to operate within range of land-based strike aircraft.

Operational experience had shown the weakness of such a philosophy. Carriers not only could operate under land-based air; they were frequently required to do so. Therefore, the FAA ideal of a two-seat fighter—pilot and navigator-radioman—underwent radical revision. Two-seaters such as the Blackburn Roc and Skua or Fairey Fulmar were simply not competitive against enemy fighters. Modified RAF types such as the biplane Sea Gladiator and more modern Sea Hurricane and Seafire filled the gap for a time, but they were inherently ill-suited for the strains of carrier operations. The Seafire in particular, though possessed of excellent low-level performance, was too delicate for rough deck landings.

Thus did the Royal Navy turn to Uncle Sam—and Leroy Grumman.

The F4F Wildcat, originally called Martlet by the Fleet Air Arm, was the first U.S. carrier aircraft used by the Royal Navy. Its rugged struc-

A map of the European-Mediterranean-North African area superimposed on a map of the Pacific Ocean. With Moscow resting on Hawaii, note that the entire landmass is swallowed in mid-Pacific.

ture and reliable nature endeared it to the British, who by 1945 had purchased nearly 1,100 F4Fs and FM Wildcats.

When more modern fighters became available, naturally the British were interested. During the summer of 1943 the Fleet Air Arm received its first F4Us and F6Fs. In all, some 2,000 Corsairs served in the Royal

Navy, more than any other U.S. aircraft type. The first British F4U squadron was formed at Quonset Point, Rhode Island, in early June.

The Hellcat entered British service a month later when Number 800 Squadron, Fleet Air Arm, exchanged its Hawker Sea Hurricanes for F6Fs. Under the British designation system of the time, the F6F-3s were named Gannet Is, after the large white sea birds which nest among the rocks of northern waters. But in January 1944 all U.S. aircraft in the Royal Navy adopted the American names. Gannets reverted to Hellcats, Martlets became Wildcats, and TBM Tarpons became Avengers. The Corsair had always been known by its original name, so no change was necessary.

Number 800 Squadron's F6F-3s were the first of 252 received by the FAA, but 930 -5s were later obtained as Hellcat IIs. The Gannet's first combat occurred in December 1943, when 800 Squadron flew from the escort carrier HMS *Emperor* in antishipping strikes off the Norwegian coast. It was the first in a long line of missions against Norwegian targets —a series of strikes which would form the bulk of British F6F operations in European waters.

Unlike the Seafire or Sea Hurricane, the Hellcat had considerable potential as a long-range strike fighter. And owing to minimal Luftwaffe opposition over Scandinavia, that is largely how the British Hellcats were employed: flak suppression and bombing.

The 42,000-ton battleship *Tirpitz* was a constant source of concern to the British Navy. Holed up in the Kaafjord of Norway's rugged coast, the ill-fated *Bismarck's* sister represented a considerable danger to Allied shipping even as she swung around her anchor. By simply existing, she posed a threat which could not be ignored.

That is why in April of 1944, four British carriers were dispatched to the North Sea in hopes of destroying her. Again 800 Squadron's Hellcats

The British Fleet Air Arm originally called the F6F the Gannet, but adopted the name Hellcat in January 1944.

were involved, as the *Emperor* was one of two escort carriers assigned to the mission, while Fairey Barracuda dive bombers—the ungainly, unlikely-looking strike aircraft—were poised aboard the HMS *Victorious* and *Furious* for the main blow.

Two strikes were planned, approximately equal in composition, with 21 Barracudas escorted by 20 Hellcats and 20 Wildcats. The first strike launched at 0415 on 3 April, 120 miles west of Kaafjord. The British pilots flew as low as 50 feet most of the way to the target, successfully evading radar detection as they approached the rugged coastline. There were snowcaps on many of the peaks dimly visible in the early northern light—surely a new sight for Hellcat pilots.

Tirpitz was sighted resting at anchor at 0527, an hour and a quarter after launch. And though the carrier planes were seen from the ground at the same time, it was much too late for the defenders. The Germans started their smoke generators in a vain effort to obscure the battleship, and AA guns began a heavy though inaccurate fire. Only 90 seconds after sighting the target, the Hellcats and Wildcats dropped into steep dives, firing their .50 calibers as they pressed their strafing runs to minimum range. They were more successful than anyone had hoped. In the one minute required for the Barracudas to attack; only one fell to some of the most concentrated flak in Scandinavia. *Tirpitz* was rocked by nine direct hits and five near-misses.

The second wave, which went in at 0640, did nearly as well. Five more direct hits were obtained by the awkward Barracudas as the Grumman fighters kept the AA gunners' heads down. One Barracuda and a Hellcat were lost over the target, but *Tirpitz* would be out of commission for the next four months.

Seven more *Tirpitz* attacks were attempted in August, but achieved considerably less success due to wretched weather. Two were canceled outright and two more were aborted en route. The next-to-last, on 24 August, was covered in part by the Hellcat Is of No. 1840 Squadron from the *Furious,* and light damage was inflicted.

Two antishipping sweeps during May of 1944 brought the only aerial victories won by British Hellcats in Europe. Again, No. 800 Squadron was involved, still flying off the *Emperor,* in company with the *Furious* and *Searcher.* An 800 Squadron formation was escorting a Barracuda strike when it was bounced by a mixed formation of Luftwaffe fighters—Messerschmitt 109s and Focke-Wulf 190s.

They were formidable adversaries. Both were faster than the Hellcat —the 109 by 30 mph—and both could stay with an F6F through most of a long dive. The Grumman's great advantage was a tighter turning radius, and the *Emperor's* pilots used it as best they could. Though one Hellcat went down immediately, and another shortly after, three German fighters were destroyed. The lone FW-190 claimed fell to Lieutenant B. Ritchie, an experienced fighter pilot who already had 3½ victories to his credit flying Sea Hurricanes.

Six days later, 14 May, the *Emperor* Hellcats found German aircraft again but had a much easier time. Ritchie pounced upon a twin-engine Heinkel 115 floatplane and shot it down. Then he joined Lieutenant Commander S. G. Orr, commanding the sister 804 Squadron on the *Emperor*, and helped send another HE-115 into the cold North Sea.

The Hellcat's next and last European appearance would occur 1,500 miles to the south, in the warm waters of the Mediterranean.

Seven British escort carriers were assigned to support the invasion of southern France in August 1944. One was the well-traveled *Emperor*, with Lieutenant Commander G. R. Henderson's veteran 800 Squadron embarked with two dozen Hellcat Is. Two carriers flew Wildcats while the other four operated Seafires.

Deployed in two task groups, the British carriers were reinforced by a pair of American CVEs. These were the *Tulagi* and *Kasaan Bay*, each with a 24-plane squadron of F6F-5s. The *Tulagi* embarked the unique Observation-Fighter Squadron One of Lieutenant Commander William F. Bringle, a 30-year-old from Tennessee. Originally equipped with F4U-1s on commissioning in December of 1943, VOF-1 acquired Hellcats in March and was carrier qualified in April.

Bringle's pilots were to direct the shipboard gunfire of the invasion fleet, and had received an intensive week's training from the U.S. Army Artillery School at Fort Sill, Oklahoma. There the carrier pilots learned spotting technique, use of maps and grids, and photo interpretation. The logic behind this seeming contradiction was that it was easier to teach a fighter pilot how to direct naval gunfire than to indoctrinate a spotter pilot in fighter aircraft and tactics.

The *Kasaan Bay* operated VF-74 under Lieutenant Commander Harry B. Bass. It was intended to work as a conventional fighter squadron, but in this combat these pilots would almost exclusively fly strike-recon missions, a function for which they were poorly equipped. They were not trained for tactical reconnaissance or artillery spotting, and had fired only three or four rockets apiece before embarking at the end of June. Nevertheless, they would run up bombing and rocket scores of nearly 35 percent in combat.

In all, the nine Allied CVEs had 220 fighters: 97 Seafires, 71 Hellcats, and 52 Wildcats. The F6Fs, with longer range and provisions for rockets, would prove the most valuable carrier planes available. They could fly to Toulouse in the west, to Mâcon 200 miles up the Rhone River, and over to Cannes and Nice near the Italian border. Additionally, a seven-plane night-fighter detachment of VF-74 would be ashore at Ajaccio, on Corsica's west coast. These F6F-3Ns were intended to provide protection over ships retiring from the beachhead at night.

D-Day for Operation Anvil-Dragoon was 15 August. It was a misty morning and it began with a strike by both U.S. Navy squadrons against four coastal defense guns at Isle de Perquelles. Low-lying clouds prevented any definite observation of the results. Nevertheless, the Hellcats kept up the pace with armed recons throughout the landing area, employing bombs, rockets, and even impact-fused 350-pound depth bombs.

One problem which became immediately obvious was the intrinsic difference between soldier and airman. Supporting the U.S. Twelfth Army, the observation pilots received numerous requests for "pinpoint attacks against enemy strongpoints."[2] Frequently no more details were provided, an exasperatingly indefinite description even with grid references. From the air, it was nearly impossible to discern exactly which obstruction was the most troublesome to advancing infantry. Description by a flier was needed to pick out the target to be attacked.

Other missions, such as a "rail out" between Arles and Mirenas, proved easier to accomplish. Communications cuts were a major factor in supporting the invasion, as the Germans rushed all available troops and vehicles to the area. Hellcat pilots found many roads leading to the invasion beaches clogged with advancing Germans. To Lieutenant Fred Schauffler, one two-lane road looked "like five o'clock traffic back in Boston."[3]

In all, the *Tulagi* and *Kasaan Bay* fighters recorded 100 sorties on D-Day, with VF-74 contributing 60. The only casualty of note was a Fighting 74 aircraft which was shot up by light AA in the afternoon and could not extend its tail hook. It was diverted to St. Catherine Field on Corsica for repairs.

Two *Kasaan Bay* planes and pilots were lost on the 17th seeking targets of opportunity in the valley country far inland. Flying in low visibility that afternoon with electric storms in the vicinity, a division leader and his wingman got separated from the other six Hellcats and never turned up.

So far the Luftwaffe had failed to put in an appearance. But the first indication that the swastika-marked aircraft were about came on the morning of the 19th. Eight VOF-1 Hellcats spotted three Heinkel 111s northwest of Tarascon, but owing to low fuel could not attack. As it was, two F6Fs landed aboard the HMS *Emperor* with near-dry tanks.

Late that evening another two *Tulagi* divisions had better luck. On a tactical recon of the Rhone River, the VOF-1 exec ran across two more

Ensign Alfred R. Wood and Lieutenant (jg) Edward W. Olszewski with the VOF-1 Hellcat in which they shot down four German aircraft over southern France. On 20 August 1944 Wood destroyed two HE-111s near Lyon. The next day Olszewski shot down a pair of JU-52s in the same F6F-5. Photo: Olszewski via R. S. Fletcher

Heinkels. Lieutenant Commander John H. Sandor's division jumped the pair of low-flying bombers heading south near Vienne. The Heinkels split up and Lieutenant Rene E. Poucel with Ensign Alfred R. Wood flamed one from astern. It crashed in the same region Poucel's parents had been born.

Sandor and Ensign David Robinson closed in on the second Heinkel at 700 feet and hit it at full deflection from starboard. The stricken bomber crash-landed in a field, where the two Hellcats came down low to burn it. The surviving crew members were killed when they ran into Sandor and Robinson's line of fire.

Continuing the reconnaissance, Ensign Wood spotted a third HE-111, still south of Vienne. He peeled off from 2,000 feet and closed in behind, setting both engines afire. The Heinkel exploded and crashed in some woods. Besides three German aircraft, Sandor's two divisions also destroyed 21 trucks camouflaged with leaves and branches, wrecked a locomotive, and left ten freight cars burning.

Fighting 74 also scored on the 19th. The skipper, Lieutenant Commander Bass, led his division down on a Junkers 88 at 0805 near the Rhone River. It was more an execution than a fight. The Junkers attempted only the slightest evasive maneuvers and all four pilots shared in the victory. Nearly eight hours later, south of Lyons, six of eight *Kasaan Bay* Hellcats went after a lone Dornier 217. Most of the pilots fired too soon but Lieutenant (jg) E. W. Castanedo and Ensign C. W. Hullard waited until the range was correct and split the kill.

Next day, D-Plus Five, was the worst of the campaign for the American Hellcats. Fighting 74 lost three aircraft and two pilots, including Harry Bass. The CO's F6F was hit by flak while strafing near Chamelet and went out of control.

Two VOF-1 planes were also shot down. Lieutenant David S. Crockett was spotting gunfire over Toulon Harbor when he was forced to bail out. He parachuted safely just north of the city to become one of the shortest-term POWs of the war. Held in a fort, he was released four days later when the garrison surrendered to Allied troops, and he was back aboard the *Tulagi* on the 26th. The other VOF-1 pilot, Lieutenant James Alston, was hit while strafing a column of motor and horse-drawn vehicles near Villefranche. He pulled up to 5,000 feet and jumped just as one wing broke off. A radio report monitored in the task force indicated Alston was safe, but an estimated 75 vehicles were destroyed or damaged.

Allied Hellcats. An F6F-5 of VOF-1 from the USS *Tulagi* departs the HMS *Emperor* during the invasion of southern France. Photo: C. F. Shores

The 21st saw more air combat and more losses. Lieutenant (jg) Edward W. Olsewski and Ensign Richard V. Yentzer found three Junkers 52 transports over the Rhone River. The tri-motored Junkers were apparently evacuating German VIPs from Marseille, and though both Hellcats were damaged from earlier combat, the *Tulagi* pilots gave chase. Olsewski attacked from starboard on the V-formation and dropped the number three man in two passes. With only one gun firing he then took out the other wingman. Yentzer got the lead Junkers by making three runs from 9 o'clock and sent it down burning.

As if to offset this success, the only Hellcat loss on D-Plus Six was also from VOF-1. Lieutenant (jg) J. H. Coyne's plane seemed to disintegrate in a dive on a truck convoy near St. Anastasie. His parachute opened just before he hit the ground. It was the ninth U.S. Hellcat lost in the operation.

That evening the U.S. CVEs withdrew for two days to resupply and returned on the 24th. In their absence, the *Emperor* lost three Hellcats on the 22nd, probably all shot down by flak.

The last six days of Anvil-Dragoon were notably safer than the first seven. Only two F6Fs were lost from the 24th to 29th, both *Tulagi* planes which made water landings. One was flown by Lieutenant Commander Bringle, who caught a load of flak over Marseilles and couldn't stretch his fuel back to base. Both splashed pilots were rescued and safely returned.

Operating for 13 days, the *Tulagi* and *Kasaan Bay* lost 11 Hellcats, nearly one-quarter of their number. In exchange, they were credited with destroying 825 trucks and vehicles, damaging 334 more, and wrecking or immobilizing 84 locomotives. They also shot down eight Luftwaffe aircraft, and the number of rail and other communications cuts numbered in the scores.

Rear Admiral T. H. Troubridge, RN, commanding the escort force, had high praise for the fighters' strike capabilities. But he singled out the F6Fs in his action report, saying in part, "The U.S. aircraft, especially the Hellcats, proved their superiority."[4]

Hellcat Squadrons in Combat: Europe, December 1943 to August 1944

VOF-1	USS *Tulagi*	Lieutenant Commander W. F. Bringle
VF-74	USS *Kasaan Bay*	Lieutenant Commander H. B. Bass (KIA), Lieutenant H. H. Basore, Jr.
800 Sqn.	HMS *Emperor*	Lieutenant Commander G. R. Henderson
804 Sqn.	HMS *Emperor*	Lieutenant Commander S. G. Orr
1840 Sqn.	HMS *Furious*	

Hellcat's Day

Battle history accounts permit but limited reference to the essential between-engagements routine upon which combat itself depends. For the Hellcat, and indeed, for all its counterpart carrier aircraft, that routine was inherent to shipboard flight operations. All carrier-based F6s—wherever their ship, whichever their squadron, or whatever their side-number—shared the same turbulent environment of sound and motion.

The following sequence of photographs offers a composite view, not of a single Hellcat, but of *any* Hellcat, on any carrier, on any ocean during W.W. II. The unusual series of photographs, of many different F6s, on many ships, over a time span of several years, depicts a truly homogeneous Hellcat.

As such, the scenes perhaps may recall other Hellcats for those who built them, for those who serviced them, for those who were pridefully fortunate to have flown them, and for those who have since come to know the legend of this remarkable airplane.

The day begins with "Pilots man your planes!" And pilots scramble to the flight deck where . . .

. . . plane captains and flight deck crewmen have already manned stations for preflight preparations.

The bullhorn bellows its admonition to "Check all chocks and tiedowns; check all loose gear about the deck; stand by to start aircraft; stand clear of propellers; start aircraft." The carrier turns into the wind, and the first plane moves out of the pack to spread its wings and move to Fly One, where . . .

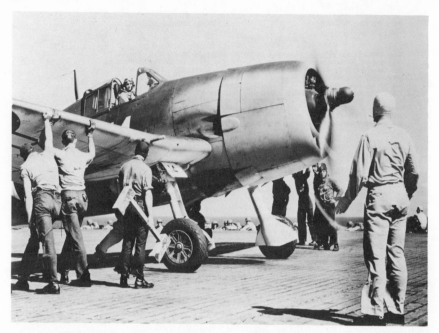

. . . the Flight Deck Officer will signal his two-finger turn-up to the pilot . . .

. . . and launch him . . .

... down the deck and off the bow for a clearing turn, join-up, and climb-out into the not-always-blue, where for the next two or three hours or more, the Hellcat occupies itself with such routine matters as ...

... Combat Air Patrol and fighter cover (and getting shot at) ...

. . . strafing enemy air fields (and getting shot at) . . .

. . . bombing ships and shore installations (and getting shot at) until . . .

. . . the return to the carrier, for the welcome: "Your signal, Charlie," and . . .

. . . for the carrier pilot, the most demandingly satisfying part of his routine as, "Gear down, hook down, flaps down," he follows the LSO's signals . . .

. . . to the "cut" and . . .

. . . hopefully, to engage the Number 3 wire . . .

. . . be disengaged by the incredibly fearless hookmen . . .

. . . and taxi forward to join the pack and secure.

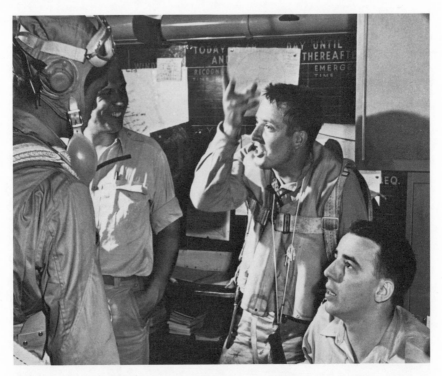

But even as the pilots jubilantly recount their exploits . . .

. . . the Hellcat's day isn't over, for on the flight deck there's respot, refuel, and rearm, and . . .

... on the hangar deck the work also goes on ...

... until preparations are completed for tomorrow ...

. . . or sooner. And the Hellcat's day ends as it began: Ready for launch.

119

6 To the Philippines

No one can guarantee success in war, but only earn it.
Winston Churchill

To the pilots flying at an airspeed of more than 200 knots and at an altitude of only a few hundred feet, the beach came up fast in the early morning light. While division leaders checked their navigation, the wingmen kept eyes alert, looking for the Japanese fighters which did not appear.

Three task groups had launched their Hellcats only 50 miles off Mindanao that morning, 9 September. Farther east, Task Group 38.4 was striking the Palaus, but the main blow fell on the southernmost of the Philippine Islands. The briefed targets were Mindanao's nine known airfields.

Surprise was complete. The Japanese had no idea American aircraft were anywhere near until they swept over the beach. When the low-flying Hellcats burst out from behind jungle foliage in shallow dives, strafing, bombing, and rocketing parked aircraft and facilities, there was nothing to do but dive for cover. Only a handful of enemy planes got airborne, and they were quickly shot down by the wide-ranging F6Fs.

One such squadron on the prowl was VF-19, led by the CAG, Commander T. H. Winters. Air Group 19 had relieved Air Group 16 aboard Vice Admiral Marc Mitscher's flagship *Lexington* in late July, and now Hugh Winters took his Hellcats to Lumbia and Del Monte airfields in the Cagayan Valley. No airborne Japanese were seen, but Fighting 19 claimed the destruction of 27 aircraft on the two fields. This was nearly half the total enemy planes destroyed on the ground during the two-day Mindanao strike.

Fighting 15 shot down the only four enemy planes it saw: two Topsys and a pair of Vals. Then the *Essex* fighters worked over a convoy of 42 ships off the east coast—all coastal freighters. Joined by other planes from Air Group 15's sweep-strike, they played a large role in sinking 18 vessels and damaging several others. But as usual, there was a price for such a victory. Lieutenant John E. Barry, Jr., a determined North Carolinian, pressed his strafing run so low on an ammunition ship that he was killed instantly when his F6F was caught in the huge explosion.

The Philippines campaign was underway.

General Douglas MacArthur's amphibious troops were to make their initial landings in Leyte Gulf the next month, and with Mindanao's air power neutralized Mitscher's three task groups raised their sights several notches. During 12 and 13 September, fighter sweeps and strikes were flown against the middle Philippines—Leyte, Samar, Negros, and Cebu.

The *Hornet* still operated Air Group Two, despite frequent assurances that relief was on the way. "Just one more operation"[1] had become the half-cynical, half-humorous byword in VF-2's ready room, but Bill Dean's pilots found that this particular "last time" afforded good hunting. The

Rippers claimed 16 kills on the 12th, including 10 in the morning when 24 Hellcats escorted 17 bombers to Negros. The fighter leader, Lieutenant Charlie Harbert, called out 10 to 12 Zekes near Cebu and two divisions engaged. Harbert chased one Zeke "halfway across the islands"[2] before he splashed it. Lieutenant (jg) C. P. Spitler downed four Zekes in about five minutes, making the Ohio pilot VF-2's 24th ace. Three more Zekes and two Irving twin-engine fighters were also claimed.

Lieutenant (jg) Andy Skon nearly got another Irving flown by a cool-headed Japanese pilot. Skon set the port engine afire at low level but was astonished to see the Irving land safely on a nearby airfield and taxi directly into a revetment, engine still ablaze!

Air Groups 15 and 19 were accustomed to working together by now in Task Group 38.3, and both the *Essex* and *Lexington* put up two divisions for an early sweep over the Visayas in extremely poor weather. Commander Winters of Air Group 19 was the sweep leader with VF-15's CO, Lieutenant Commander James F. Rigg, the *Essex* leader. These 16 Hellcats found an estimated 80 Japanese fighters taking off from Cebu and Opon airdromes and immediately engaged.

It was a wild, widespread fracas fought under low clouds. Rigg saw two Zekes taking off from Opon and dropped one from ten o'clock high. It crashed near the south end of the runway. Next he saw two Tojos climbing and flamed the leader from eight o'clock low. By now the 29-year-old squadron commander was alone and, looking for an F6F, he saw another Zeke low over the water of Cebu Harbor. Rigg made an overhead run and saw it splash. Next he dove from 5,000 feet on a Zeke over Cebu town and literally shot it in two. His fifth victim was seen jinking low among trees and houses, fleeing the area, and Rigg hit it from astern. The Japanese glided down to a water landing.

Still hungry, Rigg joined two *Lexington* fighters and went after a lone Zeke extremely low over Mactan. This Zero was flown by an expert who avoided all but a few hits and evaded the three Hellcats after nearly ten minutes.

While Rigg was becoming Air Group 15's fourth "ace in a day," Hugh Winters was destroying three fighters himself. The top VF-19 score was turned in by Lieutenant Albert Seckel, who claimed four. In all, Winters' pilots were credited with 14 kills and Rigg's with 17, but with the loss of two F6s. The fact that Commander Dave McCampbell waded in with some of the strike's escorting F6Fs and bagged ten more—four by the CAG himself—did little to alleviate the feeling of loss. A comment from Rigg is noteworthy: "We lost two experienced pilots for *only* 17 (emphasis added) and one probable."[3] Ensign Claude W. Plant, an ace with eight-and-one-half victories, and Lieutenant (jg) W. V. Henning were VF-15's fifth and sixth pilots known lost to enemy aircraft.

The next day, 13 September, was more of the same. The *Essex* fighters claimed another 29 kills during two missions, including 21 during the dawn fighter sweep over Cebu and Negros. Three VF-15 divisions ran into nearly 50 airborne bandits, a curious mixture of 20 to 25 fixed-gear Nates, 15 to 20 Zekes and Oscars, and four Bettys. The Nates were small, open-cockpit monoplanes, slow and lightly armed but incredibly maneuverable—presumably used for advanced training. McCampbell got two Nates early in the fight, then separated and called for rendezvous ten miles south of Bacolod airdrome. His wingman, Roy Rushing, had bagged two Oscars and was covering Ensign J. W. Brex, who had force-landed. Therefore, McCampbell was alone when attacked from above by a Nate which he did not see until too late. The nimble Japanese fighter pulled up quickly out of gun range without doing any damage, but McCampbell wanted the kill. He dropped his belly tank and went to War Emergency Power, climbing hard but still losing ground.

Noticing its advantage, the Nate rolled over to begin an overhead pass. McCampbell was having none of that. He pushed his nose down and dived to safety. After dropping an Oscar he returned to the *Essex* and reported: " (1) Nate is even more maneuverable than Zeke. (2) Nate can outclimb F6F at 110-120 knots airspeed. (3) This 'operational student,' if he was such, will have no trouble completing the course."[4]

Most of the other "operational students" were spared the trouble. Eleven more Nates fell to VF-15, including three each to Ensigns Wendell Van Twelves and Larry R. Self. Nineteen Japanese planes were also thought destroyed on Bacolod.

The *Essex*-class air groups drew most of the juicy assignments during this period, but one of the more fortunate CVL squadrons was VF-31 off the *Cabot*. During the dawn fighter sweep of the 13th, 21-year-old Lieutenant (jg) Arthur R. Hawkins put his previous experience to good use. He had claimed three kills during the Turkey Shoot and another in July, but exceeded his previous total by knocking down five enemy fighters in this, his third combat. His squadron mate "Conny" Nooy got three more as the *Cabot* pilots ignored heavy AA fire over their airfield targets to pursue enemy aircraft to extremely low level. But during the 13th and 14th most damage was done on the ground. As before, VF-19 enthusiastically went after parked airplanes and returned to the *Lexington* with another big tally. The 30 burned or wrecked on Negros and Panay brought Fighting 19's three-day total on the ground to 110.

The mid-September strikes were an unqualified success. Over 170 aerial victories and over 300 ground claims went into the files, this against a loss of eight carrier planes attributable to enemy action. The fast carriers were therefore ordered to hit Luzon on the 21st and 22nd, where an estimated 500 Japanese aircraft were thought to be based. On the night of

20 September, Admiral John S. McCain radioed the squadrons of his Task Group 38.1: "Tomorrow will be hot fighting over land and water."[5]

He was right. But for a change the heaviest action was found by the CVL units. Morning launch was delayed due to bad weather and heavy seas, but the first strikes were in the air by 0700. There were two fighter sweeps by three CVL squadrons each, led by Lieutenant Commander Roger Mehle of Air Group 28 and Lieutenant Commander Fred Bardshar of Air Group 27, respectively.

Bardshar took his 48 Hellcats to Nichols Field and Neilsen Field, where his 16 *Princeton* fighters accounted for 38 kills, which was 8 more than VF-27 claimed in the Turkey Shoot. The four *Princeton* divisions were low cover at 12,000 feet when Bardshar spotted a lone Nick at 10,000 over Neilsen. The combined fire of Bardshar and his wingman's guns shattered the twin-engine fighter. Then the dogfight began.

Bardshar had a tough battle with some Zekes which shot out his right aileron and arresting hook. He downed two of them before disengaging and making a barrier landing aboard a big carrier. But all his other planes returned to the *Princeton*.

Lieutenant Carl Brown almost didn't get back. He shot down a Hamp and a Tony, but one Zeke got in a good burst which stopped his engine. Brown split-essed to evade and decided to bail out while he still had altitude. He was ready to jump when "I thought better of it. . . . I hit the primer and pumped the throttle. The darned thing roared."[6] Upon landing aboard, the Texan found two 20-mm holes in one propeller blade.

Nor was that all. After Brown reported to the ready room, his plane captain called him back up to the flight deck. There Brown saw his seat-pack parachute in tatters. Unknown to him, another 20-mm had exploded and fragments had shredded the 'chute. He commented, "Had I bailed out, my descent would have been faster than I planned."[7]

Lieutenant Commander Mehle's formations attacked Clark Field, where a remarkable performance was again turned in by VF-31. The *Cabot* Hellcats were launched with 500-pound bombs but were intercepted near the target. Conny Nooy and his wingman, E. W. Toaspern, engaged several bandits, but both pilots retained their bombs. It was in direct contrast to normal procedure and—some may have argued—not good sense. But Nooy and Toaspern "fought their guns" so successfully that they shot down seven planes between them. Nooy bagged two Zekes, two Tojos, and a Tony; Toaspern got a pair of Tonys. Then they dropped their bombs on Clark Field hangars. This impressive display of skill and courage won Nooy his second Navy cross, and boosted his aerial score to 15 kills. Other *Cabot* fighters claimed 22 more.

Late that afternoon Lieutenant Charles M. Mallory led six VF-18 Hellcats as top cover for an *Intrepid* strike to Clark. The weather had improved, and as Mallory led his F6s towards 24,000 he could see the bombers beginning their dives towards the green fields of Luzon between breaks in the fluffy clouds. At that moment Japanese fighters bounced the bombers, and Mallory prepared to lead the way down when his wingman called out two dozen bandits five miles away. They were converging from port, about 5,000 feet below.

Thankful for his division's extra altitude, Mallory attacked. He exploded a Tony on his first pass. "The next few minutes were a free-for-all," he recalled.[8] Covered by his wingman, whose guns were inoperative, Mallory shot down three more bandits. Then he saw one of his pilots boxed in by five Tojos, one only 100 feet behind the F6. With so little room for deflection, Mallory rolled in to an aiming point ahead of the Hellcat and loosed a burst. The Tojo rolled over in flames, his fifth kill of the engagement.

In the pull-out another Tojo boresighted Mallory and hit his plane solidly. The port elevator was shot off, the landing gear partially extended due to loss of hydraulic pressure, and several holes were punched in the wings. The CO evaded by feinting a split-ess, then gathered his troops en route home. All five other F6Fs were badly damaged and two pilots wounded, but each landed safely. When Mallory climbed out of his cockpit and dropped to the hardwood deck, his plane captain informed him there were 67 bullet holes in his airplane. "My Grumman had brought me home safely," he recalled.[9]

There was less air combat during the 22nd. Fighting 15 had to settle for a single kill, though VF-19 claimed six Tonys and three probables during an escort. And at long last, Fighting Two's four victories during two strikes proved the end of their long string. Lieutenants (jg) M. W. "Tex" Vineyard and Wilbur "Spider" Webb got the last pair of Tonys during the *Hornet*'s second strike of the day. It raised VF-2's aerial claims to 261 in ten months of combat, of which 224 were officially allowed. Bill Dean's pilots flew their final mission two days later and anxiously looked forward to getting back to "Uncle Sugar." Not a few of the original VF-2 contingent wondered if Wave Ensign Marie Thompson would be on hand to welcome them back. She had gone to Atlantic City to bid farewell to Lieutenant Jack Holladay, the personnel officer, when the squadron left the East Coast the previous October. Aviators being what they are, every pilot kissed Ensign Thompson goodby. Admiral McCain must have understood, for he wished the squadron, "luck, ladies, and the good time they have earned."[10]

Upon its retirement to Ulithi and Manus, the task force received replacement air groups and one new carrier. When Fighting Two finally departed the *Hornet*, it left a mixed batch of F6F-3s and -5s to

VF-11 under tough, aggressive Lieutenant Commander E. G. Fairfax, captain of the 1939 Annapolis boxing team. Two CVL air groups were also rotated; the *Cabot* and *Langley* welcomed VF-29 and VF-44 respectively. Fighting 31 departed the *Cabot* with 146 aerial victories. It would remain the top score for a CVL fighter squadron in one tour.

The new addition to the force, the *Hancock* with Air Group Seven, brought the total fast carriers to 17. Lieutenant Commander Leonard J. Check was skipper of VF-7, which with 41 F6F-5s including four night fighters, was equipped entirely with late-model Hellcats. So were VF-18, VF-20, VF-21, and VF-22.

By now the two F6F types had been flown together long enough to form an opinion of their relative merits. The consensus held that it was undesirable to operate both -3s and -5s in the same formation because the former were usually slower than the latter and used more fuel to keep pace. Some said the -5 climbed faster than the -3; others said the heavier -5 lost some vertical performance. But the F6F-5's primary attribute was its greater offensive capability, and that was what was most valued.

The first half of October was devoted to a feint at the Ryukyus and preliminary strikes upon Formosa and Luzon. In attacks against Okinawa on 10 October surprise was achieved, and most enemy planes were attacked on the ground. For instance, Fighting 19 found no airborne opposition, and VF-14 off the *Wasp* claimed only two enemy planes damaged in the air. The *Essex* Hellcats were more fortunate. After an unopposed early sweep, VF-15 tangled with a mixed bag of Tonys, Oscars, Zekes, and Nates at midday and bagged eight. One of the Tonys was credited to Lieutenant Bert DeWayne Morris, Jr. The blonde, handsome 30-year-old Californian was better known as movie star Wayne Morris, one of several Hollywood actors who flew off to war. Jimmy Stewart became a B-24 squadron commander in England; Tyrone Power flew Marine transports; Robert Taylor was a naval aviator, and Clark Gable flew a few missions as a B-17 gunner. But Bert Morris—who was married to Dave McCampbell's niece—became a genuine "Hollywood ace." The Tony was his fifth confirmed victory in air combat. The top VF-15 score of the day went to Lieutenant (jg) Arthur R. Singer who shot down three Frances bombers that afternoon.

Fighting 11 had suffered relatively light casualties during its 1943 tour on Guadalcanal with F4Fs, but quickly found out how things had changed. Pressing through heavy flak to get at shipping in Miyako Jima anchorage, the Sundowners were credited with probably destroying two of the ten vessels sunk during the day. Nineteen-year-old Ensign Ken Chase, the baby of the squadron, skipped his 500-pounder directly into

Hollywood ace. Movie actor Bert D. (Wayne) Morris, Jr., became a fighter pilot with VF-15 aboard the USS *Essex*. On 10 October 1944 he shot down his fifth Japanese aircraft, a Tony fighter. Two weeks later he gained his last two victories, a pair of Zekes in the Battle of Leyte Gulf.

the side of a 5,500-ton transport. Then, while following his division leader Lieutenant Jimmie E. Savage off the target, Chase's Hellcat was hit by flak and crashed into the water. "Doc" Savage remembered how Chase's young mother had kissed Savage goodby and asked him to take good care of her son. How did one explain there was no way to protect a pilot from hidden, anonymous antiaircraft guns?

The strikes continued until dusk when approximately one hundred enemy aircraft had been destroyed—mostly by strafing—against a loss of 21 carrier planes to all causes. On the next day a strike against northern Luzon met very little opposition, and results were equally slight. The Hellcat CAP found only three snoopers to handle. But the following day, 12 October, would more than compensate. The target was Formosa.

There were almost 350 Japanese aircraft on Formosa, nearly half of them fighters. Though the Fast Carrier Force steamed within launch range undetected by enemy patrol planes, the dawn fighter sweep which launched before 0600 was picked up on Japanese radar. Two hundred and thirty bandits immediately scrambled for one of the most sensational fighter battles since the first Truk raid.

Commander Dan F. "Dog" Smith's Air Group 20 aboard the *Enterprise* had had no significant air combat since its tour began in August. The sweep-strike to Einansho changed all that. The skipper of VF-20, Lieutenant Commander Fred Bakutis, led three divisions which met an estimated 30 fighters. Young Ensign Doug Baker, barely a year out of flight school, shot down three Tojos and a Zeke in his first dogfight. Bakutis claimed one of the other seven victories. Then Dog Smith, leading ten Hellcats with the *Enterprise* strike, arrived and knocked down a bold Zeke trying to surprise an Avenger formation. One VF-20 pilot bailed out to become a POW.

The *Lexington* and *Essex* provided the Hellcats of Task Group 38.3, which fanned out to cover central Formosa from Kagi to Taichu. They ran into large numbers of Zekes and Tojos with a few Oscars and Jacks observed nearby. Fighting 15 knocked down 20 bandits, losing none in air combat, but had two pilots forced down either by AA fire or engine trouble. Ensign Clarence A. Borley had the best shooting, with two Oscars, a Zeke, and a Tojo destroyed.

Fighting 19's sixteen fighters were not as lucky. When the four divisions became separated from one another, small formations of Hellcats were sometimes outnumbered as much as six to one. The *Lexington* pilots fought tenaciously, claiming 27 kills in the frantic, fearful minutes the battle lasted. Three Hellcats were lost, as were two pilots: VF-19's skipper, Lieutenant Commander F. E. Cook, and the flight officer, Lieutenant D. K. Tripp. A New Jersey pilot, Lieutenant Joseph J. Paskoski, got four kills, then ditched his shot-up F6F near the task force. Nearly all the planes that returned to the *Lexington* bore significant battle damage. Lieutenant B. L. Garbow claimed three victories, but he earned them the hard way; he counted 48 holes aft of his cockpit.

Lieutenant (jg) Luther D. Prater had a similar experience. He shot one Zeke off Cook's tail, then saw the CO crash on the airfield he was strafing. Prater was jumped by more Zekes, evaded into some clouds, and shot down one on the way home. But upon his return to the *Lexington*, he discovered his arresting hook would not extend due to battle damage. Yet he managed one of the trickiest feats in naval aviation—a carrier landing without a tail hook—and caused no further damage.

Though the *Essex* and *Lexington* Hellcats claimed nearly 50 victories between them, the most spectacular battle was fought by 32 F6Fs of VF-8 and VF-18 in Task Group 38.2. The targets were Shinihi and Matsuyama airfields, which the *Intrepid*'s Hellcats attacked with 500-pound bombs. Fighting 18 pushed over into 60-degree dives and hit

Shinihi's hangars, then rendezvoused at 8,000 feet north of the target and headed for Matsuyama. En route, four Lillys and one Sally were seen preparing to land at Taien airfield. Lieutenant Cecil E. Harris, a South Dakota school teacher with two previous kills in Wildcats, led his division down. Inside of two minutes all the bombers were destroyed, including a Sally and Lilly by Harris.

Then 15 to 20 Zekes hit the top rear cover from a cloud layer at 12,000 feet. These Zekes were well flown; they were unobserved until they attacked and maintained their altitude advantage through most of the combat. With a professional eye, the *Intrepid* pilots commented on "the beautiful way the Japs flew."[11] Smaller enemy formations arrived in several minutes until about 40 Zekes were engaged.

The combat area was some eight square miles from 10,000 feet down to the trees. All that the Hellcats could do was weave, keep a sharp lookout, and shoot straight. It was enough. Repeatedly, F6Fs with Zekes on their tails led their pursuers across the noses of section leaders or wingmen, who shot the Japanese off. Ensign Arthur P. Mollenhaur had bagged one of the bombers and in the next few minutes fired at ten Zekes. He expended 1800 rounds and received confirmation on four Zekes, becoming an ace in his first combat. Lieutenant (jg) F. N. Burley got three Zekes, while Cecil Harris and Lieutenant F. C. Hearrell both added a pair of Zeros to the bombers they had shot down.

Fighting 18 lost four Hellcats and three pilots in this combat against a claim of 20 fighters and five bombers. Returning pilots said there was never less than one parachute in the air, and at one time there were perhaps five.

Fighting Eight also had an observation, but of a different nature. Scotty McCuskey, the squadron's chief G-suit booster, noticed that it was easy to identify Japanese aircraft at a distance because of the fine streamers of vapor trailing from their wingtips. The Zeke vapor trails were thin and continuous, while those from the F6Fs were blunt and irregular.

The *Bunker Hill* pilots got into the hassle when Nick twin-engine fighters were seen taking off from Taien. Twelve Hellcats went down to have a look while the CO, Commander W. M. Collins, kept his division as top cover. His number four, Lieutenant (jg) W. E. Lamoreaux, called out a large gaggle at 12,000 feet, which was several thousand feet above the Hellcats. Collins looked up to see an estimated 50 to 75 fighters.

In the ensuing combat, Collins methodically shot down two Zekes and two Oscars; Lamoreaux, guarding his tail, got two more Zekes. Then Collins's plane was hit, and as he jinked violently he blacked out momentarily despite his G-suit. But the Zekes had been unable to follow his high-speed maneuver. When Collins emerged from a cloud he found a Betty dead ahead, apparently unaware of him, and he shot it down.

The other VF-8 pilots had also joined the combat. Scott McCuskey shot at five planes, killing a Nick and two Zekes. Five other *Bunker Hill* pilots also claimed triples, frequently joining the *Intrepid* Hellcats as elements of both squadrons became separated from their friends. Back aboard the *Bunker Hill*, Fighting Eight counted 32 destroyed and three probables for one F6F jettisoned with heavy damage. The grand total for this fighter sweep was 57 kills for five Hellcats lost.

Combat continued throughout the day, though at a considerably lessened tempo. Fighting 8 and 18 ran their scores for 12 October to 49 and 40 respectively during further sweeps and strikes. Final claims showed 188 aerial victories for the Hellcats. But not all of the combat occurred over the island. One hundred enemy sorties were flown against the task force which, counting snoopers downed by the CAP, accounted for 40 of the Japanese losses. Fighting 29, off the *Cabot*, splashed six Bettys during an unsuccessful dusk torpedo attack, the last action of the day.

There was considerably less air combat on Friday the 13th. Fighting 19's new CO, Lieutenant Roger Boles, shot down a Tojo, the only bandit his squadron saw. Other *Lexington* pilots occupied themselves by shooting up a large primary training field. The delicate Willow biplanes, which reminded the F6F pilots of N2S Stearmans they had flown back at Pensacola or Corpus Christi, made easy targets.

Air Group 11 found tougher going against Takao city. The *Hornet* pilots reported extremely intense AA fire from ships, the shore, and the hill that rose above the harbor. Young Lieutenant (jg) Blake Moranville, a Nebraska boy who had quit college when the flying bug bit him, was astonished by the volume of gunfire from "Ape Hill." "It lit up like a bunch of blinking Christmas tree lights," he said.[12] The *Hornet* CAG, Commander Fred Schrader of the Annapolis class of '35, was strafing a moored seaplane when his F6F was hit heavily by flak and crashed from low level.

The dusk torpedo planes were back again that evening. Three low-flying Bettys got within gun range of Task Group 38.4 and went after the *Franklin*. A VF-13 pilot in the landing circle spotted the threat and splashed one Betty with the help of gunners on nearby ships. The remaining two released their torpedoes, which narrowly missed the *Franklin*.

The cruiser *Canberra* lacked "Big Ben's" luck. She took an aerial torpedo and slid to a stop only 90 miles off Formosa and 1,300 miles from the nearest Allied base, Ulithi. She was ordered towed from the area, and two CVLs were detached to provide air cover—the *Cowpens* from TG-38.1 and the *Cabot* from TG-38.2.

As expected, the 14th brought intense action as Japanese aircraft made determined efforts to sink the damaged *Canberra*. Nearly 200 enemy aircraft approached or actually attacked the task force, and another 225 tried to find it but failed.

Though 250 carrier sorties were flown against Formosa, the heaviest combat occurred out at sea during the afternoon and evening. Seven *Hornet* Hellcats under Lieutenant Nelson Dayhoff were vectored onto an incoming raid of about 12 Judy dive bombers escorted by 15 to 20 Zekes and Tonys. Dayhoff's radio quit before the interception, then Lieutenant Doc Savage's compass failed, so tactical command passed to Lieutenant Charles R. Stimpson, entering his first combat since Guadalcanal.

Savage called the tally-ho at 17,000 feet. Charlie Stimpson climbed to tackle the top cover, leaving Savage to deal with the Judys. Experienced, deadly "Skull" Stimpson "tiptoed up behind three Zekes"[13] and exploded them before they could even drop their external tanks. His wingman, Ensign Fred Blair, also bagged one. Then they dived behind the other Zekes attacking Savage's flight, and Stimpson exploded one with a short burst. Savage had dropped two Zekes himself, only to find a Tony on his tail, which Stimpson hit and saw fall away smoking. It went unclaimed, but Blair shot a Zeke off another Sundowner's tail for a confirmed kill. By now three Hellcats had also gone down, including Dayhoff.

Stimpson and Blair were attacked from both sides and scissored on one another. Stimpson hit another Tony chasing Blair, who in turn

Commander Emmet Riera, CAG-11, ready for takeoff from the USS *Hornet*. Originally a dive bomber pilot, Riera's first flight in an F6F was while at sea. Photo: R. E. Riera

flamed yet another Zeke. But as Stimpson reversed again, a Zeke hit Blair's belly tank which burst into flames. Pulling wide deflection, Stimpson blew one wing off this bandit and fired his final rounds at another which tried to follow Blair down. The last Zeke broke off, but it was too late. Blair's burning Hellcat splashed headlong into the sea.

Fighting 11 had completely broken up the attack, claiming 14 definite kills against the loss of three pilots and four F6Fs.

Fred Bardshar led two divisions of VF-27 into a covey of 16 Fran torpedo planes approaching TG-38.3 that afternoon. The skipper splashed three and his pilots gunned down ten more as the survivors jettisoned their torpedoes and fled.

Fighting 19 from the same task group had 20 fighters up on CAP and search missions that evening and claimed 10 of 30 hostiles encountered between 1600 and 1700. Lieutenant (jg) R. W. Blakeslee was escorting a *Lexington* SB2C when 19 Japanese twin-engine bombers passed below on a reciprocal heading. The Helldiver pilot lost track of Blakeslee when the F6F turned to attack, and minutes later heard Blakeslee on the radio. He had shot down two bombers but had a badly damaged aircraft and zero oil pressure. Blakeslee added he was making a water landing. It was the last thing heard from the courageous Michigan pilot.

Despite the efforts of VF-11, VF-19, and VF-27—and other fighter squadrons—the Japanese tenacity brought results. The light cruiser *Houston*, which had replaced the *Canberra*, was torpedoed at dusk. A "cripple division" was formed of the two damaged cruisers and their escorts, and it began the long, slow haul out of air range. The *Cabot*'s VF-29 downed three Japanese planes near the vulnerable ships, losing one plane and pilot.

On the next day, 15 October, three task groups withdrew southward to refuel and resume attacks on Leyte. But Task Group 38.1 stayed behind to cover the four-knot retreat of the two cruisers being towed slowly to safety. Fighting 14 off the *Wasp* claimed 31 kills during the day, raising four pilots to ace status, but losing one pilot in combat. Fighting 11 claimed only three Judys and, like VF-14, lost a pilot who bailed out but was never rescued. Meanwhile, Fighting 29 flamed three snoopers near the plodding "CripDiv One."

On the 16th the Japanese tried harder.

Over 60 enemy planes went after the "bait" group, now guarded by only the combined 46-plane strength of the two CVL fighter squadrons. Most of the combat fell upon VF-29. Lieutenant Alfred J. Fecke's division joined that of Lieutenant Max Barnes about 20 miles north of the ships, then headed west at 10,000 feet. They sighted the enemy at 1335, a mixed formation of twin-engine Frances bombers, Jill torpedo planes, and Val dive bombers covered by about 20 Zekes at 11,000 feet. Barnes took his pilots into the bombers while Fecke climbed to starboard to draw off the fighters.

But the Zekes held back, apparently covering the rearmost bombers, and both *Cabot* divisions quickly got in among the leaders. Barnes splashed two Frans, then was chased into some clouds by a half-dozen late-arriving Zekes. His wingman, Ensign Robert E. Murray, also got a Fran on the first pass and then, separated from Barnes, joined Lieutenant (jg) Irl V. Sonner of Fecke's division. Murray got two Jills, and as he passed the second one he saw the Japanese pilot stand up and shake his fist at the Hellcat, just before the Jill hit the water. Murray then bagged a Zeke while Sonner dropped two Jills and two Frans.

Fecke's division rang up 15 kills. Seeing the Zekes hanging back, Fecke went after the rearmost bombers and shot a Frances down in flames. He quickly splashed three Jills, then chased a fourth with two other F6Fs and finished it as well. Fecke's wingman, Ensign R. B. Williams, became separated after the first pass and though he shot one Zeke off a Hellcat's tail, his plane was badly shot up and he dropped the F6F into a safe water landing. Williams was rescued shortly.

Meanwhile, Fecke's number four, Ensign Robert L. Buchanan, bagged two Frans and a pair of Jills. Heading home he attempted to join about 16 "friendly" Zekes. Recognizing his error, Buchanan scooted for some protective clouds at 17,000 feet while two Zekes chased him, one high and one low. But the second Japanese stalled 800 feet below the Hellcat, giving Buchanan a safe opening against the other. He attacked from three o'clock, saw his tracers hit the cowl, and the Zeke exploded in midair.

Eight Hellcats had broken up a major attack, downing 26 planes for the loss of one F6F. Buchanan and Fecke were both credited with five victories, Sonner and Murray with four each.

Fighting 22 picked over the remainder of the Japanese. The *Cowpens* Hellcats claimed a dozen kills, including four torpedo planes by Lieutenant Clement M. Craig. One torpedo-packing Japanese pressed on to hit the *Houston* a second time, but the battered cruiser remained afloat. Both ships survived their ordeal, thanks to the spirited defense put up by their Hellcat guardians.

Some 500 Japanese replacement aircraft intended for the Philippines were destroyed on Formosa, so the next week passed in relative quiet as the fast carriers roamed east of Luzon. Wednesday the 18th was the busiest day of that week, with small but violent fighter battles over land and water. On the morning sweep Fred Bakutis took three of his VF-20 divisions to the Manila area, prowling high at 25,000 feet. The *Enterprise* Hellcats found seven Tojos climbing out of Clark Field, and Bakutis took two divisions down after them. But more bandits arrived, the F6 top cover came down, and a close-in, milling dogfight ensued. Lieutenant (jg) Bill Foye bagged two fighters, then radioed he was going down near Subic Bay. He bailed out, unseen by his friends, and was found by Filipino guerrillas.

Ensign John Hoeynck collided with an Oscar in a turning contest, losing three feet of his port wing. The Japanese fighter tumbled out of sight, and Hoeynck limped towards home under close escort by Bakutis and another Hellcat. After a persistent Oscar made five or six passes at Hoeynck, Bakutis reversed his usual turn in the defensive weave and shot it down for his third kill of the fray. Ensign Doug Baker, continuing to score in multiples, also shot down three as did Ensign Chuck Haverlund. In all, VF-20 claimed 18 kills in this combat and added another 11 later in the day, but lost two more Hellcats.

Fighting 14 flew two sweeps over central Luzon, meeting strong opposition. When enemy fighters jumped Lieutenant E. B. Turner's division and shot down his section leader, Turner "went berserk"[14] and destroyed five. The other *Wasp* pilots got 11 more.

But most squadrons saw little air combat on the 18th. Fighting 15 scored six victories in an early morning sweep over the Visayas, including a Dinah and a Nate by Dave McCampbell, who became the first Navy pilot to reach 20 kills. "Fabled Fifteen" then burned a medium-sized transport. And though VF-19 got two Kates in the same area, Hugh Winters's Hellcats were mainly engaged in trying out their new, fast, shallow masthead bomb attacks against cargo vessels.

Three of the four fast carrier task groups were steaming in Leyte Gulf the morning of 24 October. Task Group 38.1 was headed for Ulithi, but the other 11 carriers prepared to launch searches and CAPs. It was a routine beginning to a most unroutine day.

Northernmost was Rear Admiral Fred Sherman's TG-38.3—the *Essex*, *Lexington*, *Princeton* and *Langley*—100 miles east of Luzon. Upon these ships' air groups would fall nearly all the major combat in this, the opening day of the Battle of Leyte Gulf. Air Group 19 aboard the *Lexington* had most of the task group's search responsibility, and 37 aircraft were sent off to scout the western quadrant to a distance of 300 miles. Five search sectors, from 245° to 295° True, were assigned to 19 Hellcats and 18 Helldivers. Another division of F6Fs was sent out to 200 miles, south of Manila Bay, to act as radio relay.

The *Lexington* search teams launched at 0607, but several F6Fs and SB2Cs lost track of each other in heavy clouds between the task group and Luzon. While search teams to the south were locating the major Japanese surface forces between Mindoro and Mindanao, the *Lexington* planes found only coastal shipping. Lieutenant Bruce Williams, formerly a Willamette University law student, led a three-plane division which was the only team to sink anything. Ammunition barges were found underway in Lingayen Gulf and Williams attacked. Known as "Willy Mohawk," for the *Lexington*'s call sign, the exuberant Oregonian put his 500-pounder on a 35-foot barge and "blew it to bits,"[15] but the explosion tossed his Hellcat 200 feet upward through the debris. Returning to base, Williams's flight was bounced by Tojos and one F6 had to duck into cloud cover. Almost immediately, however, Williams and Lieutenant (jg) Larry Cauble pursued several twin-engine Sallys in a tail chase through a valley and shot down five before their ammunition ran out.

In the adjacent search sector, Lieutenant Elvin Lindsay's division was flying by sections near Clark Field when they were jumped by 17 Tojos. Lindsay and Ensign W. H. Martin had ten to themselves. Lindsay claimed a kill and two probables while Martin got two kills, the Japanese displaying little coordination or air discipline. Though Martin's F6F was damaged in the fight, he and Lindsay each dropped a Val shortly thereafter. Martin ditched his faltering plane near a destroyer upon returning to the task group and was rescued. The second section bagged three of seven Tojos. The division had claimed eight victories for one F6F.

The biggest haul was made by Lieutenant (jg) William J. Masoner's division, which found 20 twin-engine bombers in four groups along its search route. Masoner already had two kills from his days with VF-11 on Guadalcanal and put his experience to superb use. His gun camera recorded the destruction of a Betty, a Dinah, and four Nells, while the other three pilots accounted for another seven bombers. In all, 15 Fighting 19 pilots claimed 30 kills from this five-hour mission while VF-15 splashed seven hostiles during similar searches in the same area.

Meanwhile, the Japanese were on the offensive. Some 450 naval aircraft had been flown into the Philippines during the night, and beginning at 0750, TG-38.3's radarscopes glowed brightly with multiple contacts. Three attack waves of 50 to 60 aircraft each, 15 miles apart, were headed towards Sherman's four carriers. For the moment, any thought of launching strikes against enemy surface units to the southwest was forgotten. All available fighters were scrambled immediately.

Aboard the *Lexington*, where 11 Hellcats were ready for launch, a peculiar thing happened. The "Lex's" gunners—hard-bitten veterans of a full year of carrier war—actually cheered as VF-19 pilots charged down the flight deck to man their planes. It was as if the fighter pilots were running onto a football field to the applause of the hometown crowd. And never could there be a more appreciative rooting section. For in this contest, when the opposition scored it meant the loss of friends, a place to sleep, of one's home away from home.

Lieutenant Roger Boles led his VF-19 pilots away from the task group on a vector of 215°, climbing at maximum power in response to the FDO's order for "Gate" speed. The Grummans arced up into a three-tenths cloud cover dotted with thunder showers, indicating 250 knots as the big Pratt and Whitneys burned four gallons per minute. Twenty miles out, the lead division spotted some lone bogeys and bagged two Zekes. Boles chased down a Nick and splashed it from a height of 100 feet.

Meanwhile, Lieutenant H. V. Bonzagni, Jr., took his second division into a formation of Vals with Zeke top cover as the third division of three Hellcats tailed behind. Bonzagni's four made high side passes, ignoring the Zekes which turned west and left the Vals unprotected. Bonzagni burned three Vals from 17,000 feet down to 8,000 and his pilots got four more plus one shared with a *Langley* Hellcat of VF-44. The third division claimed one Jill shot down but returned minus Ensign F. P. Hubbuch, who had reported engine trouble and was last seen chasing a hostile. Thus, the *Lexington*'s fighter scramble claimed 11½ kills for one loss.

At the same time, VF-27 was already engaged. Three divisions were up on CAP before the scramble was ordered, including those of Lieutenants James A. Shirley and Carl A. Brown. "Red" Shirley received two vectors to investigate bogeys and shot down two snoopers. Carl Brown also got two vectors but both times found Avengers with their IFF off.

Shortly thereafter, Shirley's division was at 20,000 and Brown's at 10,000 when both were given the same vector at Gate speed. Shirley's flight pulled ahead while Brown clawed for altitude. "When both of us got the same vector," Brown said, "I knew it had to be trouble."[16] He was right.

Still climbing at Gate, Brown repeatedly asked how many bandits were up ahead. The busy FDO ignored the questions several times, then rasped out, "Many, many, many, many."[17] The lower division had reached 18,000 feet when Shirley tally-hoed two hostiles in succession and dropped them both. Brown had now closed up, and saw a huge enemy formation straight ahead, stacked from about 20,000 to 23,000 feet. Notifying the *Princeton*, Brown said, "Hatchet Base, estimate 80."[18] He got a roger and good luck as he prepared to engage. At almost the same time Shirley called out, "Hundreds of bogeys, high, low, and in the middle. Am attacking 'til ammo runs out."[19]

For the next several minutes, airplanes fell into the sea at a terrific rate. To the men on the *Princeton*, Red Shirley had always been "a real killer,"[20] and certainly he was this day. He spent the last of his ammunition on his fifth victim of the mission. It brought his total to 12 in only three combats.

Another division rushed to the scene, and the battle intensified as casualties were inflicted on both sides. Ensign Thomas J. Conroy paced the squadron with six and a half kills while Lieutenant Gene Townsend splashed five planes. But Lieutenant Ralph S. Taylor was shot in the leg and returned to the *Princeton,* and Ensign Oliver Scott never got back at all.

Carl Brown had a rugged five minutes. He began the fight with an altitude and airspeed disadvantage, attacking from below. His F6F was repeatedly hit in a series of dogfights with numerous Zekes. But he gave better than he got, and claimed five destroyed and two probables. He recalled, however, that "I finished the fight with four Zekes on my tail arguing who'd kill me."[21] Before they decided who would do the honors, Brown shoved his stick full forward, two-blocked the throttle with prop in full low pitch, and made a hard right spiral. This violent maneuver shook his pursuers and, despite his damaged plane, he requested a steer back to the combat. But by then the raid had dissipated.

Brown's instrument panel was shot up, and a cut fuel line spilled about three inches of gasoline onto the cockpit floor. Approaching the task group, he discovered his arresting hook would not extend. Then he heard that the *Princeton* had a fouled deck, and neither the *Lexington* nor the *Langley* would take him aboard, fearful he would crash and close their decks, too. The Texan had just resigned himself to a water landing when the *Essex* came on the air: "Hatchet 7, if you'll land immediately, we'll take you."[22] Immensely relieved, Brown prepared to land without an airspeed indicator or tail hook. Yet despite two leg wounds, he plunked his battered Cat down on the *Essex*'s deck, the hook jarred loose, engaged the first wire, and he was safe.

The saga of Fighting 27 was not yet over. The CAG, big Fred Bardshar, had been scheduled to lead a strike when his division was scrambled to meet the emergency. That made 20 *Princeton* fighters airborne during the raid. The flight was placed in a rather vulnerable orbit at 7,500 feet about 75 miles from the force, barely above the overcast. Bardshar tried to get permission to climb higher but the voice circuits were jammed. Then the roof fell in.

Some 30 Oscars dived on the division from 5,000 feet above. But they were unaggressive and most dived into the clouds rather than face VF-27's delayed weave. Two Oscars disappeared trailing smoke, and though Bardshar's plane had taken hits in the engine, smearing his canopy with a film of oil, "the old R-2800 ran well."[23] On the way home the CAG's wingman, Ensign Arthur Munson, drew blood for the division by shooting down a stray Val.

Vectored to base, ten VF-27 pilots had been taken aboard when Bardshar and the remaining eight learned that the *Princeton's* problem was

Lieutenant Carl Brown's VF-27 Hellcat is pushed forward on the USS *Essex* after combat with Japanese aircraft attacking the light carrier *Princeton*. Fighting 27 claimed the destruction of 36 attackers, but one broke through and hit the *Princeton*, starting her fatal fires. Photo: R. M. Hill

more serious than a fouled deck. At 0938 a lone Judy had dropped out of the low clouds and put its bomb into "Sweet P's" flight deck, near the aft elevator. Other Hellcats destroyed the Judy but the *Princeton*'s fires proved uncontrollable. Six hours later she exploded and sank—the only U.S. Navy fast carrier lost in the last three years of the war.

The *Princeton* orphans were made most welcome aboard the *Essex*. No pilots had ever fought harder for their ship. The shark-mouthed Hellcats had shot three dozen Japanese planes into the water in only a few minutes. Of the seven pilots who destroyed five or more enemy aircraft this day, four were from VF-27. And though they were now effectively out of the action, many of them would be back.

Spotted on the port catapult aboard the *Essex* that morning was Dave McCampbell's F6F-5, "Minsi III," named for his friend Mary Blatz of Milwaukee. Originally scheduled to lead a strike, McCampbell was shot off at 0820 to meet the imminent threat, and two divisions followed. His section leader's plane was unable to launch, however, giving the CAG seven fighters including his own.

Over the *Essex* at 6,000 feet, McCampbell was Buster-vectored north to a radar plot 38 miles out. Three minutes later he saw a large formation about 25 miles away. At first the disposition looked like a TF-38 strike group, but "shortly thereafter the planes were definitely identified as enemy and reported to be composed of at least 60 rats, hawks, and fish."[24]

Most of the "rats" (enemy fighters) were well above McCampbell's altitude of 14,000 feet. But as he led his Hellcats towards them, the Japanese reversed course, causing the formation to string out. It was now vulnerable and the CAG ordered his second division after the "hawks" and "fish" (dive bombers and torpedo planes) while his three worked over the fighters.

At this moment communications failed. The F6Fs had to change radio frequencies, and McCampbell lost tactical control when five of his fighters dived on the enemy below, chasing the bombers down through the overcast. Four of the VF-15 pilots eventually gunned down six planes, but the main event was fought topside.

Dave McCampbell and his regular wingman Roy Rushing were the right men in the right place at the right time. The 21 Japanese flags below McCampbell's cockpit testified to his experience and proficiency. In all, there were about 40 bandits—mostly bomb-carrying Zekes and a

Commander David McCampbell in his personal F6F-5, "Minsi III," aboard the USS *Essex* on 22 October 1944. Two days later he shot down nine Japanese fighters while defending his task group from heavy air attack, a feat which earned him the Congressional Medal of Honor. Photo: R. M. Hill

few accompanying Oscars. They maintained a large, orderly Lufbery circle which guarded the tail of each plane. After three or four passes to seek an opening, McCampbell and Rushing pulled up and each lit a cigarette. Time was on their side.

McCampbell figured the Japanese "probably were not too flush with petrol,"[25] knowing that when they dispersed there would be confusion and easy pickings among the stragglers. There were.

For 95 minutes Dave McCampbell and Roy Rushing played out their waiting game. They sat above the Japanese, harrying the large formation as it finally headed back towards Manila—two wolves biting at the flanks of a dangerous herd. The two Hellcats were careful not to expose themselves to unnecessary risk, but concentrated on enemy planes which attempted to climb to their altitude, those which lagged behind or went too wide on their weaving turns. Working this way, McCampbell could see it was going to be a long day. "It was not until we had destroyed five and business was beginning to get good that I decided to keep a box score by marking on my instrument panel with a pencil,"[26] he recalled.

McCampbell spent 30 minutes screaming for help before he got through to the *Essex* FDO—a future Secretary of the Navy named John Connally. One VF-15 F6F flown by Lieutenant (jg) Albert C. Slack finally joined up. Now able to take on larger groups, the *Essex* Hellcats pressed their attacks and flamed three planes on each of two passes. Slack used up all his ammunition while downing four Zekes and withdrew, leaving McCampbell and Rushing to finish the job.

Between them, the CAG and his wingman made 18 to 20 passes, and there were only 18 planes left in the formation when ammo and fuel shortages forced them to disengage. Dave McCampbell had nine definite kills: seven Zekes or Hamps and two Oscars, plus two probables which were last seen spinning towards the water. Roy Rushing splashed five Zekes or Hamps and an Oscar, damaging three others. The only damage to their two F6Fs was some superficial dents and scratches caused by the debris of exploding airplanes.

In this mission McCampbell set a record for American and Allied fighter pilots: nine kills in one sortie. He ran his score to 30, temporarily sharing the U.S. "ace of aces" title with Army Air Force Major Richard Bong. Rushing had doubled his own tally, from 6 to 12.

McCampbell and Rushing returned together to the task group but the CAG had to set down on the *Langley*. His fuel tanks had not been topped off before the scramble, and he couldn't wait for the *Essex* to recover aircraft already in the pattern. But Dave McCampbell had the luck of the Irish. His engine died when he tried to taxi out of the arresting gear, and the *Langley* deck crew told him he had two rounds of .50 caliber remaining.

Meanwhile, a second scramble had been ordered. Two full divisions, led by Lieutenant Bert Morris, intercepted a mixed fighter-bomber-torpedo formation 50 miles out. In a 25-mile running battle the eight Hellcats destroyed ten bandits. The two *Essex* scrambles, involving 15 F6Fs, had shot down 35 Japanese aircraft. In all, the task group had claimed over 85 attackers, allowing one to get through—the lone Judy which hit the *Princeton*. It was proof enough of what the other carriers had been spared.

By mid morning the fast carriers were on the offensive. Powerful Japanese surface units, reported earlier in the Sibuyan Sea and Surigao Strait, were tracked for the rest of the day and subjected to several air strikes. The first was a 36-plane group from the *Intrepid* and the *Cabot*, including 21 Hellcats, which went after the larger force in the Sibuyan Sea. The TG-38.2 planes attacked Admiral Kurita's 26 warships at 1026, pushing through intense AA fire, but meeting no aerial opposition. On this strike, as on most of the others, many Hellcats were armed with bombs.

Once Rear Admiral Fred Sherman's northern task group was free to do so, the *Essex* and *Lexington* began launching 16 Hellcats, 20 SB2Cs, and 32 Avengers at 1050. The strike coordinator was Commander Hugh Winters, leading his squadrons through terrible weather across southern Luzon and out over the sea. Low overcast and five-mile visibility plagued the attackers most of the day.

Fighting 19 carried no bombs, anticipating enemy air cover, but instead engaged almost entirely in strafing. Lieutenant J. J. Paskoski, Winters's section leader, had just pulled out of a firing pass when he saw a Jake being overrun by other F6Fs. Paskoski turned in behind the floatplane and sent it down burning after a single burst, one of only four enemy aircraft seen over the Kurita force.

Arriving back at the task group around 1500, Winters noted AA bursts in the air. He was about to call Mohawk Base to ask the *Lexington* what was happening when he saw a Judy fleeing from two Helldivers low on the water; another raid was in progress. Winters peeled off, got on the Judy's tail and exploded it with one well-aimed burst.

Lieutenant Elvin Lindsay, a wheat rancher from Palouse, Washington, was on his second flight of the day. He led two divisions into an estimated 30 Zekes at 4,000 feet only 15 miles out. Lindsay flamed two from dead astern, his third and fourth confirmed kills of the 24th. Five other VF-19 pilots splashed seven more, and the raid was dispersed.

Meanwhile, TG-38.4, farthest south, had launched search-strikes from the *Enterprise* and *Franklin*. The "Big E's" planes, under Commander "Dog" Smith of Air Group 20, found Vice Admiral Nishimura's seven ships near Mindanao. Smith's 18 F6Fs and 12 Helldivers were not enough to sink either of Nishimura's two battleships, but they could do considerable damage. Lieutenant Commander Fred Bakutis, skipper of VF-20, led his Hellcats down in a rocket attack and took hits in his engine. Losing oil pressure, he shucked his belly tank and splashed down to a water landing. He spent the next seven days floating in the Sulu Sea before rescue by a U.S. submarine.

The other missions were all flown against Kurita, since he represented the greater threat. By the time the last Grummans and Curtisses departed after 1500, the giant battleship *Musashi* had taken three dozen bomb and torpedo hits. She sank that evening. But unknown to the Americans, Kurita doggedly continued east during the night, heading for San Bernardino Strait.

In all, 259 carrier sorties had been flown against this powerful surface force, nearly half by Hellcats. Eighteen TF-38 planes were lost to the formidable flak put up by the battleships and cruisers. Ten more went down on search or CAP sorties, but upwards of 150 Japanese planes had been destroyed—over three-quarters of them by the F6Fs of TG-38.3. The *Lexington* fighters led the way with 52 claims.

Air combat was one thing; attacking battleships was yet another. But the next day would make many of the aviators' fondest wishes a reality. Japanese carriers were again at hand.

All during the night of the 24th and into the wee hours of the 25th, the fast carriers pounded north. Admiral Halsey, commanding the Third Fleet, had no intention of letting the hated Japanese flattops escape as they had from the Marianas. He had no way of knowing that the four enemy carriers steaming off Cape Engano were sacrificial decoys in classic Japanese fashion, with only 29 planes.

Thus diverted, Halsey left San Bernardino Strait open to the determined Kurita's battleships and cruisers, which would fall upon the escort carriers off Samar. But to the aviators of TF-38 all this was both unknown and irrelevant. Long before daylight the ready rooms were full of eager fliers, anxious to see and strike Japanese carriers. Few of Mitscher's aviators had ever seen one; only three air groups remained from TF-58 and that long-ago evening of 20 June.

Search teams of F6Fs and SB2Cs were launched as soon as practical, probing west and north for the enemy carriers. To save time, strike groups were also sent up, orbiting about 50 miles north of the task force waiting for the enemy's location. A VF-15 radio relay team led by Lieutenant John Collins made first contact, passing the word at 0735 that four carriers, two hermaphrodite battleships, and eleven escorts were 150 miles north of Mitscher.

Task Group 38.3's heavy punch from the *Essex* and *Lexington* went in first. Eighteen to 20 Zekes were airborne to meet the strike. Fighting 15 got to them first and shot down nine. Four Zekes fell to Lieutenant J. R. Strane, who bailed out over unfriendly water after his engine was hit. He was fished out that afternoon by a U.S. destroyer.

Dave McCampbell set up as target coordinator, call-sign "99 Rebel," and prepared to oversee the first two strikes. He directed his own planes and those of other squadrons against the light carrier *Chitose,* which took several bomb hits. Lieutenant Roger Boles, at the head of VF-19, shot down one Zeke which got in his way en route to the *Chitose* and the "Lex's" planes also piled in. The *Chitose* went down at 0937.

McCampbell remained as target coordinator until relieved by his counterpart Hugh Winters who arrived with the third strike. By this time two more light carriers and one of the flight-deck-equipped battleships had also been damaged.

Winters's strike was the largest of the day—over 200 aircraft. The *Lexington* CAG directed a torpedo attack against the only remaining CV, the veteran *Zuikaku,* which sank on the spot. Subsequent missions finished off the two damaged CVLs.

Well over 500 carrier sorties were flown in the course of six strikes, but nearly all the damage was done in the first four. The strain began telling by 1700 when the fifth strike went in, as many pilots were then on their third mission. A full 200 of the task force sorties were flown by F6Fs, which accounted for a goodly share of the bomb hits. It was in contrast to the Marianas where bomb-toting Hellcats fared poorly in the strike role. But here, off Cape Engano, there was no shortage of time or daylight; nor was there effective fighter interception.

Finally deprived of any effective carrier force, the Japanese Navy had become desperate. Yet exactly how desperate was not to be evident for a few days.

On 29 October Task Groups 38.2 and 38.4 were assigned airfield targets on Luzon, and four of the air groups met with considerable success. The *Hancock, Franklin, Intrepid,* and *Enterprise* Hellcats claimed some 70 aerial victories during the strikes, and left about a dozen more wrecked on their parking aprons. Ten Hellcats were lost to enemy action. Fighting 18 had the best of the action, with a tally of 42 kills during the day's four missions, losing two in combat and one operationally. Lieutenant Cecil Harris bagged three Tojos and a Zeke, the third time he had downed four planes in one day.

During the noon hour a large Japanese formation was intercepted too close to the task force to prevent a lone intruder from sneaking past the CAP. Taking advantage of the poor weather, this plane intentionally dived into one of the *Intrepid*'s starboard 20-mm gun sponsons. The "Evil I" was not seriously hurt, and remained with the task group. But her slight damage did nothing to alleviate the fact that the first suicide attack against the fast carriers had been successful.

The kamikazes had arrived.

The next day, Task Groups 38.2 and 38.4 were operating off Leyte. The sustained pace of combat had depleted operational F6Fs to a dangerously low level, and several kamikazes either penetrated the CAP or evaded interception entirely. Five of them dived on TG-38.4, but were spotted by the AA gunners, who fired at them. Three fell into the water.

The surviving pair lived long enough to die as they intended. One smashed into the *Franklin,* tearing a large hole in her flight deck, destroying 33 aircraft, and causing over 100 casualties. The other plunged down on the *Belleau Wood* and made a direct hit, inflicting 150 casualties and wrecking a dozen planes. The task group was forced to return to Ulithi because of these setbacks, leaving only the under-strength TG-38.2 covering Leyte for the moment.

During the short breather at Ulithi, Vice Admiral John S. McCain relieved Mitscher as Commander Task Force 38, and the new staff began considering suicide attack countermeasures. An analysis of the Philippines reports showed that kamikazes always came from the nearest land, usually in two groups—sometimes three—numbering from three to six planes in the first group and three to 15 in the next two. They nearly always flew at mixed altitudes up to 18,000 feet.

For the moment, the only possible action was to restore the fighter squadrons to their full authorized strength of 54 Hellcats on CVs and 24 on CVLs. But McCain decided to retain more fighters for ForceCAP while sending fewer to escort strikes. And while sailors and airmen traded rumors about an unfathomable enemy—suicide pilots were reported locked in their cockpits or shot down by other Japanese if they returned to base —McCain's staff went to work on an effective kamikaze doctrine.

By the end of October 1944 the Fast Carrier Force had evolved to its penultimate form. Over a year of combat and practical experience had brought the force to its current high level of proficiency. There were full-time night carriers, enabling round-the-clock operations against nearly any target in range. The importance of fighters had been recognized to the extent that F6Fs comprised 60 percent of all aircraft in the task force. Consequently, they were performing virtually every function but torpedo attack. Directed by experienced controllers with the best electronics available, the Hellcats had made their flight decks almost immune to conventional air assault.

The battle against the kamikazes would sorely test all previous skill, knowledge, and experience.

Hellcat Squadrons in Combat: September to November, 1944

VF-2	*Hornet*	Commander William A. Dean, Jr.
VF-3	*Yorktown*	Lieutenant Commander W. L. Lamberson
VF-4	*Bunker Hill, Essex*	Lieutenant Commander K. G. Hammond
VF-7	*Hancock*	Lieutenant Commander Leonard J. Check
VF-8	*Bunker Hill*	Commander William M. Collins, Jr.
VF-11	*Hornet*	Lieutenant Commander Eugene G Fairfax
VF-13	*Franklin*	Commander William M. Coleman
VF-14	*Wasp*	Lieutenant Commander R. Gray, Lieutenant Commander H. H. Hassenfratz
VF-15	*Essex*	Lieutenant Commander James F. Rigg
VF-18	*Intrepid*	Lieutenant E. J. Murphy
VF-19	*Lexington*	Lieutenant Commander F. E. Cook, Jr. (KIA), Lieutenant R. Boles (KIA)
VF-20	*Enterprise*	Commander F. E. Bakutis, Commander James S. Gray
VF-21	*Belleau Wood*	Lieutenant Commander V. F. Casey
VF-22	*Cowpens*	Lieutenant L. L. Johnson
VF-27	*Princeton*	Lieutenant Commander Frederick A Bardshar
VF-28	*Monterey*	Lieutenant Commander Roger W. Mehle
VF-29	*Cabot*	Lieutenant Commander W. E. Eder
VF-31	*Cabot*	Lieutenant Commander D. J. Wallace, Jr.
VF-32	*Langley*	Commander Eddie C. Outlaw
VF-44	*Langley*	Commander Malcolm T. Wordell
VF-51	*San Jacinto*	Commander Charles L. Moore

7 Interim

If I go away to sea,
I shall return a corpse awash.
Thus for the sake of the Emperor,
I will not die peacefully at home.

Ancient song of the Japanese warrior

Vice Admiral John S. McCain began his first cruise as ComTaskForce 38 with three task groups ready to launch a series of strikes against Luzon. The four-day operation was to begin on 3 November, but mindful of the new suicide threat, McCain decided to assign fewer F6Fs to escort missions. He preferred to retain more Hellcats for ForceCap. His judgment proved correct, for aerial opposition over Luzon was scattered and largely ineffective.

The one exception came early in the morning of 5 November when the CV fighter squadrons of Task Groups 38.1 and 38.3 tangled with large gaggles of Zekes, Oscars, and Tojos around Clark Field. The fighter sweeps netted a total claim of 58 aerial victories, nearly half of which fell to the Sundowners of VF-11.

The sweep was led by VF-11 CO Gene Fairfax, since *Hornet's* new CAG was not yet qualified in the F6F. Commander Emmett Riera had only been aboard a few days as CAG-11, hastily transferred from his previous slot as skipper of *Enterprise's* VB-20 to replace Commander Schrader, killed at Formosa. A dive bomber pilot since 1939, Riera soon obtained permission from Captain Artie Doyle to check out in the F6F while at sea. It would have been unthinkable in an F4U or SB2C, perhaps, but the Hellcat was so easy to fly that Riera's first flight in an F6F was made from the *Hornet's* deck.

Meanwhile, at 0615 on the fifth, Gene Fairfax led 52 Hellcats and 35 bombers from TG-38.1 on a 160-mile strike to the Clark Field complex. The F6Fs arrived at first light and dispersed to shoot up parked aircraft at Tarlac and Mabalacat, since apparently no Japanese were airborne. But at the latter field, one of Fairfax's division leaders, Lieutenant James S. Swope, called out Bettys taking off. Swope's section leader, Lieutenant (jg) Blake Moranville, rolled over and made a fast run on one Betty and shot it down.

Almost immediately the Sundowners found themselves in a pretty good dogfight. Fairfax, Swope, and Moranville each bagged a pair of Tojos, and seven other VF-11 pilots shot down nine more fighters. "Rabbit" Moranville, with only one gun firing, got his second Tojo at zero feet by forcing it to catch a wingtip on the ground. The *Hornet* Hellcats' only loss was Ensign W. W. Mann, flying an F6F-5P. Mann was attacked by an Oscar which set his drop tank afire, and his section leader in an F6F-3 without water injection was unable to weave fast enough to drive the Japanese off. It was a bitter point with many pilots that -3s should remain at sea when F6F-5s were being assigned to some operational training units. The fact was, it took time for the new fighters to reach combat squadrons, but it was small consolation.

The *Hornet* and *Wasp* fighters escorted their Helldivers and Avengers back to the task group without further loss, but the unexpected opposition of the first strike forced a change in plans. Strike Baker, with more VF-11 and VF-14 Hellcats, pounced upon Clark Field North and found more Oscars airborne. The Sundowners bagged ten without a loss as Lieutenant Charles R. Stimpson continued his two-tour standing as VF-11's top gun. The tall, thin ace got three kills to run his total to 14.

Fighting 14 bagged 21 enemy aircraft during two sweeps and three strikes, but lost its top scorer, Lieutenant W. M. Knight, who had seven and one-half victories to his credit. The *Wasp's* fighters also lost their perfect escort record as a straggling bomber fell out of formation and was shot down by two Zekes.

Later during the day Air Groups 15 and 19 went to Manila. Target coordinator was Dave McCampbell with one division of *Essex* fighters. McCampbell found time to shoot down a Zeke and a Val, while his wingman Roy Rushing bagged a Zeke for his own 13th and last kill. Elsewhere during the day Fighting 15 claimed another ten victories, but otherwise the TG-38.3 fighters had little shooting. Fighting 19 got four kills during an afternoon strike but lost its CO, Lieutenant Roger Boles, to AA fire south of Manila. He was VF-19's second commanding officer killed in action in three weeks.

Nor was that all. Later that afternoon several Zekes attacked Task Group 38.3 with little warning. The *Lexington* fighters shot down one, but four broke through the CAP. Three were shot to pieces by the *Lex's* highly practiced AA gunners, but inevitably the fourth proved to be a kamikaze. It hit the *Lexington* on the starboard side of her bridge. Resulting fires were controlled in 20 minutes, but when the tally was made, 182 men were dead or wounded.

The *Ticonderoga's* brand-new VF-80 broke into combat for the first time this same day, during strikes upon Manila. Lieutenant John W. Fair scored the first kill for Lieutenant Commander Leroy W. Keith's squadron, and five other enemy aircraft also fell. Two were splashed by Keith himself and by Lieutenant Patrick D. Fleming, later the squadron's top scorer. But it was a costly introduction to combat as four Hellcats were lost.

The next day, 6 November, was the fourth and last of the operation. The final combat of VF-19's tour came when two divisions gunned down 12 Japanese fighters around Clark Field. A thirteenth was literally hacked down. Ensign Robert A. Farnsworth, Jr., flew according to sound fighter doctrine and stubbornly refused to break off from a head-on run by a Tojo. The Japanese pilot pulled up too late to miss, and glanced off the Hellcat's wing. Incredibly, the F6 stayed in the air, but the Tojo cartwheeled down, minus one wing. Farnsworth returned to the *Lexington* with a large hunk of Japanese aluminum lodged under his own wing. It was a fittingly spectacular end to Fighting 19's combat career, raising the squadron's aerial tally to 167 kills.

The sixth also saw the last combat of VF-14, which had been aboard the *Wasp* since mid-May. The Iron Angels had accounted for 140 planes in the air and 242 on the ground but had lost 20 pilots and 43 aircraft in six months of combat. That included the first two COs, both shot down in July, and there had been four acting skippers since. Having flown both Hellcat models in combat, VF-14 concluded that the F6F "has proven itself to be the best all-around plane yet developed."[1] The F6F-3's tail problems—wrinkling of the empennage skin and partial stabilizer failure —drew comment, but the *Wasp* pilots still considered the Hellcat beyond praise.

Admiral McCain had some praise of his own. In bidding farewell to Fighting 14, he called the squadron "a great fighting organization" and wished everybody "plenty of luck, liquor, and ladies."[2]

During the four-day November raids, carrier planes claimed 439 enemy aircraft, the large majority on the ground. Flying low over the lush green Philippine landscape, F6F pilots reported numerous Japanese planes hidden in revetments many miles from the nearest airfields. Some were found as far as 35 miles out, evidently towed along narrow roads. The Japanese were abandoning their airdromes.

Additional strikes were conducted through mid month, with only spotty opposition. Japanese air power in the Philippines was being systematically destroyed on the ground, though VF-15 found fair hunting on Armistice Day. During a convoy strike near Ormoc Bay by the *Essex* and *Ticonderoga* squadrons, Dave McCampbell's 16 Hellcats tangled with about 20 Japanese fighters. "Fabled Fifteen" knocked down ten Oscars, including one by the CAG. Again experimenting, McCampbell reported, "It is worthy of note that the F6F-5 with War Emergency Power was able to overcome a 3,000-foot altitude disadvantage and catch Oscar in about three minutes at his best altitude, 11,000 feet."[3]

Three days later Dave McCampbell and Air Group 15 finished their tour. The CAG was the only one to score, shooting down one Oscar and damaging another. It brought his aerial score to 34 confirmed, only two behind Air Force Major Richard Bong as the top American fighter scorer. Bong remained in combat until mid-December, running his string to an even 40, but McCampbell's personal and unit records were landmarks.

In six and one-half months of combat, VF-15 had been credited with 313 enemy aircraft destroyed in the air and an equal number on the ground. These figures, along with the shipping losses Air Group 15 inflicted on the Japanese, were the highest in the U.S. Navy. Fighting 15 produced 26 fighter aces—another record, for it was one more than the

Rippers of VF-2. The squadron's pilot losses totaled 21, attributed equally to air combat, AA fire, and operational or unknown causes.

Dave McCampbell's 34 kills, though exceeded by two Army Air Force pilots, were the most ever scored by an American flier in one tour of duty. He was also credited with seven probables in the air and 21 planes on the ground. At the Turkey Shoot and Leyte Gulf he became the only American to achieve five or more aerial victories in one day on two separate occasions. For this personal record and the leadership of a highly successful air group, McCampbell became the only carrier pilot awarded the Medal of Honor in the last three years of the war.

Strikes continued almost until the end of November, with Manila the focal point. On the 19th, 116 enemy planes were reported destroyed, including eight shot down near the task force. The *Lexington* now operated Lieutenant Commander Fred Bakutis's VF-20, which burned 70 planes on a well-camouflaged field near Del Carmen while VF-11 shot up the large airdrome itself.

Six days later the Japanese mounted their first large air attack since the end of October. Task Groups 38.1 and 38.2 were back on station off Luzon, their Hellcats shooting 26 bandits out of the air. But after noon, radar picked up a bogey too close to analyze sufficiently, only 30 miles out. A hasty interception was made, but three Zekes got through. It was the same new-old story. Two were shot down by AA and the third dived into the *Intrepid*. Five minutes later another pair dived on the "Evil I." One splashed and one crashed. The *Intrepid* burned for two hours, and over 150 men died or suffered serious injuries. She was pulled off the line, forcing an end to VF-18's eleven-week combat tour in which 187 enemy aircraft were shot down. Fighting 18's top scorer, Lieutenant Cecil Harris, downed four planes during the day to raise his total to 24, of which 23 were scored in Hellcats. His spot as the Navy's second-ranking fighter ace was secure.

The kamikazes were not yet finished. The light carrier *Cabot* was also hit, and the *Essex,* with Air Group Four newly embarked, was nicked by one of two Judys which attacked her. At a cost of 32 Japanese aircraft shot down or expended in suicide dives, two carriers had been hit and one badly damaged. Only the *Intrepid* was put out of action, but the Fast Carrier Force returned to Ulithi. It was now apparent that at least three task groups were required to operate together against kamikazes with any hope of prolonged time on station.

Sufficient time had passed for the task force staff to evolve an anti-kamikaze doctrine, and it was laid out at the end of November. It became known as "The Big Blue Blanket," after the phrase coined by Admiral McCain's chief operations officer, Commander John S. Thach. There were four factors:

First, a "blanket" of all airfields within range of carrier-based F6Fs was called for, particularly those identified as posing a kamikaze threat. Nocturnal heckler missions would make this plan effective round the clock.

Second, the local CAP was increased and redisposed, with 20 to 24 Hellcats over each task group. Additionally, four pairs of fighters were positioned at low level (up to 3,000 feet) just outside the AA screen. The two F6Fs on each side of the task group were called "Jack Patrols." Their job was to intercept low-flying suiciders or snoopers that got in under the radar coverage.

Third, pairs of radar picket destroyers, identified as "Tomcats," were stationed in the two or three most likely directions of attack at least 40 miles from the task force. Each Tomcat station had a minimum of one fighter division overhead to provide forward interception, since by this time most ships in the task force had FDO capability. In addition to providing early warning, the Tomcats allowed "delousing" of returning friendly formations. Any "Sneaky Petes" trying to tag along with the flow of traffic could be identified and disposed of by the Hellcats on Tomcat CAP.

Finally, task force fighter direction was relaxed in order that it be better coordinated with task group FDOs. The new doctrine allowed any ship with available fighters and a bogey on the screen to assume the contact and direct an interception. It allowed much more flexibility and saved time when seconds counted.

Obviously, the demand for more Hellcats also required more fighter pilots. Each large-carrier fighter squadron was doubled in size, with authorized pilot strength increased from 54 to 105 aviators. The envisioned 73-plane fighter squadrons automatically meant fewer dive bombers and torpedo planes. Therefore, SB2C and TBM squadrons were reduced to 15 planes each. This situation was still considered unacceptable to Admiral McCain, who pressed for even more fighters. The Hellcats could perform adequately in the dive bomber role, and he seriously considered eliminating all SB2Cs from the CVs and all Avengers from CVLs. Under this plan, the Fast Carrier Force would operate only Hellcats and Avengers, with the CVLs having all-fighter air groups.

The plan was never fully implemented, but one ship had already experimented with a similar arrangement. Near the end of October, the *Bunker Hill* was an all-fighter carrier; VF-8 and VF-4 were both aboard with 50 Hellcats each. But there were complications. Recalls Scott Mc-Cuskey, "The plan resulted in a bad morale problem involving VF-8 pilots. We had already flown three 'last missions' and then were asked to go again. But this time the plan, as I recall, involved using the experienced personnel of VF-8 and dispersing us among the inexperienced personnel of VF-4. This would have destroyed our team tactics which we all felt so strongly about."[4]

As it was, the joint operation was very short-lived. Fighting Eight had already been in combat for seven months, and most of the air group was flown stateside from Manus in the Admiralty Islands before the end of October. The last contingent was 20 officers and men under McCuskey who "had actually boarded the aircraft for return to the States, but were kicked off because of the Battle of Leyte Gulf. To make a long story short, we hitch-hiked home from New Guinea."[5]

Despite such problems, when Task Force 38 departed Ulithi on 11 December, the F6F buildup was well underway. At least five *Essex*-class carriers now operated 70-plane fighter squadrons: VF-3 in TG-38.1; VF-7, VF-11, and VF-20 in TG-38.2; and VF-80 in TG-38.3. Additionally, Air Group Four had been reunited aboard the *Essex* in TG-38.3 and had operated at least 64 fighters since mid-October. The usual composition of the enlarged fighter squadrons was 69 F6F-5s, including four photo birds, plus four night fighters for a total of 73.

In order to meet the demand for additional fighter pilots, numerous SB2C pilots transitioned to F6Fs during late November. First to do so was Bombing Seven under Lieutenant Commander John Erickson on the *Hancock*. His SB2Cs were put "on the beach" while the transition to Hellcats was accomplished. Erickson was killed in a take-off accident while experimenting with the F6F conversion, but no further problems developed and the plan was well received at all levels.

It had been a long time coming. McCain, never enthusiastic about the SB2C to begin with, had planted the idea of using F6Fs as fighter-bombers before leaving Washington that summer. West Coast training squadrons experimented with Hellcats and Corsairs as dive bombers and found they compared favorably with the SB2C's bombing scores. McCain went to sea believing his plan was in effect behind him in the training and ordnance pipeline.

But sometime between summer and fall, the plan fell apart. Various forces were blamed: the politically powerful Curtiss-Wright organization which built the SB2C, some munitions boards machinations, anonymous partisans at various levels. The first indication McCain had of the reversal was in early November when one of his new operations officers reported aboard. Lieutenant Commander Bill Leonard later recalled, "First sentence after 'howdy' on my initial meeting with McCain was, 'How is the F6F/F4U bombing score?' I told him it was better than ever, but. . . ." When McCain learned the Helldiver would not be fully replaced, he exploded. "I thought he was going to stomp me," Leonard said. "He smiled sweetly in a minute and told me to get with Jim Thach and write some blue dispatches for him to vent his ire and get the program back on track."[6]

The fast carriers were to support the Mindoro landings in the Philippines, scheduled for 15 December. Hellcats opened the campaign at dawn on the 14th with a series of fighter sweeps, finding relatively little airborne opposition then or during the next two days. The one big scrap of the 14th involved VF-80, whose two divisions tangled with 27 Zekes and Oscars attempting to reinforce Mindoro from Luzon. The eight *Ticonderoga* Hellcats caught the Japanese at low airspeed in loose formation and had things entirely their own way. In a swirling dogfight, the VF-80 pilots claimed 19 kills for no losses and no damage. Top scorers were Lieutenants Robert H. Anderson with five victories, "P.D." Fleming with four, and Richard L. "Zeke" Cormier with three.

Meanwhile, the Big Blue Blanket was going into effect. The 500-plus day and night fighters covered every enemy airfield within range and smothered nearly every Japanese attempt to get up. Sixty-nine enemy aircraft were known to have taken off on the 14th and two-thirds of them—46 to be exact—were shot down. Jimmy Thach's blanket proved so effective on its first outing that no attacks were made upon the carriers, though Japanese aircraft from elsewhere in the Philippines sank two ships of the invasion force and damaged four.

Approximately 200 enemy planes had been destroyed, largely on the ground. In exchange, 27 U.S. carrier aircraft were downed. Most of them fell to AA guns at heavily defended airfields, and three of the missing Hellcats were flown by aces.

On the dawn fighter sweep near Clark Field, newly promoted Lieutenant (jg) Doug Baker shot down three Zekes in scattered encounters and was last seen destroying a fourth. With 12 kills in five combats during VF-20's service aboard the *Enterprise* in October and November, Baker was one of the most successful fighter pilots in the task force. But when noses were counted back aboard the *Lexington,* the young Oklahoman was not there. Credited with a total of 16 victories, he was the highest scoring Navy fighter ace killed in action. Filipino guerrillas found his wrecked Hellcat and took his dogtags, knowing the Americans would soon be ashore.

Fighting 29 off the *Cabot* lost two planes in a mid-air collision. Both pilots bailed out, one being Lieutenant (jg) Walter D. Bishop, with five kills to his credit. He was seen the next day on a beach along Subic Bay, waving to low-flying carrier planes, but could not be rescued.

156

The third F6F ace downed on the 14th had better luck. He was Alex Vraciu, back for a third tour. In his previous deployments Vraciu had been the top scorer of both VF-6 and VF-16. During his short stateside trip he married pretty Kathryn Horn, a brunette from East Chicago, but he soon returned to the Pacific.

Quiet and friendly, Vraciu was one of the "tigers" whose demeanor on the ground bore little resemblance to his personality in a fighter plane. He retained his stamina and enthusiasm at a time when others began feeling the strain of prolonged operations. This was partially due to the different nature of the Pacific War at this time. Over a year before, when Vraciu first entered combat, most carrier actions had been hit-and-run affairs. Of this period Vraciu said, "You went out, flew a few hops, saw a little combat, and went back to Pearl or the states."[7] Now it was different. Since the Marianas, the trend had been toward longer periods in combat.

But there were always a few who seemed to thrive on combat, who were less susceptible to fatigue or stress. There were fighter pilots like Charlie Crommelin, torpedo pilots like Bill Martin, and dive bomber pilots like Stockton Birney Strong. Each had already done all that was expected or required of him. Each, for diverse personal reasons, came back for more.

Vraciu had arranged for a return to the *Lexington* where VF-20 was the resident fighter squadron. His tenure with Fred Bakutis's outfit was very short lived, however. On his second mission with the squadron, Vraciu's F6F was hit by AA fire over Bamban airfield, and he bailed out when his engine seized from lack of oil. Vraciu always said he was Grumman's best customer; he'd already put two Hellcats in the water.

Almost as soon as he hit the ground he was surrounded by Filipino guerrillas. Uncertain of their intentions, and not knowing how well they spoke English, he uttered the first phrase which came to mind. "Believe it or not, I actually said, 'Take me to your leader,'" Vraciu recalls.[8]

The Japanese were reported closing in from three sides, searching for the pilot they had seen parachuting. There was no choice but to flee. But Vraciu's concern for his immediate future was temporarily distracted when one Filipino jogged alongside and said in good English, "There are just two things I want to know. Has Madeleine Carroll married the second time? And has Deanna Durbin had a baby yet?"[9] Cut off from outside contact for nearly three years, the Filipinos still found Hollywood the main topic of interest.

During the next five weeks Vraciu, as a brevet major in the guerrilla army, found himself the chief of a 180-man band. They looked more like a gang of Mexican bandits. When Vraciu met U.S. Army troops in January,

many of his men were mounted on horses, complete with a troop of bu-
glers. Vraciu himself, astride his steed, sported an inch-long beard, and
was armed with his .45 automatic, a Japanese pistol, and a trophy saber.
Upon his return to the *Lexington* he handed over Doug Baker's dog tags,
given to him by the Filipinos. But his request to remain in combat was
denied, and Al Vraciu's long war was over.

While at Ulithi in late December, the F6F's 16-month dominance as
the fast carriers' only fighter came to an end. Two Marine F4U squadrons
joined Air Group Four aboard the *Essex*, displacing her dive bombers.
The *Essex* embarked 54 Hellcats and 36 Corsairs, leaving only 15 Avengers
for heavy attack duty. Admiral McCain was pleased.

But the Marine fliers were new to carriers, and suffered accordingly.
Seven pilots were lost in operational accidents in the first nine days aboard.
It would be several weeks before F4Us operated in any strength with con-
sistent safety, but in the next two months four more fast carriers took on
F4Us. The Hellcat's days as *the* carrier fighter were over.

The task force departed 30 December, embarked upon an ambitious
and wide-ranging cruise which would visit Formosa, the Ryukyus, Luzon,
back to Formosa, and then into the South China Sea. The entire deployment would take nearly a month, and would be characterized by almost
uniformly bad weather.

Early on 3 January 1945, the customary fighter sweeps departed the
task force over an arc from Formosa and the Pescadores in the south up to
Okinawa in the Ryukyus. Launched 140 miles from their Formosan targets, the strike groups encountered a thick front off the east coast. Those
planes which got through to the objective had to fly on instruments
through the "soup" but were rewarded with lucrative targets.

The *Ticonderoga*'s VF-80 once again benefited from the best hunting
as three of its divisions swept the area searching for airborne targets. They
found them. Fifteen Japanese fighters were engaged by the *Ticonderoga*
Hellcats, which downed a dozen for the loss of Ensign P. J. Manella, who
was shot by enemy fighters as he hung in his parachute. Lieutenant Pat
Fleming, now VF-80's top gun, accounted for three kills, raising his score
to ten.

The weather clamped down that afternoon, precluding further flight
operations. More strikes were flown the morning of the fourth but a dis-
couraging meteorological outlook dictated an early departure for Luzon.

Two days of strikes were conducted back in the Philippines, where the
Japanese had restocked some 500 aircraft on Luzon. Again poor weather
prevented complete dispersal of the Big Blue Blanket. Carrier pilots flying under leaden gray skies found nearly all of northern Luzon obscured
by heavy clouds on 6 January. Reported ceilings were as low as 200 feet,

This flak-damaged F6F-5 returned from a mission over Luzon and broke in half from the strain of a carrier landing. As can be seen, the pilot climbed out without assistance.

resulting in fighter claims for only 14 aerial kills and 18 on the ground. Perhaps the best illustration of the weather was provided by VF-3 Hellcats returning to the *Yorktown* after strafing trucks on a road near Manila. At least one F6F landed aboard with mud spattered on its wings and canopy.

The seventh offered better visibility over the large target area, but as if attempting to even the odds, nature placed a rough sea and high winds in the launch area. The carriers lost 18 aircraft in accidents, but got through to Japanese airfields and destroyed an estimated 75 planes on the ground. The blanket was working again; only four bandits were shot from the sky. Most of the others had been unable to take off because of the Hellcats' and Corsairs' air superiority over the airfields within range. From 3 to 9 January the Big Blue Blanket had allowed fewer than 100 kamikazes and 40 escorts to take off.

Another strike was flung at Formosa on the ninth, but again aerial opposition proved almost nonexistent. Low-flying carrier pilots reported the Japanese using even more dummy aircraft than before, so an accurate tally of strafing claims was almost impossible. It did, however, seem that the enemy now regarded Formosa as largely untenable.

French Indochina, however, was another matter. It had been ruled since 1940 by the pro-Vichy government and was occupied jointly by French and Japanese forces, the former entirely dominated by the latter.

159

Strikes were ready to fly off at dawn on 12 January, the first time since the earliest days of the war that Allied surface vessels had turned a wake in the South China Sea.

Gray cloudy skies greeted the first sweep-strike, but U.S. air supremacy was established almost immediately. Throughout the day only 15 Japanese aircraft were claimed shot down while the air groups roamed along a 400-mile stretch of coastline, as far south as Saigon. Antishipping strikes found many more targets; an amazing 1,500 sorties were flown by the aircraft of the 14 fast carriers, resulting in 46 enemy ships being sunk.

About 20 twin-float Japanese aircraft were burned on the water at Cam Ranh Bay by strafing Hellcats in the morning, and throughout the day about 70 were destroyed on the ground. Mainly these were based at Saigon Airport, better known in a later war as Tan Son Nhut.

This famous airfield figured in one of the day's interesting footnotes. Fighting 11 had already launched a morning sweep-strike against the area, when a call was put through for three divisions to work over Saigon's airdrome in the early afternoon. Lieutenant Jim Swope volunteered his division which launched with seven other *Hornet* Hellcats, all armed with rockets.

Sweeping low over the big field, the VF-11 pilots each made three to six passes, firing their rockets at hangars and other buildings. Twenty-one-year-old Lieutenant (jg) Blake Moranville had just fired his last rocket into a hangar, when he was startled by his wingman's cry, "Hey Rabbit, you're on fire!"[10]

"Rabbit" Moranville's plane was not actually aflame, but his engine was losing a steady stream of oil which resembled smoke. His F6F had been hit by 20-mm fire. Jim Swope regrouped the division and led Moranville southwards, hoping to make the coast where presumably he could ditch near a lifeguard submarine. But Moranville's engine gave out over the swampy river delta and he splashed down to a safe wheels-up landing in a rice paddy 75 miles southwest of Saigon.

Moranville got out of his Hellcat and detonated the IFF destruct package by flipping a switch on his electrical panel. Circling overhead, Swope looked down at his section leader tromping around the F6, wondering why he didn't walk away from it. Swope wanted to strafe the plane and burn it, but developed a rough engine and was forced to return to the task group. The last the Sundowners saw of Moranville he was standing knee-deep in the rice paddy beside his airplane, surveying the damage.

The young Nebraskan shortly made contact with friendly natives who took him to a village where he waited until dark. Then a French count, a Vichy official, arrived and delivered him to a French army garrison. Thus did Blake Moranville, who had shot down all six Japanese aircraft he fought, become the only U.S. Navy fighter ace prisoner of war.

Lieutenant (jg) Blake Moranville (gesturing), with six planes to his credit, was the only Navy fighter ace captured by the enemy. His F6F was shot down near Saigon in January 1945 and he was held by the Vichy French, but he later made his way to safety in China. Photo: H. B. Moranville

But he was not alone in captivity. Ten other Hellcats were lost during the day. One of the *Hancock*'s three missing F6Fs was piloted by Lieutenant (jg) Elmer G. Stratton, assigned to McCain's photo-mapping unit. Stratton, with a Marine pilot off the *Essex* and a *San Jacinto* TBM crew, was thrown in with Moranville at Saigon's central prison. Once arrived, their status became less definite but more bearable.

The political situation was changing in Indochina. Since 1940 the Vichy regime had collaborated with the occupying Japanese, but now that American forces were operating freely in the region, the wisdom of continued close cooperation seemed dubious at best. Therefore, the French prison warden looked upon his new inmates more as guests than prisoners. He had previously been marked by the Free French for trial and execution, so his treatment of the Americans was guided by a strong dose of Gallic pragmatism; they were his ticket home.

Members of the anti-Vichy movement were permitted to deliver food, books, magazines, tobacco, even a radio. Not to mention liquor—lots of it. Moranville, not yet 22, was senior in the group and realized they were

161

much better off than one might imagine for POWs in Asia. The fliers were allowed to roam much of the prison and exercised in a small court-yard each evening. They amused themselves by terrorizing a tiger shark kept in a cement tank, and considered it grand sport to watch the beast snap broom handles in two. The main restriction was that they should never be seen or heard by any Japanese.

Eventually, however, the Japanese learned that Americans were being held somewhere in Saigon. Inquiries were made, searches commenced, and the warden began to feel the heat. So arrangements were made to truck the fliers north to Hanoi. They were turned over to a French Foreign Legion unit in the hills outside the city, where conditions were considerably less pleasant. The men had little to eat but rice, were kept in dirty quarters, and most came down with dysentery. But things only got worse. A few nights later, Japanese troops massacred a French army garrison nearby. Realizing how attitudes had shifted, the Japanese were eliminating all sources of possible resistance.

There was only one course of action available. The 200 Legionnaires decided to march over the mountains westward to Dien Bien Phu, one of the few strongholds remaining. The Navy fliers were turned loose, issued rifles, and invited to come along. It was not a cheerful prospect, but the alternative was clearly less attractive. The group walked nearly 300 miles in 13 days across some of the roughest geography in Southeast Asia. Only a quarter of the troops made it. The rest fell victim to disease or were killed in a nocturnal ambush while crossing a rice paddy. Moranville and Stratton's group survived the trap only because of the quick thinking of a German sergeant who led them to safety in the jungle.

When the men arrived at Dien Bien Phu on 22 March, they were in poor shape. Sick, exhausted, and hungry, they now had to wait for clear weather so they could be flown to safety in China. They waited nearly a week, with the Japanese steadily drawing nearer. Casualties straggled in daily, testifying to the bitterness of the fighting. And each day the weather prevented any landing on the rough airfield.

Finally on the 28th the clouds lifted enough for a C-47 to fly down from Kunming. The Americans scrambled aboard, most of them clutching souvenir teapots they had purchased along the way. While recovering their health at Kunming, they learned that Dien Bien Phu had been over-whelmed by the Japanese. Blake Moranville summarized, "I wouldn't take a million dollars for the experience, but you couldn't pay me that much to do it again."[10]

Three days after the Indochina raid the task force was preparing to strike the huge enemy-occupied harbor facilities at Hong Kong. On 15 January strikes were flown over Formosa and the China coast, encountering surprisingly little air opposition. Sixteen Japanese planes were shot down. Five fell to a VF-11 division led by the squadron commander, Gene Fairfax, while he was leading 20 other Hellcats on a sweep near the next day's target.

About 50 miles east of Hong Kong, Fairfax spotted a Tabby transport —a Japanese-built DC-3—escorted by four Zekes. He correctly reasoned the escort meant a VIP aboard the Tabby and ordered his pilots to "leave the transport alone till we have the escorts."[11] The Tabby had no chance of outrunning the F6Fs.

Fairfax recalled the short combat: "One Zeke turned toward us and I had a head-on shot but didn't get him. He went over me or I went under him. The other escorts stayed with the transport and as I made a run from behind the formation, one started turning left, all wrapped up. I got inside his turn and flamed him with a deflection shot of about 45 degrees. When I came around, the four escorts were all burning in the water, so we lined up on the transport and probably overkilled it. My wingman, Ensign Jack Suddreth, and I both thought we flamed it first so we tossed a coin and he won."[12]

A wire-service reporter, Keith Wheeler, was aboard the *Hornet* at this time and wrote a dispatch speculating that one less Japanese admiral might be around as a result of VF-11's action that day. He was right. The VIP was Vice Admiral K. Hatakeyama, commander of the South China Sea frontier, who had been on an inspection trip to Hong Kong.

Next day Hong Kong itself was hit, and again hunting was sparse with only 13 claims of enemy aircraft shot down. But the flak was the most vicious the carrier pilots had yet seen. They characterized it as "intense to incredible,"[13] and it was responsible for nearly all the 22 aircraft losses over the target.

Fighting 11 again figured in the day's activities, losing two Hellcats to AA fire. The executive officer, Lieutenant Commander Robert E. Clements, with two fighter divisions, escorted a strike of four TBMs and four SB2Cs against shipping in the harbor. Bombs, rockets, and torpedoes were used against Japanese tankers and merchantmen. But, as Clements recalled, "The AA fire was bad. Of the four TBMs making low-level runs in the harbor, one was shot down on the run-in, another as he pulled over the target, another couldn't make it back to the ship, and the fourth was considerably shot up."[14]

After the attack, Clements led his wingman, Ensign Matt Crehan, back to take damage assessment photos. Crehan's Hellcat took a direct hit and started burning behind the cockpit. Hoping to clear the harbor, Clements led Crehan towards the offshore islands where the ensign bailed out just as his crippled F6 broke in two.

What did you do in the war, Daddy? Fighting Squadron 11 pilots engage in a popular pastime between missions. Photo: H. B. Moranville

Crehan was safely down in the water but his life raft drifted away. Circling overhead, Clements summoned aid. "I found a bomber crew who came over and dropped a life raft to Crehan," he recalls. "But this one blew up as he pulled the cord. After that I couldn't find any more VB aircraft so I disengaged my own life raft and threw it in to Crehan. This time it worked and he climbed in. Incidentally, it *ain't easy* to stand up in your seat, fly at about 200 feet to keep a man in the water in sight, pull off your harness and seat pack to get to that raft in the bottom, and throw it to a man in the water."[15]

But the exec's problems—not to mention Crehan's—were far from over. Despite a rapidly diminishing fuel supply, Clements remained overhead, radioing for a submarine while scaring away small vessels heading towards Crehan. Clements finally contacted a sub but learned the offshore waters were too shallow to attempt a rescue. Then his radio quit, but still the Sundowner exec remained overhead, hoping to attract attention.

Finally, with only 30 gallons registering on his fuel gauge, he reluctantly turned away and found a friendly straggler who homed in on the task group. When Clements caught the arresting wire with his tail hook, his tanks all showed empty. No other aircraft found Ensign Crehan, and he was listed Missing In Action.

Clements finishes the story: "After the war, Crehan himself came down to Annapolis to see me and told me that a Chinese sampan picked him up and landed him safely on shore and put him in contact with guerrillas. He walked to Kunming with a group of people, having a somewhat similar experience to that of Rabbit Moranville."[15] Actually, Crehan and Moranville found each other while at Kunming; they could hardly believe it themselves.

On 21 January the fast carriers were back at Formosa, operating 100 miles offshore while air strikes went after shipping and airfields. Only three enemy planes were seen in the air and two were shot down, though strafing fighters claimed about 100 destroyed on the ground.

Then the kamikazes appeared. Until now the fast carriers had been free from air attack, but as usual the Japanese arrived during the noon hour in three groups. The *Langley* took a bomb hit which interrupted air ops for three hours, then minutes later a lone Zeke got past the CAP and dived into the *Ticonderoga* with a 550-pound bomb. The explosion caused wild fires, and only 40 minutes later another threat appeared. This attack involved eight bandits, two of which evaded the CAP and one of which fell to AA fire. The survivor lived long enough to crash his target, already marked by smoke and flame. He hit the *Ticonderoga*'s island, bringing already serious casualties to 345, including 143 dead.

Several VF-80 pilots had manned AA guns after the first hit, replacing wounded gunners. Pat Fleming was at a 20-mm battery when the Zeke hit. He was struck on his helmet by a piece of debris and knocked overboard. Efficient rescue work by a destroyer prevented the bizarre loss of one of the U.S. Navy's outstanding fighter pilots, but the *Ticonderoga* retired towards Ulithi under close escort.

Meanwhile, the suicide attacks continued. Fighter direction had been hampered during the first assault by cluttered radio channels, and pilots were advised in the strongest of terms that strict radio discipline must be maintained. During the afternoon two more kamikaze groups neared the task force, one composed of seven suiciders and six fighter escorts. This group was intercepted by two divisions of VF-22 under the acting CO, Lieutenant Clement M. Craig. Fighting 22 was one of the senior squadrons in the task force, with one tour completed in the fall of 1943, and its second tour aboard the *Cowpens* since September. Craig's pilots backed up their reputation as veterans by shooting down or chasing off all the raiders. The skipper, a graduate of Butler University's journalism school, claimed five kills and raised his personal total to an even dozen. The feat earned him a Navy Cross, as five victories in one day was now an established requirement for fighter pilots to qualify for the service's highest decoration.

The day's third enemy attack proved no more successful than the second, as 13 more hostiles were broken up and prevented from attacking. This proved the last kamikaze formation to take off from Luzon, only 220 miles from the southern tip of Formosa. After striking the Ryukyus the next day in a preliminary raid to gather information, the task force shaped course for Ulithi.

What might be termed the first kamikaze campaign was now over. It had lasted three months, from 25 October to 25 January. In that period, according to Japanese sources, 447 kamikaze sorties, of which three-quarters were Zekes, had taken off for Philippine or Formosan waters. The Japanese claimed that 201, or 44 percent, had actually dived on American ships and that only one-sixth of the total sorties were shot down or lost to weather, operational accidents, and so forth. It is significant that 40 percent of the total—179 aircraft—returned to base, either unable to find any targets or chased away by the combat air patrol.

These figures are at variance with the American reports, but the damage was real enough. Six fast carriers, four CVs, and two CVLs had been tagged by kamikazes. The heaviest damage was done to the invasion fleet: the troopships, escorts, and CVEs, which of necessity operated close to shore.

While the anti-kamikaze measures had proven effective, it was now evident that they needed to be virtually 100 percent effective all the time. As Marine F4U squadrons and the enlarged Navy F6F units arrived in the new year, the stronger fighter force would be better able to handle the problem of fleet defense. And it was a good thing that more fighters were becoming available at this time.

The next target was Japan.

Hellcat Squadrons in Combat: November 1944 to January 1945

VF-3	*Yorktown*	Lieutenant Commander W. L. Lamberson
VF-4	*Bunker Hill, Essex*	Lieutenant Commander K. G. Hammond (KIA), Lieutenant L. M. Boykin
VF-7	*Hancock*	Lieutenant Commander L. J. Check (KIA), Lieutenant J. A. Duncan
VF-11	*Hornet*	Lieutenant Commander E. G. Fairfax
VF-15	*Essex*	Lieutenant Commander James F. Rigg
VF-18	*Intrepid*	Lieutenant Commander E. J. Murphy
VF-19	*Lexington*	Lieutenant Roger S. Boles (KIA)
VF-20	*Enterprise, Lexington*	Commander Fred A. Bakutis
VF-21	*Belleau Wood*	Lieutenant Commander V. F. Casey
VF-22	*Cowpens*	Lieutenant L. L. Johnson, Lieutenant C. M. Craig
VF-28	*Monterey*	Lieutenant Commander Roger W. Mehle
VF-29	*Cabot*	Lieutenant Commander W. E. Eder
VF-44	*Langley*	Commander Malcolm T. Wordell
VF-45	*San Jacinto*	Commander G. E. Schechter
VF-51	*San Jacinto*	Commander Charles L. Moore
VF-80	*Ticonderoga*	Lieutenant Commander Leroy W. Keith
VF-81	*Wasp*	Commander F. K. Upham

8 Hunters in the Night

The bright day is done, and we are for the dark.
Shakespeare
Antony and Cleopatra

It is said that bad news travels fast, and certainly it was true in late 1943. The word quickly spread that Butch O'Hare was dead, lost on some sort of night mission in the Gilberts.

Beyond that, little was immediately known. Famous as the Navy's first fighter ace and a Medal of Honor winner, in November O'Hare had taken command of Air Group Six aboard the *Enterprise*, temporarily operating VF-2 as the fighter squadron. O'Hare had taken a personal interest in flying night fighters from carriers, and when he disappeared the night of 26 November, he was on a "bat patrol" with another conventional F6F-3 in radio contact with a radar-equipped TBF.

Some theorized that O'Hare was shot down by a Japanese bomber which was trying to attack the task force; others thought he fell to American gun fire. But the fact was that nobody really knew. It had been only the second night of the experiment, and while it resulted in two kills by the Avenger, it demonstrated in tragic terms the problems inherent in operating single-engine fighters from carriers at night.

The U.S. Navy had been working on carrier-based night fighters for nearly a year before O'Hare's death, making use of British technological and operational experience. However, the initial Air Interception radar sets installed in experimental F4U-2 Corsairs were custom-built by the Massachusetts Institute of Technology and were "all-American."

The Navy's night fighter program was coded Project Affirm, begun at NAS Quonset Point, Rhode Island, in early 1942. The first squadron produced by the program was the Corsair-equipped VF (N) -75 which was flying in the Solomons that fall, though half the unit was redesignated VF (N) -101 and went to the fleet carriers in four-plane detachments. The second and third squadrons, equipped with F6F-3Es, likewise went to the fast carriers in four-plane detachments, becoming operational in early 1944.

There was relatively little difference between the Corsair and Hellcat in adaptability to night fighting, as both had good visibility and could accommodate the radar equipment. The F4U had a slight speed advantage and a somewhat better altitude performance, but the F6F was much easier to land and was considered a more stable gun platform. For these two reasons, primarily, the Grumman was identified early on as the more promising night fighter.

Initial enthusiasm was such that half of the subsequent Hellcats produced were to be night fighters, but both technical and human resources precluded anything of the sort. The AI Model A sets were still being virtually custom built, and the 29-week specialized pilot training course ensured that night fighters would remain a limited commodity for quite some time.

Experimental installation of airborne intercept radar on an early F6F-3. Photo: R. P. Gill

Still, there was reason for optimism. Mounted in a bulbous pod under the starboard wing, the AN/APS-4 (Army-Navy/Airborne Pulse Search Equipment) weighed only 180 pounds and gave coverage out to four miles. It was designed with simplicity in mind, being operated and monitored by the pilot without undue diversion from his more immediate task of flying the airplane.

The F6F-3E, using APS-4, had a very limited production run. Barely two hundred -3 Hellcats were completed with AIA fittings, and of these a mere 18 were actually equipped with APS-4. They were allotted to the detachments of VF (N) -76 and -77 which went aboard various fleet carriers at the end of 1943 and in early 1944. The remaining F6F-3 night fighters became the -3N variant, with the newer APS-6 radar.

Though heavier than the earlier unit by some 70 pounds, APS-6 in the search mode gave the night fighter pilot a search radius of five to five-and-one-half miles. Its blind-fire control capability was considered unreliable and its use was proscribed in some squadrons. In search mode, APS-6 was effective as close as 400 feet, and could usually detect a large ship at over 20 miles. A fleet formation such as a task force could be picked up as far out as 60 miles.

APS-6's greatest improvement over previous AI sets was its new "double dot" display system. Besides the true blip reflected from the target, a "ghost" dot was painted on the screen immediately to the right of the bogey, and this second image indicated relative height above or below the night fighter. Thus, height and bearing were presented simultaneously on one scope. This feature, coupled with the set's simplicity of operation —only six dials or knobs besides the on-off switch—made APS-6 highly popular with pilots. Many frankly considered it superior to the sets which followed for several years.

The -3 Night Hellcats became a proving ground for night fighter equipment and techniques. Cockpit lighting was a primary feature, and red instrument panel lights, coupled with flat windscreens in place of the standard curved variety, helped reduce glare. A radar altimeter provided the exact height information so crucial in instrument flying, and an APS-13 tail-warning radar provided 60° coverage behind the fighter at 800 yards. With a top speed of about 360 mph at 18,000 feet and a climb rate of almost 3,100 feet per minute, the Hellcat night fighter was well matched against its opposition.

The -3Es and -3Ns aboard the *Hornet, Yorktown, Bunker Hill, Wasp, Essex,* and *Lexington* in the first half of 1944 helped establish night fighters in the fleet, but acceptance was slow in coming. Largely this was due to the inherent contradiction involved in operating night fliers aboard daytime carriers. The flight schedule aboard a fast carrier often called for 15 hours of operations, usually from 0430 to 1930. By dark, the deck crews were exhausted from spotting and respotting aircraft for numerous launches and recoveries. It hardly seemed worth the effort to recover a few night fighters when radar-controlled gunfire could presumably deal with nighttime raiders.

As a result, the night fighter pilots spent an inordinate amount of time sitting in their ready rooms, chafing at the inactivity. And with idleness their skills lost the sharp edge so essential to success. It was a vicious circle which tended to feed on itself, and early night fighter actions hardly

Nocturnal fighter protection for the Fast Carrier Task Force was provided by detachments of F6F-3Ns in the early 1944, as by this VF-(N)-76 aircraft aboard the USS *Essex.* The squadron also had detachments aboard the *Yorktown, Lexington, Bunker Hill,* and *Hornet.*

inspired confidence. During the two-day Truk raid in February, 1944, a *Yorktown* Night Hellcat pursued a Japanese torpedo plane into gun range of the task force, causing the AA director to hold fire for fear of hitting the Grumman. Result: the *Intrepid* limped back to Pearl Harbor with a hole in her stern.

The situation was not improved by an incident at the end of March. During an operation near the Palaus, the *Lexington* launched four F6F-3Ns in response to bogeys on the scope in the early morning. Almost three hours later, well after sunrise, a conventional Hellcat mistook one of its nocturnal kin for a hostile and, as one might say, shot the living daylights out of it. The night fighter plopped down to a water landing, though happily the pilot was rescued.

Three Night Hellcat squadrons were at sea from January to September of 1944: VF (N) -76, VF (N) -77, and VF (N) -78, with detachments spread among nine carriers. The most successful was Detachment Two of VF (N) -76 aboard the *Hornet*. From April to September, Lieutenant Russell L. Reiserer's team accounted for 25 confirmed kills, over half of all F6F night fighter kills during this period. But only eight were actually made in the hours of darkness, seven of which came in a single spectacular offensive mission.

Lieutenants (jg) Fred L. Dungan and John W. Dear were launched at 0030 on 4 July to conduct an intruder strike against Chichi Jima in the Bonins. Their primary mission was to locate and attack enemy shipping with 500-pound bombs, since no Japanese aircraft were expected on the island.

The two Hellcats remained on station four hours before a large procession of vessels departed the harbor. Dear had just attacked a destroyer when "Buck" Dungan radioed for help; three Rufe float fighters were on his tail.

In all, there were nine or ten Rufes airborne. Dear quickly splashed two, but the next half-hour was one long, dark dogfight. Dungan shot down four and Dear bagged another before the surviving Rufes disengaged, leaving both Hellcats badly damaged. Dungan, with a bullet in his shoulder, landed aboard the *Yorktown*, and Dear was right behind. His engine ran out of oil just as his hook engaged the wire. Nor was that all. Chichi Jima proved just as rugged a target for Russ Reiserer, who returned to the *Hornet* with face wounds inflicted by the spectacular, intense flak.

Though night fighters demonstrated their potential in such missions, problems remained. There were too few Night Hellcats available at any one time due to the continuing maintenance schedule for electronics. And task group commanders were loath to interrupt their nightly routine with the unpopular chore of launching and recovering BatCaps. Furthermore, many captains still put their faith in evasive shiphandling and AA guns to counter the nocturnal bomber threat.

But even the most expert seamanship couldn't prevent a snooper from tracking a task force with near impunity in the absence of defending night fighters. It therefore became plain that the most logical solution to all these problems was a full-time night air group operating from a night carrier.

Enter Lieutenant Commander Turner F. Caldwell. Out of the Naval Academy Class of '35, Caldwell was something of a legend from the Guadalcanal campaign, where he won three Navy Crosses as an SBD squadron commander. He commissioned VF (N) -79 at Quonset Point on 20 January 1944 and moved the infant unit to NAAF Charlestown, Rhode Island, at the end of the month. Charlestown became Project Affirm's permanent home.

Caldwell set about building his squadron around three lieutenants, all former Dauntless pilots like himself with combat experience in the Solomons, vintage 1942. His executive officer was William E. Henry, a husky blue-eyed Californian who would finish as the most successful night fighter pilot in the U.S. Navy. The rest of the squadron was filled out with hand-picked ensigns fresh from operational training. One of them was Jack S. Berkheimer, an engaging 20-year-old New Yorker who could fall asleep on his feet after two beers. He would become one of the Navy's most proficient night hunters, but he would never reach 22.

After four months at Charlestown, VF (N) -79 moved to San Diego in preparation for deployment to the Pacific. Arriving in Hawaii in early June, Caldwell's Hellcats and the attached Avengers went through Captain J. Griffin's "finishing school" at Barber's Point, home of the Night Combat Training Unit. The night fliers were now at their peak readiness: highly proficient in instrument flying, carrier-qualified for day and night, and versed in gunnery and radar interception. Even their night vision was improved with constant practice. By using only the peripheral area of their eyesight, night fighters could better distinguish forms rather than details in darkness.

Most of the pilots now had close to 300 hours in Hellcats, much of it on instruments. In preparation for three- to four-hour missions, they had to be able to read the gauges by second nature and force themselves to disregard totally what their natural senses tried to tell them. Vertigo could be fatal, as one's inner ear might demand corrective measures for a right turn when the needle and ball said the aircraft was perfectly level.

Meanwhile, the energetic Caldwell, now a full commander, had been selling his concept of a "pure" night air group to anyone who would listen. The prospect improved with the availability of the light carrier

Independence, recently returned to Hawaii from a six-month overhaul in the States. The flattop's skipper, Captain E. C. Ewen, found Caldwell's enthusiasm infectious, though the squadron commander was not without reservations. He characterized the project as "a new experiment in suicide,"[1] and much later confessed he felt a bit like the steward who said, "Man was never made to fly, nohow. And if he was made to fly, he was never made to fly off a ship. And if he was made to fly off a ship, he was never made to fly off a ship at night."[2]

Despite any uncertainties, in late August Turner Caldwell got what he most wanted. Fighting 79 was dissolved to reform as VF (N)-41 while the enlarged TBM contingent was designated VT (N)-41. Caldwell assumed new duties as Commander, Night Air Group 41, while retaining personal command of the fighter squadron, enlarged to 14 F6F-5Ns and five "straight" -5s. On 29 August the experiment began when the *Independence* sortied from Eniwetok with Task Force 38.

Disappointment followed fast upon departure. The air group was employed almost entirely in a conventional role, the Night Hellcats having their radomes removed so as not to lose one over the Philippines. It was bothersome for pilots because with the bulb off the wing, the aircraft was out of rig and the stick not centered.

Daylight CAPs and fighter sweeps occupied much of VF (N)-41's time, and bitter resentment began to set in. Though dawn and dusk CAPs were flown, it was obvious the specialized training was going largely to waste. Similar feelings were shared by the night fighter detachments aboard

The first full-time night air group was Air Group 41 aboard the light carrier *Independence* from September 1944 to January 1945. Here a batch of F6F-5Ns warm up their engines prior to launch in October 1944. Photo: R. M. Hill

Essex-class carriers. The original Hellcat night fighter squadrons were decommissioned and absorbed into the fighter units of the carriers upon which they were based. Many—possibly most—of these pilots found themselves flying routine day missions. With the *Independence* in the task force, there was not enough night work for other VFNs to obtain flight pay or remain current.

Things picked up a bit on 12 September when two of Caldwell's pilots shot down a Betty snooper near the task force in early daylight. But the unit's first genuine night fighter success came that evening when Bill Henry, now a veteran of over 2,100 hours flight time, was returning with his division from a dusk CAP. The *Independence* radar picked up a bogey and vectored the four Hellcats towards it, but not before the intruder got within gun range of the fleet.

Henry recalled what happened next: "When the ships fired at the Jap, he turned and headed for Leyte and started to climb. We were vectored after him, and I finally got him on my radar at 21,000 feet almost over Samar. We were required to identify planes before firing, and I ended up almost on top of him. It was a Dinah. I dropped back and fired. The plane started to burn so I eased off to the left. Jack Berkheimer on my wing also fired, and I fired again and he blew up. After that action we kept our radar installed for all flights."[3]

But this initial success by the first night air group failed to change the situation very much. A few days later eleven day fighter pilots were brought in to augment VF (N)-41's strength, and the month's remaining combats were all conventional daylight engagements. Caldwell's Hellcats finished their first month of operations with ten confirmed kills, including four on 22 September during a sweep over Luzon in which Henry bagged two Vals and Berkheimer destroyed a Zeke. September also saw numerous heckler missions assigned, the F6Fs rotating with the Avengers, but like the squadron's air combats, much of this activity was under the glare of the sun instead of the dark of the moon.

October was to be the decisive month for Caldwell's pilots. The strikes on Formosa and the invasion of the Philippines gave the Night Hellcats plenty of opportunity to prove their worth under conditions for which they were trained. Of the 12 kills credited to VF (N)-41 during the month, 10 were destroyed in completely dark or semidark conditions. And once again, Bill Henry was in the right place at the right time.

Shortly before 1900 on 12 October, Henry's division was in the landing pattern after a dusk CAP off Formosa when a scattered group of Bettys initiated an attack on the task group. "We were vectored out and just as I passed over one of our DDs I picked up a target on my radar," Henry recalled. "We were about 500 feet with low clouds and light rain. I closed to about 700 feet and saw the Betty. I fired and the plane burned at both wing roots and dove into the water and exploded. The controller turned us around and I picked up another target. We ran up on two more Bettys. I got one and my wingman, Ensign Jim Barnett, got the other."[4]

But it wasn't one-sided. Two other *Independence* pilots, Ensigns G. W. Obenour and J. F. Moore, lost radio contact and were never heard from again. The night wasn't over, however, for at 0500 "Berky" Berkheimer and R. W. Klock came across three Emily flying boats during a heckler mission over Formosa. Berkheimer shot down two and Klock splashed the third.

Early on the 15th the task force was still off Formosa. Bill Henry was sitting in his Hellcat, call sign Cupid 13, taking his turn at the Condition Two watch. A bogey was reported, and the exec was catapulted off at 0245, almost immediately picking up a target three miles ahead. The blip entered a rain shower, so Henry turned down his radar to keep the scope from "flooding," for rain as well as aircraft painted on a scope. Coming out of the squall, Henry turned up his set again and regained his target. He closed in at 700 feet, identified the bandit as an Emily, and fired into the port wing. Personnel on the carrier saw the giant flying

Lieutenant William E. Henry, executive officer of VF (N)-41, was the Navy's top night fighter pilot. He was credited with six and one-half nocturnal victories and four by day. Photo: W. E. Henry

boat explode and hit the water. Perhaps better than any other victory scored by the squadron, this one exemplified their complete mastery of both instrument flying and the technical knowledge necessary for success as a night fighter pilot.

The night concept was now truly well proven, and it was a mark of confidence when Fighting 41's daytime fighter pilots were transferred back to regular F6F squadrons in the middle of the month.

From Formosa the fast carriers returned to Philippine waters, and while there VF (N) -41 almost suffered another casualty. Before leaving the West Coast, Ensign Harry Johnson's wife had told Bill Henry to "take care of Harry," so the exec made Johnson one of his wingmen. During the first strike on Clark Field near Manila, Johnson's F6F was shot up by Zekes and he ditched en route back to the task group. After he was picked up and returned to the ship, Johnson went straight to Henry and advised him, "You're not taking very good care of me."[5]

The sprawling, confused Battle of Leyte Gulf began on 24 October, and VF (N) -41 may have fired the first shots in this, one of the greatest of all naval engagements. At 0215 Jack Berkheimer shot down an Emily and splashed a Mavis an hour and 20 minutes later. Ensign W. E. Miller and his wingman got a pair of snoopers later in the morning.

But that night the snoopers were back. One Mavis in particular proved troublesome when the *Independence* Hellcats tried to corner it long after sunset. Most scout planes departed when their presence became known, but this one seemed intent on tracking the Third Fleet all through the night. It was imperative to shoot her down, lest she report Halsey's position at daylight.

Finally, at 0135 on the 25th, two *Enterprise* night fighters of VF-20 were launched. One was flown by the skipper, Commander James S. Gray, Jr., a veteran fighter pilot from the early days of the war. He had just taken command after the previous CO had been shot down attacking Japanese shipping during the day.

Gray and his wingman were vectored 40 miles to the southwest, where radar contact was quickly established. But it was obvious why the *Independence* fighters hadn't bagged this snooper yet. In the black moonless sky, even using binoculars, Gray acquired and lost visual contact three times. It seemed Jim Gray's luck as a night fighter was no good. At the end of August he had lost a sure kill as CO of VF (N) -78 because tracer ammunition had erroneously been loaded in his guns, giving away his position to a Betty he was stalking.

But this night the situation was reversed. The persistent Mavis might have escaped had not the enemy tail gunner opened fire. His tracers provided Gray with a point of aim, and the Hellcat opened fire from 300 yards astern. Struck squarely in the fuselage, the big Kawanishi fell burning into the sea.

Jim Gray later recalled with pride, "Admiral Halsey said this was the second most important single kill of the war. (The first was the interception of Yamamoto.) Without it, the Third Fleet would have been pinpointed for kamikazes the next morning."[6]

Earlier that same night an *Independence* Hellcat located the Japanese battleship-cruiser force in the Sibuyan Sea, heading east for San Bernardino Strait. It was one of the most valuable bits of tactical recon in the war, but it went unheeded. Admiral Halsey was after the enemy carriers.

Fighting 41 proved useful in a decidedly different manner a few days later. At dusk on the 29th a large strike was returning to the task force from Luzon when a sudden squall came up, drastically reducing ceiling and visibility. Landing operations came to an immediate halt and the strike planes could only mill about, doing little more than keeping straight and level. Few air groups were night qualified, so Caldwell's Hellcats rounded up the strays and herded them back to their respective ships. Had the night fighters not been available, many aircraft would have been lost to fuel exhaustion.

November brought nine more victories to VF (N)-41, including one in daylight. Bill Henry bagged another Emily on the 19th, becoming the first Navy pilot with five or more kills at night. Only an hour later, at 0545, Jack Berkheimer became the Navy's second night ace by downing an Oscar during a heckler mission over Luzon.

Still in the Philippines through December, the *Independence* Hellcats clawed down five more victims, including three on the 16th. But the law of averages was finally catching up. There had been no pilot losses since mid-October, but mid-December changed all that. On the 14th two F6F pilots were shot down, and one was lost in an operational accident. Harry Johnson's plane was hit by AA fire and he ditched in a lake. This time it took Johnson considerably longer to get back and remind his division leader of the promise made to his wife, but Filipino guerrillas eventually escorted him to safety. The other two pilots were not recovered.

Two nights later Jack Berkheimer was leading his wingman over Luzon. Berky radioed, "I see a plane with its lights on over Manila. I'm going after it."[7] Shortly thereafter the wingman saw a large explosion in the sky and could get no response from Berkheimer. It was thought the young New Yorker had collided with his intended victim or was hit by AA fire. With a total of seven and one-half confirmed victories, including five and one-half at night, Berkheimer was second only to his friend Bill Henry among VF (N)-41's top hunters.

Night Air Group 41 finished its tour in January, knocking down ten more planes for a career total of 46. Squadron records credited Henry with ten and one-half, of which six and one-half were at night. Wally Miller and Jim Barnett followed Berkheimer with four and one-sixth and three and one-third respectively. Caldwell's belief in his methods and personnel had been entirely vindicated, though at a price. Ten of the 35 night fighter pilots were lost from August through January—nearly 30 percent. Six pilots (excluding Johnson) and seven aircraft had been lost to enemy action, but only three pilots were lost in operational accidents. Turner Caldwell had proved that after the careful selection of pilots and meticulous training, the night squadrons could operate with a better safety record than most day squadrons.

Flying from the 70-foot-wide deck of a CVL in adverse weather and darkness for five months, Turner Caldwell heaved an audible sigh of relief upon his return to the States. His final word on the affair: "All I can say is, we got away with it!"[8]

As Caldwell's air group rotated home, Night Air Group 90 arrived to take its place. Led by Commander William I. Martin, a long-time advocate of night carrier operations, Air Group 90 was the first such unit embarked on board a full-sized fleet carrier, the tireless *Enterprise*. With a strength of 34 Hellcats and 21 Avengers, Martin's group would be better able to perform offensive missions than Caldwell's more limited resources had allowed from a CVL. The fighter squadron was under Lieutenant Commander Robert J. McCullough, with 19 F6F-5Ns, eleven -5Es and two photo birds.

The first combat for VF (N) -90 came on 6 January 1945 when Lieutenant Carl S. Nielsen shot down a Dinah, an Oscar, and a Zeke during the day. A fourth daylight victory followed before Lieutenant James J. Wood made the unit's first successful night intercepts. Flying alone, he shot down a Frances in the pattern over Tainan airfield on 21 January and a Helen on 19 February. But there were still lessons to be learned. Near the end of January a four-plane heckler flight to southwestern Formosa strafed an airfield. Afterwards, a brilliant orange light was chased a considerable distance before the Hellcat pilots decided they were pursuing a star.

Meanwhile, yet another night air group was making its debut in February. This was Air Group 53 aboard the venerable *Saratoga*, which included a mixture of night and day aircraft. VF (N) -53 had F6F-5Ns and VT (N) -53 had TBM-3Ds, but there was also VF-53 with conventional F6F-5s. The air group began operations on 17 February, intending to provide round-the-clock air cover for the Iwo Jima invasion. This bold experiment was cut short on the fifth day when poor old *Sara* was clobbered by five kamikazes. Though she survived, this was the third and last time she was knocked out of the war. It left the *Enterprise* as the only night carrier in the task force, and Martin's crews proved equal to the challenge. From 23 February to 2 March, more than one solid week, the Night Hellcats of Air Group 90 remained continuously on station over the Volcano Islands with CAPs, sweeps, and heckler missions. In 175 hours, only one accident occurred when Ensign Rex Milton landed his plane in three distinct pieces.

Lieutenant Kenneth D. Smith made the squadron's only kill during this period, downing a Helen in the darkness of the 24th. He would be heard from again.

Following the Iwo Jima operation, VF (N) -90 provided 14 night fighter pilots to other carriers on a sort of "lend-lease" basis. Selection for this potentially unrewarding duty was effected by drawing lots. But for some it was an unexpected opportunity. Flying from the *Bennington* with Air Group 82, Lieutenant Smith and Lieutenant (jg) William G. Piscopo accounted for three confirmed and a probable between them during the first week of April, all at night. Ensign Waldo West, detached to the *Bunker Hill*'s VF-84, splashed three bandits by himself during the same month.

Night fighters were unusually active in the early morning hours of 18 March, prior to a large strike on Kyushu. *Enterprise* Hellcats engaged in numerous pursuits which resulted in four kills and a probable. Dodging in and out of low clouds and rain squalls, Japanese aircraft were able to remain within sight of the task force for several hours before the F6Fs caught them. Lieutenant (jg) R. C. Wattenberger chased a Helen "all over the Western Pacific"[9] and once around the task force but finally called in a splash. Lieutenant (jg) W. R. Williams, a persistent New Hampshire pilot, had an even tougher time. He repeatedly drove off one pesky snooper for nearly three hours, then cornered it and sent it down. A Frances and a Jake were also splashed and a Tabby went unconfirmed. It was VF (N) -90's best night thus far, marred only by the loss of Lieutenant (jg) John Cole's F6F, shot down by "friendly" AA fire. Cole was fished out of the water by a U.S. destroyer.

Meanwhile, a division of *Hornet* night fighters launched at 0400 to conduct a predawn heckler mission to Kanoya. The VF-17 pilots patrolled with their navigation lights turned off, and enjoyed a profitable half-hour. Between them, the four Hellcats claimed six kills over Kanoya's airdromes. One was a Japanese-built DC-3, code-named Tabby, which became the first victim of Lieutenant Robert J. Humphrey. In the next three months Humphrey would add four more nighttime victories.

Other night fighter pilots found numerous targets during April and May. On 6 April Lieutenant Donald E. Umphres of VF-83 scored four kills in two sorties. The first was a Betty which he chased by himself for a half-hour before dawn near the north tip of Okinawa. Early that evening Umphres was headed to the rendezvous spot for a dusk CAP with two other Night Hellcats when he was vectored onto three small groups totaling five Oscars and three Vals. Despite low clouds and diminishing visibility, the night fighters conducted a daytime engagement, splashing all eight hostiles without damage to themselves. Umphres dropped a Val and two Oscars while Ensign J. M. Barnes got a pair of each and Ensign W. K. Somers downed the other Oscar.

Also near Okinawa on 4 May, Lieutenant (jg) John Orth of Fighting Nine engaged three large targets in a row. The 23-year-old reservist shot down all three in rapid succession before they could reach the task force, winning a Navy Cross in the process. This predawn intercept raised Orth's personal total to six night victories, a figure exceeded in the U.S. Navy and Marine Corps only by Bill Henry's six and one-half nocturnal kills.

While the night fighter detachments of day fighter squadrons were enjoying their successes, Commander Bill Martin had retrieved his pilots out "on loan" to other carriers and planned an exceptionally ambitious intruder mission over southern Kyushu for the night of 12-13 May. Martin led 16 of his Avengers to designated targets in the Sasebo and Nagasaki areas, bombing airfields and harbor installations with the intention of disrupting enemy plans to attack the fast carriers as they entered Japanese waters. As the TBMs withdrew in the first grey light of the 13th, VF (N) - 90's Hellcats were already on the prowl, finding the best shooting of their entire tour. Seven of Lieutenant Commander Bob McCullough's F6F-5Ns launched at 0230 and flew to the target area.

First blood was drawn by Lieutenant Owen D. Young who spotted the exhaust flame of a Tony over the water off Kanoya. Young dived too rapidly, overshot his target, and had to extend his wheels to slow down enough to turn in behind his victim, which he shot down in flames.

Young and Ken Smith then proceeded to Kanoya East where the lights of taxiing aircraft were visible. But it was still too dark for visual shooting so they made repeated dummy strafing runs to keep the Japanese from taking off until visibility improved. Smith and Young shot up four fighters on the ground, but Smith's plane took several hits in the port wing, and he broke off to return to the ship. Not far from the airfield he was bounced by a pair of Tonys, but one of them made the fatal error of pulling up directly in front of the Hellcat. Smith couldn't miss, and he didn't. The other bandit was last seen making knots for home, a course of action the *Enterprise* pilot wisely emulated. The Tony was his fifth victory, and his only one in daylight.

Meanwhile, Owen Young staged a miniature turkey shoot at the expense of three Jake floatplanes taking off from Kagoshima Bay. He bagged four victims in this, his only combat. In all, Fighting 90 claimed ten kills during this mission, a conglomeration of six Japanese aircraft types. No

Enterprise planes were lost, and not a single enemy aircraft bothered the task force during its run-in to launch strikes against the Japanese home islands.

Late the night of the 13th, Lieutenant (jg) Charles Latrobe added a Betty to the pair of Petes he'd collected some 20 hours previously. It was the 34th victory credited to a VF (N) -90 pilot—the 16th and last at night.

At 0300 on the 14th, the *Enterprise* sent 15 night fighters to Kyushu and Shikoku. The ten over Kyushu tangled with three Oscars, and Lieutenant (jg) L. F. Harrison got one. When the intruder divisions returned to the task force, they found an enemy attack in progress and were ordered to orbit. Lieutenant (jg) G. P. Taylor was vectored onto an incoming single Zeke and shot it down for the squadron's final victory. For at 0700 another bomb-laden Zeke dropped out of the clouds and, despite intense AA fire, split-essed directly into the *Enterprise*'s forward elevator. The "Big E," veteran of every carrier battle but Coral Sea, holder of 20 battle stars, was turned into an inferno. From nearby ships it seemed she could hardly stay afloat another hour, but superb damage control pulled her through with only 80 casualties. Next day she set course to the east under her own power.

Since early January VF (N) -90 had been credited with 36 Japanese planes in the air and 19 on the ground, losing 14 Hellcats to all causes. Five of these were attributable to enemy action, but only one was known shot down by enemy aircraft.

Six-plane night fighter detachments remained aboard most daytime CVs till the end of the war, generally in the ratio of four F6F-5Ns to two -5Es. Over 1,500 Hellcat night fighters were produced during the war, including 80 for Britain, but not all the others went to the U.S. Navy.

The Marines were also to be heard from.

The first Marine F6F night fighter squadron engaged in extensive combat was VMF (N) -541. Originally based in the Palaus, which had become the backwater of the war by the fall of 1944, the squadron had to content itself with a single Jake splashed by Major N. L. Mitchell on the night of 31 October. But the Army's misfortune in the Philippines turned to the Marines' advantage when single-engine Japanese fighter-bombers proved too fast for P-61 Black Widows. To deal successfully with these nuisance raiders, mainly Oscars, a faster plane was needed, and the P-61 squadron at Tacloban traded places with 541 in the Palaus.

Five-Forty-One arrived at Tacloban on 3 December 1944. Once established, however, the "Bat Eyes" CO, Lieutenant Colonel Pete Lambrecht, discovered that his 12 Night Hellcats would not be flying typical Marine missions. Instead of "pure" night fighter patrols, their primary assignment was to provide dawn and dusk CAP. And to complicate things, the

Army radar crews were inexperienced and unfamiliar with the Navy-Marine procedures. In one early mission they steered a 541 pilot *away* from his intended victim and temporarily got him lost!

But the squadron's first success came only two nights after arriving in the Philippines. Lieutenant R. E. Montgomery caught and destroyed an Oscar in the dark on 5 December, and two more bandits were shot down the next night.

These were 541's last night kills. The remainder of the month brought 17 daylight victories, including 11 on a dawn patrol over a convoy on the 12th. By 3 January 1945, 32 days after its arrival, VMF (N)-541 had shot down 22 planes in six combats. The remaining eight days at Tacloban brought no further claims, and the Bat Eyes returned to Palau on 12 January. General Douglas MacArthur was so grateful for their assistance that they became the only Marine squadron to receive an Army Distinguished Unit Citation.

Perhaps the unknown poet was thinking of 541 when he penned this bit of doggerel, "With the help of God and a few Marines, MacArthur returned to the Philippines."

If the Philippines proved the happy hunting ground for VMF (N)-541, then the Ryukyus were an outright game preserve for the night hunters of 533, 542, and 543. The last two arrived at Okinawa on 7 and 9 April respectively, each with 15 Night Hellcats launched from escort carriers.

The night fighters were badly needed. Okinawa was well within range of home-based enemy aircraft, and there were frequent night raids. Major William C. Kellum's 542 at Yontan Airfield on the island's west coast became the Tactical Air Force's (TAF) first operational night fighter squadron, but had to scrounge for itself until the ground echelon caught up on 1 May. Even then it was rough going, for what facilities existed were unfinished or makeshift. It was much the same for the Night Hawks of 543 who set up shop on nearby Kadena.

Unlike their counterparts in the Philippines, the Okinawa night fighters flew both day and night missions regularly. The standard tactical organization called for a pair of F6F-5Ns to fly in the daytime or on night strike missions, and for a single night fighter on NCAP. Both squadrons had an early opportunity to put these procedures to work, for they each broke into the scoring column the same night, 16 April.

Second Lieutenants A. J. Arceneaux and W. W. Campbell of 542 were on dusk CAP that evening when they tagged on to a pair of single-engine fighters 45 miles west of "Point Bolo" on Okinawa's southwest coast. In a short combat Arceneaux claimed a Zeke and Campbell a Frank, both at 1845 hours. Only ten minutes later Captain James A. Etheridge made 543's first kill almost directly over Kadena. Outbound on a CAP with his wingman, Etheridge spotted a Frank attempting to attack the field and pulled into it, firing at wide deflection from port. The Frank smoked, then flamed, and went into the beach from a right-hand slow roll. American AA fire hit Etheridge's Hellcat but he landed safely.

The next night Second Lieutenant C. A. Engman of 543 destroyed a Sally near Naha Airfield but his propeller struck the water on pulling up from his low-level attack. With his engine stopped, Engman quickly zoomed to 50 feet, locked his canopy back, lowered his flaps and dead-sticked the Grumman into a water landing. He was rescued by a passing vessel four hours later. The worst was not over, however, as both squadrons lost a pilot and an aircraft in a takeoff collision resulting from the closely spaced traffic patterns of the two airfields in the early morning.

Yontan was bombed almost every night in April, despite the fact that by month's end 542 claimed five kills and 543 a pair. Both units added two more before Lieutenant Colonel Marion "Mac" Magruder brought VMF (N)-533 into Yontan on 10 May. The "Crystal Gazers" had spent the previous 12 months at Eniwetok without so much as a sniff of Japanese aircraft. But their fortunes were changing. They would eventually own almost every record worth having in Marine Corps night fighter circles, due in no small part to their own gunsight modification.

The Mark VIII reflecting sight projected a ring of dots around the center pipper as a means of gauging range and deflection. But the luminescence from these dots caused excessive glare, and the rheostat could not be turned low enough to cure the problem. Therefore, 533 soldered over the dots leaving only the pipper for sighting. It considerably enhanced a pilot's visual acuity.

Five-Thirty-Three's first score was recorded at 0300 on the 16th—a full 30 days after the TAF's first night fighter successes—when First Lieutenant R. M. Wilhide shot down a Betty in flames over Kume Shima Island. The next night he was killed by U.S. antiaircraft fire while chasing two bogeys closing on Ie Shima.

On the 18th Magruder's pilots set a record by splashing five enemy aircraft in less than two hours. First Lieutenant E. N. LeFaivre was vectored by Ringtail GCI into a head-on approach to his first victim and the pilot gained radar contact at three miles. After reversing his course, LeFaivre pursued the bogey for 25 miles before closing in and identifying it as a Hamp. He exploded his unsuspecting target with two bursts. Shortly another contact was made, but it evaded at high speed. But only half an hour after the Hamp went down, LeFaivre got his third chance of the night and bagged a Betty.

The stellar performance this night was turned in by First Lieutenant R. E. Wellwood. Between 2200 and midnight he exploded one Betty, shot a second into a graveyard spin, and chased a third into thick U.S. antiaircraft fire, which put 18 holes in his F6F-5N and knocked out his radio. Turning back from his final pass, Wellwood saw the burning remains of the Betty floating on the sea. He had made three definite kills with only 517 rounds of .50-caliber ammunition.

By splashing five of their six contacts that night, "Black Mac's Killers" amply demonstrated the deadly efficiency which radar-guided fighters had attained since the early period of experimentation. Highly trained pilots and well-drilled GCI officers in six radar stations were making Okinawa a much quieter place to sleep at night.

But the Japanese, as was their custom, had a new variation on an old theme in the wind.

On the night of 24-25 May, Major R. B. Porter landed at Yontan at about 2200 after taking his turn in the flight schedule of VMF (N) -542. Porter was the new CO, the day before having relieved Major Bill Kellum who was to fill a staff vacancy. At 25, Bruce Porter was one of the youngest squadron commanders in the Corps. He came to 542 with three victories from his 1943 tour in the Solomons as a Corsair pilot with VMF-121, and had previously served as exec of 533 and 511 aboard the escort carrier *Block Island*. The Japanese would have a spectacular welcome for the new CO.

Meanwhile, Magruder's pilots had the western quadrant that night, and Lieutenants J. E. Smurr and T. B. Trammell each splashed a Betty shortly after 2100. Another 533 pilot, First Lieutenant A. F. Dellamano, shot down a Betty and a Jake near Ie Shima in the 20 minutes before Porter landed at Yontan.

At 2220 Dellamano got another contact on his screen and identified it visually as a Sally. He pursued from 13,000 feet down to 10,000, finally dropping his wheels to match the target's speed as he closed in from astern and slightly below. One long burst torched the Sally, which dived into the water. Five-Thirty-Three had bagged five victims in about 90 minutes. And a Betty fell to 543.

But these planes may have been intended as sacrificial decoys to cover what was happening farther east at Yontan. Major Porter had just reached his tent on the hill overlooking 542's revetments when he got a call on his command phone that Japanese aircraft were landing on the field. It seemed incredible, but it was true.

The Japanese penchant for suicide tactics had taken a new turn, and five Sallys carrying members of a special airborne attack unit had attempted to crash-land on Yontan. Only one of them made it; the other four were shot down from low altitude by the field's perimeter AA guns. But that one bellied in on the runway at about 2230, disgorging a dozen

VMF-511, a mixed Hellcat-Corsair Marine squadron, flew from the escort carrier *Block Island* in early 1945. The unit included eight F6F-5Ns.

suicide commandos who immediately ran to parked aircraft, clamping on suction grenades and firing automatic weapons.

Consternation temporarily reigned in the Marine compounds. Rumors flew back and forth that a dozen or more enemy aircraft had crashed or were landing; scores of blood-thirsty Japanese were reported swarming the flight line. Pilots and ground crews jumped into their foxholes, took up small arms, and prepared to defend themselves. The aviators watched tracer bullets cutting a path back and forth on the field, saw burning aircraft, and watched incredulously as 70,000 gallons of aviation gasoline erupted like a medium-sized volcano. The firing seemed to move slowly closer and many airmen cut loose at shadowy targets, either real or imagined. The excitement lasted until dawn, by which time Marine infantry and armor arrived to take control of the situation.

When documents found on Japanese bodies were examined, they revealed the chilling nature of the commandos' intentions. The Japanese had reasonably accurate maps of Yontan and its facilities, and their two major targets were the fuel depots, which they destroyed, and the night fighter area. In a decidedly backward compliment to the Night Hellcats' efficiency, the suicide troops had orders to slip into the camps and kill as many night fighter personnel as possible.

American casualties were light, with 2 killed and 18 wounded, but 9 aircraft were completely destroyed and nearly 30 damaged, including three F6Fs. The blazing fuel dumps burned for two days, but the aircraft losses were replaced or repaired, and the first and last Giretsu raid was over, if not forgotten.

The night of 27 May saw more action, with claims for four more kills: two by 543 which splashed a Jake and a Hamp. The Jake was downed by Captain Etheridge, who had opened the squadron's account on 16 April. But the most impressive performance of the evening belonged to First Lieutenant J. E. Smurr of 533. Vectored onto a persistent bogey northwest of Ie Shima, Smurr closed head-on, turned on command of the controller and got a blip on his scope at a range of only one-eighth mile. Flying in bright moonlight the Marine almost immediately identified his target as a Jake floatplane. He followed it through a full circle to port, then into a starboard turn which allowed him to get inside and pull deflection. At only 50 yards Smurr didn't need his gunsight. He triggered one very short burst which hit squarely between the floats. The Jake folded up in an incendiary ball and fell to the water, 45 seconds after Smurr made contact. Upon landing back at Yontan, the armorers found Smurr had fired only 62 rounds. It was probably the quickest and definitely the most efficient kill ever made by a Marine night fighter.

By the end of May the three Night Hellcat units on Okinawa had added 29 more "meatballs" to their scoreboards. Magruder's Crystal Gazers accounted for 15 of these, all in the second half of the month. But conventional night fighter operations were augmented by the introduction of heckler missions, largely by 542. Carrying rockets and bombs, Porter's pilots flew 26 sorties over enemy territory in May, seeking targets of opportunity. It wasn't all one-sided, though, and Second Lieutenant W. W. Campbell failed to return after splashing a bogey on the 16th, exactly four weeks after he had scored one of 542's first two victories.

June started slowly. First Lieutenant William E. Smith of 542 got an Irving early in the morning of the third, and First Lieutenant E. P. Pendrey of 543 expended 1,200 rounds of .50 caliber on a Val the evening of the seventh. Five-Thirty-Three recorded two successes during the ninth, with First Lieutenant J. A. Stokes downing a Tony before dawn and Captain Robert Baird a Jake late that evening. The first kill had been a long time coming for Bob Baird, who had flown a complete tour in the Corsairs of VMF (N)-532 without any sightings. But he was in line for several more opportunities.

The next day First Lieutenant Fred Hilliard scored 542's only daylight victory, splashing an unidentified hostile in the afternoon; then he reported he had contact with another. Nothing more was heard from Hilliard, though a thorough search was made. He was the squadron's second and last combat casualty.

It fell to Bruce Porter to avenge Hilliard's loss. The 542 CO was up on a five-hour "nightcap" on the 15th in his personal F6F-5N named "Black Death." Unlike the squadron's other aircraft, Porter's had a mixed armament of two 20-mm cannon and four .50-caliber machine guns.

The major had drawn a time slot which included the 2000 to midnight stint, the period when half of all night fighter victories were scored. It was a cloudy, moonless night when the controller alerted the young Californian to a bogey shortly after 2100. Porter was vectored west towards an inbound aircraft at about 13,000 feet and established contact on his scope. He identified the intruder as a Nick twin-engine fighter, armed his guns, and fired twice.

"The 20s put out a load of lead that was just fantastic,"[10] Porter said, and the combined firepower seemed to chop the Nick in two. The splash was confirmed by the radar station on Ie Shima at 2118.

An hour later the same controller reported another contact. Porter was surprised. Four 542 pilots now had two kills each, but all had been made in two separate missions; a double hadn't yet been scored. But Porter began climbing to catch a bogey coming in high and fast, and barely overtook it outside the AA screen. It was 2225 when Porter lined up an unsuspecting Betty from six o'clock low, his eyes peering intently through his illuminated gunsight. He triggered one burst from all guns, and the Betty's fuel tanks exploded in an orange-yellow glare.

Two years and three days after his first confirmed victory back in the Solomons, Bruce Porter had become probably the only Marine Corps pilot to score multiple kills in both the Corsair and Hellcat. When Porter landed at Yontan, 542's flight surgeon broke out some brandy to celebrate the CO's marksmanship. The squadron average was 785 rounds per confirmed kill. Porter had used only 500 rounds of .50 caliber and 200 rounds of 20 mm for two.

Five-Thirty-Three had moved to Ie Shima on the 15th but that didn't stop Bob Baird from emulating Porter's achievement the next night by shooting down two aircraft in little more than an hour. The first was a Betty contacted near Ie Shima at 23,000 feet. Baird climbed up from his patrol altitude of 10,000 feet in ten minutes and closed to within half a

The most successful Marine night fighter squadron was VMF (N)-533, which scored 35 confirmed kills during the Okinawa campaign. This 533 Hellcat was based at Ie Shima in June of 1945.

mile by referring to his scope. The Betty had already turned on her bombing run and was nearly into the AA zone, so the controller told Baird to orbit. Baird protested, saying he had a solid contact, and requested permission to continue. His aggressiveness was rewarded. Approval granted, he moved to within 300 feet astern, verified the identification, and opened fire. Only three of his six .50s were operable, so Baird fired three or four more bursts into the bomber's fuselage. The Betty crashed in flames from 16,000 feet.

Arsenic Control was working Baird again an hour later, positioning him above another inbound bogey. The Marine dropped his landing gear to reduce speed and began a let-down from 21,000 to 18,000 feet, gaining a blip on his scope at one and a half miles. He moved off to one side to silhouette the bomber against the lighter eastern horizon and made it out as a Nell. Indicating 160 knots, he moved back astern and fired from 100 yards range, this time with only two guns working. But it was enough. The starboard engine caught fire and the Nell spun straight down.

Nearly a week later, on 22 June, 533 bagged five victims in one 24-hour period for the third time in its career. And again Bob Baird figured prominently in the night's events. From 0045 to 0233 he found another pair of bombers, blew the tail off a Frances and burned a Betty. Baird thus raised his personal tally to five, becoming the first and only Marine Corps night fighter ace. He was also the only Okinawa night fighter pilot to score two doubles. Lieutenants Karl B. Witte and J. B. Mahoney each got a Sally during this same period.

The last kill of the 22nd belonged to 533's skipper, "Black Mac" Magruder. He caught up with two Bettys at 2240, under the direction of Ringtail Control, and moved in from three miles to gain visual identification. At this point one of the bombers turned away, and Magruder continued his approach on the other. The skipper allowed 20 degrees deflection from five o'clock in a shallow right-hand turn, firing three bursts which set both engines afire. The Betty turned into the F6F "with murderous intent,"[11] but Magruder quickly pulled up and watched his victim nose straight into the water from 14,000 feet.

During June, 542 had gained five more victories and 543 a pair, but once again 533 grabbed top honors with 15. It brought the Hellcats' total to 58 since April. Northrop P-61s of the Army's 548th Night Fighter Squadron "poached" three Japanese planes during the month but were never as successful as the Marines, who had more speed and better altitude performance.

The first kill of July came before dawn on the third when First Lieutenant G. P. Anderson of the Night Hawks dispatched a Tony with only 80 rounds. The other two Hellcat outfits were otherwise occupied; 533's exec, Major S. B. Folsom, took over from Magruder on the eighth and moved the Crystal Gazers to Chimu on the 14th where they were reunited with Porter's 542. The latter had no opportunity to score during July, and even the redoubtable 533 had to wait till mid month when Bob Baird added a sixth victim to his bag, but it was noteworthy.

Baird's aircraft, Fox-Nan-Four, was chosen for a series of tests using 20-mm cannon in place of two of the .50-caliber machine guns. Though most new -5Ns arrived with two 20 mms and four .50s, the former were invariably removed because their flash suppressors unaccountably failed to arrive with them. Firing the cannon at night without the flash suppressors seriously impaired the pilot's vision, hence the weapons were removed.

"When we did reinstall the 20s they were most difficult to get into correct operation," Baird recalled. "On the day of my last kill (13 July), in which I used the 20s for the first time, I test-flew the bird and fired the guns six times before they fired without a stoppage. That was about the fifth or sixth day of working on them, and we were about to give up. Determination paid off, however, and they were magnificent."[12]

Indeed they were. Under Baywood Control, Baird pursued an inbound bogey from far below, climbing at 2,000 feet per minute, then levelled off at 18,000 feet and overhauled it from eight miles astern. The Japanese pilot seemed aware of the Hellcat's presence and took evasive action, but Baird had no trouble following the S-turns on his screen. Despite perfect weather and no clouds, Baird had to close to 100 yards in the inky darkness to verify the bogey as a Betty. It was 0441 on the 14th when, from

Captain Robert Baird, flying with VMF (N)-533 at Okinawa, shot down six Japanese aircraft to become the only Marine Corps night fighter ace.

100 feet below the bomber, Baird fired a single three-second burst which hit both engines. Burning wildly, the Betty flew straight and level for about ten seconds, then rolled inverted and went straight down. She broke in half at about 10,000 feet.

Baird found the 20 mms just as lethally effective as had his former squadron mate Bruce Porter four weeks earlier. The 533 pilot spent only 50 rounds of 20 mm and 120 rounds of .50 caliber. He described the force of this combination as "unbelievable,"[13] but Baird and Porter would remain the only two Okinawa Marines to make kills with the mixed armament.

Five-Thirty-Three scored twice on the 18th and once on the 19th, but the Marine total for the month was only eight, plus one for the Army's 548th Night Fighter Squadron. Appropriately, VMF (N)-542, which gained the first night victories for the TAF four months earlier, was also responsible for the last. Lieutenant William E. Jennings locked on to a Tony at 0308 on 8 August and sent it to destruction, the 69th confirmed kill for Marine night fighters of the Tactical Air Force.

When the score was tallied, 533 came out well on top with 35 victories, then 542 with 18, and 543 close behind with 16. The Crystal Gazers produced the top four night scorers of the campaign: Baird with six kills, then Dellamano, Hemstad, and Wellwood with three apiece.

The Okinawa Hellcats destroyed 16 Japanese aircraft types with an average expenditure of 567 rounds on each shoot-down. Again, 533 was far ahead of the pack with only 420 rounds per kill—a record which Baird attributed to the squadron's "mod six" gunsight. Black Mac's Killers had fully lived up to their name.

Five days after the last Marine F6F victory at Okinawa, the Navy night fighters scored their final success. The *Bon Homme Richard* was the fourth night carrier in combat, with Air Group 91 embarked. Night Fighting 91 included several displaced VF (N) -53 pilots who had been made homeless when *Saratoga* was damaged at Iwo Jima. But even with additional personnel, the pickings were fairly slim, and VF (N) -91 had claimed only five victories prior to the night of 13 August.

At 1740 that evening, two F6F-5Ns were launched on Tomcat Patrol, reporting to a destroyer-based FDO off Honshu. They were almost immediately vectored 25 miles west where the section leader, Lieutenant R. T. Kieling, called out two bogeys below.

The Night Hellcats bracketed a pair of Nicks at 4,500 feet and attacked. Kieling had four guns jam on his first burst, but he pursued his target right down to the water where it crashed and burned. His wingman, Ensign Philip T. McDonald, took out the second Nick with two bursts.

Climbing back through 4,500, McDonald saw a Frances three miles dead ahead. He closed in, burned the starboard engine, and dived to port as Kieling got in a short burst. One parachute came out at 100 feet, and the Fran crashed. A new vector put the section on another Fran coming head-on. As before, McDonald did most of the shooting, and the Japanese pilot bailed out.

These contacts occurred so quickly that the first Frances was still burning on the water when a third was seen. McDonald flamed the port en-

A night Hellcat of VMF (N) -534, based at Orote Field on Guam from July 1944 to the end of the war. This photo was taken in August 1944 while wreckage of Japanese aircraft still littered the field.

gine, but the Yokosuka bomber dived into some clouds and could not be found again. It was claimed a probable.

Climbing once more to rejoin "Rudder" Kieling on top, Phil McDonald found yet another target—a Nick crossing two miles in front of him. He overhauled, hit it squarely, and saw it drop into the clouds at 100 feet. Looking down, Kieling also saw flames and reckoned the Nick could not have pulled out.

Before McDonald could rejoin his leader he got two more blips on his scope and, with ammunition remaining, chased them over Honshu. But Kieling recalled the aggressive young Kansan, and they returned to the ship.

It had been a night fighter's orgy. In barely 40 minutes the two Hellcats made eight contacts, claiming five kills and a probable. Mister McDonald established an American record with four night kills on one sortie —a fitting end to the success story which was the Hellcat night fighter.

Hellcat Night Fighter Squadrons in Combat: 1944–45

VF (N)-33	*Sangamon* and *Chenango*	Lieutenant Commander P. C. Rooney
VF (N)-41	*Independence*	Commander Turner F. Caldwell
VF (N)-53	*Saratoga*	Lieutenant Commander A. N. Main
VF (N)-76	Five detachments	Lieutenant Commander E. P. Aurand
VF (N)-77	Four detachments	Lieutenant R. M. Freeman
VF (N)-78	Two detachments	Commander James S. Gray
VF (N)-90	*Enterprise*	Lieutenant Commander Robert J. McCullough
VF (N)-91	*Bon Homme Richard*	Lieutenant Commander Alphonse Minvielle
VMF (N)-533	Okinawa	Lieutenant Colonel M. M. Magruder, Major S. B. Folsom, Jr.
VMF (N)-534	Marianas	Major R. S. Mickey, Major J. B. Maguire, Jr.
VMF (N)-541	Palaus, Philippines	Lieutenant Colonel P. D. Lambrecht, Major N. L. Mitchell
VMF (N)-542	Okinawa	Major W. C. Kellum, Major R. B. Porter
VMF (N)-543	Okinawa	Major C. C. Chamberlain, Major J. B. Maguire, Jr.

9 Okinawa and Japan

Strike—til the last armed foe expires.

Fitz-greene Halleck
Marco Bozzaris

By late January 1945 the Fast Carrier Force had grown to 12 CVs and 6 CVLs. These 18 flattops embarked the staggering total of 1,365 aircraft, of which nearly three-quarters were fighters. The fleet defense problem, as far as the mere number of fighters, was solved.

The large carrier air groups averaged 102 aircraft, the light carriers 27. Hellcats still represented over 80 percent of the total fighter force with 820 in all, but 174 Corsairs were spread among the *Essex, Wasp, Bennington,* and *Bunker Hill* air groups. In fact, Air Group 84 aboard the latter embarked 71 F4U-1Ds and only six Hellcats, all photo planes.

The reliable old F6F-3 was almost gone now. Only 63 remained with the force, scattered among eight squadrons where -5s were unavailable in sufficient number. Four of these were CVL units but the largest -3 contingent was VF(N)-90's sixteen F6F-3Es.

The fighter emphasis on some ships was astonishing. The *Wasp's* Air Group 81 boasted 127 fighters with 91 Hellcats and 36 Corsairs. As a result there was no dive bomber squadron, but 15 Avengers were retained. Five other CVs operated at least 70 Hellcats, and, combined with F4Us, eight of the ten CV day air groups each had 70-plus fighters. The two exceptions were the *Hancock's* Air Group 7 with 64 Hellcats and the *Bennington's* Air Group 82 with 33 Hellcats and 36 Marine Corsairs.

Sharply contrasting with this wealth of aircraft was the depleted Air Group 22 aboard the *Cowpens.* Fighting 22 had only nine F6Fs on hand at this time, and VF-29 aboard the *Cabot* retained 16. The other three CVL fighter outfits all had two dozen F6Fs.

An administrative change had occurred earlier in the month which bore directly upon CV fighter squadrons. With an average complement of 71 F6Fs and 105 to 110 pilots, it was decided to divide the enlarged fighter squadrons into two equal parts. Thus was created the fighter-bomber squadron, designated VBF. On those ships that operated all F6Fs (or later, all F4Us), it was no problem for both squadrons to fly the same aircraft interchangeably since maintenance could be performed on a share-and-share-alike basis.

For air groups at sea, the decision whether or not to make the VF-VBF split was in some cases discretionary. Since the current executive officer would automatically take over the fighter-bomber outfit, that individual stood to gain from a professional viewpoint. But not all units split up. The *Hornet's* VF-11, for instance, was very near the end of its tour and decided to stick together. The *Wasp's* VF-81, with 91 Hellcats, had been in combat since November and also remained intact, making it the largest single squadron in the force.

But air groups on the West Coast or staging west from Hawaii divided their fighter squadrons as a matter of routine. One of the first such to reach the fleet was Air Group 12, destined for the brand-new *Randolph*

Hellcats break into four-plane divisions prior to landing aboard two *Essex*-class carriers before the first strikes against Tokyo in February 1945.

(CV-15). The CAG was an old hand around the Pacific—Commander Charlie Crommelin, who had somehow flown his riddled Hellcat back to the *Yorktown* over a year before and had landed aboard literally half-blind. Fighting 12 had been reorganized under another veteran fighter pilot, Commander Noel A. M. Gayler, who would shortly depart for staff duty with Vice Admiral McCain. When Fighting 12 was split in half, VBF-12 came under the direction of dark, good-looking Lieutenant Commander Ed Pawka.

Air Group 12 was representative of a not entirely successful experiment conducted during late 1944. The old Air Group 9 had been divided, with about half the fighter pilots transferring to form the VF nucleus of Air Group 12. It was theorized that five-man fighter teams could be "grown" from the ground up, trained as a unit, and sent to the task force to fit into any squadron with a minimum degree of adjustment and indoctrination.

By itself, it was probably a valid concept. But in implementing the experiment, another factor became evident. There were numerous Naval Academy graduates with high flight time as instructors in the U.S. who rightfully considered themselves eligible for combat assignments. Therefore, many of the five-man divisions were organized around the Annapolis men, with a combat-experienced pilot assigned as the second section leader. Three young "nuggets" filled out the division, taking turns to put four planes in the air.

An unforeseen problem that occasionally occurred was one of morale. The setup tended to push all three factions into cliques. The Annapolis graduates gravitated towards one another, the pilots with previous combat towards each other, and the youngsters frequently kept to themselves. The team concept suffered accordingly. Furthermore, some section leaders

199

with combat in their logbooks were disappointed at not having a division of their own, but the Academy men had seniority.

No one called this combat team organization a failure. It was merely argued that within some squadrons the structure added an unnecessary complication. For it came at a time when the fast carriers were experiencing undreamed-of expansion and technological advances.

For the fighter pilots, the most outstanding piece of new equipment was the gyro-stabilized, lead-computing gunsight. First available in the fall of 1944, it appeared in the task force in early 1945. The Mark 21 sight automatically showed a pilot the correct deflection when tracking a hostile aircraft and was deadly accurate. The problem was that some squadrons had too little time to practice with the new gadget before entering combat. Ed Pawka's pilots in VBF-12 would choose to leave their lead-computing sights locked in "pegged range" through most of the forthcoming tour. This in effect made a standard reflector sight which was fully adequate for a fighter pilot used to shooting by "Kentucky windage."

On the evening of 15 February, sixteen fast carriers ran northwest through heavy seas. Again under the command of Vice Admiral Mitscher, they were once more known as Task Force 58, deployed in four day task groups and one night group.

Seven of the air groups were embarking upon their first combat operation, and two others were beginning new tours. One of the latter was Lieutenant Commander D. A. Clark's VF-30 on the light carrier *Belleau Wood* in TG-58.1. Operating off the *Monterey* from November 1943 to March 1944, Fighting 30 had claimed 50 victories. This new tour would more than double that figure.

In TG-58.2 another veteran air group was returning to combat. Fighting Nine aboard the *Lexington* was still led by Lieutenant Commander Herb Houck, and the former fighter skipper, Commander Phil Torrey, remained CAG. Though the VF-9 of 1943-44 had been split to help form VF-12, many of the original F6F pilots remained. One was Lieutenant Gene Valencia, who had bagged seven planes during his first tour. Now it was almost exactly a year to the day since his last combat and the frantic tail-chase near Truk. But Valencia had used the interim well.

While the air group re-formed at NAS Pasco, Washington, Valencia found three enthusiastic "jaygees" to round out his division: Joseph H. Roquemore, his wingman; James B. French, his second section leader, and Clinton L. Smith as number four. Intensely devoted to the art of flying fighters in combat, Valencia worked his pilots relentlessly. As French recalled, "We were at Pasco for about six months, and most pilots averaged 70 to 80 hours a month. But Gene flew us over 100 hours a month." This was more than was authorized, so Valencia needed extra

The most successful fighter division in the U.S. Navy was led by Lieutenant E. A. Valencia (left) with Lieutenants (jg) C. L. Smith, H. E. Mitchell, and J. B. French. These four VF-9 pilots accounted for 50 Japanese aircraft without loss or damage to themselves.

fuel. Legend has it that he and his pilots "misappropriated" extra fuel, but Jim French denies it. "That implies we stole the gas," he says. "Actually, we sort of traded for it. We just slipped the service crews a few bottles of booze, and they filled up our airplanes for us."[1]

En route to Hawaii, Valencia's wingman Joe Roquemore died of pneumonia. After trying out several others, Valencia decided to make a young VBF-9 pilot his new number two. Lieutenant (jg) Harris E. Mitchell was a 21-year-old West Texas farmboy with a slow, deliberate drawl and a smile-when-you-say-that directness. He admitted to a certain degree of envy in watching the antics of Valencia's team at Pasco, and quickly fitted in during training in Hawaii.

Valencia not only worked his pilots hard; he developed a strong esprit de corps. He wanted to paint purple lightning bolts on his Hellcats, but since regulations forbade such markings, his division adopted flamboyant decorations for their flying helmets. Jim French had the ace of spades on his helmet, for instance. Intense, mercurial, and often short-tempered, Valencia nevertheless had a certain flair.

Once the flight line was secured, his division sipped champagne or mint julips from frosted glasses while other pilots indulged in more regulation refreshment. Gene Valencia seldom endeared himself to his superiors, but his pilots knew they would be ready the day they entered combat.

That day was less than 24 hours away on the evening of 15 February. Mitscher informed his task force that the next morning's target was Tokyo —the first carrier strike on the enemy home islands since Mitscher himself had sent the Doolittle Raiders on their way from the old *Hornet* three years before.

With so many new air groups in the task force, and the enlarged fighter and fighter-bomber squadrons, the first Japan strikes would be the initial combat exposure for a large portion of Mitscher's aviators. But he confidently predicted the greatest air victory of the war for carrier aviation, and told his young pilots that the individual Japanese was "probably more afraid of you than you are of him."[2]

Nevertheless, a good many pilots felt just as Harris Mitchell aboard the *Lexington* did, "The adrenalin, you might say, flowed very freely that night."[3]

The first fighter sweep was launched before daylight into a 20-knot northeast wind under low clouds and limited visibility. It was 125 miles to the target airfields around Tokyo, but landfall was made halfway en route as the Hellcats and Corsairs groped their way along. The ceiling was low enough—4,000 feet—but broken clouds extended down to only 1,000 feet. Some of the Hellcat pilots wore long-John underwear, some-

British Hellcat I of 804 Squadron aboard the HMS *Ameer* in the Indian Ocean early in 1945.

thing they never imagined they would need in the Pacific, because numerous F6F-5s had been delivered without cockpit heaters.

The *Lexington's* sweep, led by the VF-9 skipper, Herb Houck, crossed the Honshu coast flying through rain and snow squalls. The TG-58.2 sweeps were the only ones to meet sizable opposition, operating over the Chiba Peninsula on the east side of Tokyo Bay. About 100 Japanese aircraft were sighted there, and in a series of dogfights Hellcats claimed over 40 kills.

Most of this combat was conducted by *Hancock* fighters from Lieutenant Commander Albert O. Vorse's Air Group 80. Vorse was one of the genuine veterans of the Pacific war. He had flown F4Fs from the old *Lexington*, the *Saratoga*, and the *Enterprise* through nearly all of 1942. But VF-80's first sweep was led by the fighter skipper, Lieutenant Commander Leroy W. Keith. Nearing the coast, the ceiling raised to 7,500 feet, and Keith sighted a lone Zeke five to six miles off. The CO bent his throttle to catch up, hauled into gun range, and dropped the Zeke burning into the choppy sea. The *Hancock* Hellcats then proceeded to their primary target, Katori airfield, where they strafed and rocketed parked airplanes and facilities. Hampered only by light to moderate flak, the F6Fs started fires in the hangars on the west side of the field, then pulled off the target just as antiaircraft fire increased.

As Keith pulled up, he met an Oscar head-on and shot it down. Japanese aircraft then dropped in "from all directions and all altitudes," for the next hour and, noted the squadron diarist, "they were given a bad time."[4]

Indeed they were. Leroy Keith shot down three more planes—a Nate, another Zeke, and a Val—for a total of five. His wingman, Ensign F. F. Ackerman, dropped a Nate which seemed to stop in midair to get on Keith's tail, plus a Zeke and two Vals. Meanwhile, in the strung-out battle fought between 1,000 and 4,000 feet, Keith's second division leader, Lieutenant William C. Edwards, Jr., knocked down two Nates, two Zekes, and an Oscar by exploiting a consistent altitude advantage. Making only fast, steep gunnery passes, the F6Fs nullified the superior maneuverability of the Japanese aircraft.

Keith's disappointed third division accounted for only one of the 24 kills and 5 probables scored in this fracas. One pilot had engine trouble which prevented him from leaving the task force, and another's guns jammed in the bitter cold.

Back aboard ship the pilots tallied their scores and told their friends of the lousy weather, the crowded airfields, and the excellent hunting. Herb Houck rushed through VF-9's ready room en route to the bridge, shedding flight gear as he went. A pilot called after him, "How'd it go,

A broken arresting wire allowed this F6F-5 to collide with the island of the escort carrier *Sangamon* in early 1945. Despite spraying gasoline from a ruptured fuel cell, Lieutenant (jg) W. G. Bailey emerged from the wreck unharmed.

skipper?" As Houck disappeared through a hatch he called over his shoulder, "There are Zeroes all over the place."[5]

It remained that way for the rest of the day. The *Lexington* and *Hancock* F6Fs saw much of the subsequent action, and the second VF-9 sweep-strike included Gene Valencia's division which followed Phil Torrey up into a 200-foot ceiling on the way to Emba airfield 40 miles north of Tokyo. Torrey's 16 Hellcats climbed on instruments almost all the way to the coast, then broke out at nearly 20,000 feet.

The CAG took three divisions down towards Emba while Valencia remained above as top cover. Then Valencia's keen eyes spotted something in his rearview mirror and he called out a bogey at six o'clock high. In a hard climbing turn, he left Harris Mitchell behind momentarily and pressed a head-on attack on a Tojo. Still out of effective gun range Gene fired four of his rockets, all of which fell short. Mitchell, back in position, did likewise. Then Valencia disappeared from view to starboard. Mitchell turned up his gunsight rheostat and continued head-on at the Tojo. His first tracers hit the bandit's cowling, the engine caught fire, and as Mitch pulled up he saw the enemy pilot bail out.

The division re-formed and for the next hour hunted Japanese planes in the air and on the ground. Valencia shot down two more and French and Smith got three between them, in addition to burning several planes parked on various airfields. Valencia's "flying circus" came away from its first combat with six confirmed kills and no damage to the four F6Fs.

But as Mitchell recalled, "Our return to the ship was with mixed emotions. Phil Torrey and two other pilots were missing."[6] Torrey, the wisecracking, popular leader, had been hit by a Tojo. His Hellcat climbed and dived out of control, then disappeared when his wingman stalled and lost contact. Fighting Nine claimed 25 victories against the day's three losses.

Meanwhile, the *Hancock* fighters found more combat. Lieutenant Pat Fleming took nine planes of VBF-80 to Mobara airfield and bombed its five hangars, three hits being observed. Fleming then spotted several Zekes high over the field and climbed up beneath to take them by surprise. He burned two almost immediately and chased down another pair, exploding both at an altitude of 50 feet. Another Zeke was hit from astern, and though Fleming's Navy Cross citation credited him with five kills in this engagement, in fact the fifth Zeke was claimed as a probable.

Fleming's section leader, Ensign E. W. Parrish, low-sided a formation at 10,000 feet and exploded a Zeke and an Oscar with one burst each. He then dispatched two more Zekes in head-on passes. Lieutenant "Zeke" Cormier, a future Blue Angel leader, lived up to his nickname with three Zeros destroyed and a probable Oscar. Two other pilots were credited with three more Zekes and a Tojo. Thus, five VBF-80 pilots had accounted for 15 kills and two probables; the only damage suffered was a 7.7-mm bullet which shattered Parrish's windscreen.

Lieutenant Commander Vorse led 14 VF-80 Hellcats on this same sweep and nearly matched the fighter-bombers' bag. Some 25 to 30 bandits were found in disorganized small groups or singles and were picked off with relative ease; the Japanese displayed little aggressiveness. The 30-year-old Vorse was credited with five and one-half victories in 1942, from the early Rabaul raid through Coral Sea and Guadalcanal. But he nearly equalled his previous total when he shot two Oscars out of a formation of three, then added a Nate and a Dinah "which was fat and dumb but soon unhappy."[7] Lieutenant John W. Fair was next best, with an Oscar and a Tojo by himself, plus a Zeke and a Dinah shared with his wingmen.

Farther west, the fifth fighter sweep was the first to actually reach Tokyo. Task Group 58.2 launched *Essex* and *Bunker Hill* fighters, which found good weather. The Hellcats of VF-4 and Corsairs of VF-84 were the first carrier-based fighters over the Japanese capital, but they met little airborne opposition.

Nearly 250 kills were recorded during the 16th, of which the Hellcats claimed over three-quarters. But losses had been heavy. The *Wasp's* VF-81 alone lost five planes and pilots in dogfights with Zekes. Fighting 82 had an equally rugged combat initiation. Four *Bennington* F6Fs were shot down near Atsugi Airfield by enemy aircraft. And one of the squadron's most popular pilots, Ensign Paul K. Spradling of Buhl, Idaho, was killed by American AA fire. While attempting a water landing, he was fired upon by a destroyer of TG-58.1 which mistook his Hellcat for a hostile plane.

The weather remained a formidable enemy. On the 16th, the *Randolph's* VBF-12 lost three pilots in mid-air collisions or weather-related accidents, including the exec, Lieutenant B. P. Seaman.

On the 17th, ceilings were down to 150 or 200 feet over the task force, and many scheduled CAPs were not even launched. Lieutenant Rube Denoff, a two-tour VF-9 veteran, was standing by with his VBF-12 division when bogeys were reported approaching the task group. Cloud tops

The *Randolph* aircraft prepare to launch under rainy skies in May 1945. Thirty-five F6Fs and eight TBMs are visible in this photo. Photo: R. M. Hill

were reported at 4,000 to 5,000 feet, so Denoff led his three pilots off "Randy's" flight deck and climbed in close formation. But there was no clearing at 6,000 feet, and still none at 15,000. Denoff and his pilots had their hands full, fastening oxygen masks while flying their planes and watching their instruments, all the while staying tucked in close formation.

They climbed for another 7,000 feet before breaking out on top, 20 miles from the ship. "How we stayed together I don't know," Denoff recalled.[8] Vectored towards the unidentified aircraft, Denoff recognized them as a flight of Corsairs and asked if they required assistance. They had neglected to turn on their IFF gear, but once informed of the situation they declined the offer of help. So Denoff led his division back down into the murk, feeling his way towards the water. He regained visual contact at about 100 feet in greatly reduced visibility—only a half to three-quarters of a mile. All four Hellcats got back safely aboard, but to Rube Denoff this flight was "the only wartime experience that still gives me nightmares."[9]

Similar conditions existed over the target area that morning. Fighting Nine launched four divisions which flew just off the whitecaps all the way to the coast. Approaching the beach, a pilot called "Tally ho. Land two o'clock at five miles." Another responded, "Wonder what it is?" A third voice piped in, "It sure as hell ain't Frisco."[10]

The sweep leader was Herb Houck, who succeeded Phil Torrey as CAG-9, while Lieutenant John S. Kitchen assumed command of VF-9. Houck decided to try to climb up through the cloud layer as it was obvious that low-level navigation in reduced visibility was an unacceptable risk. It was snowing in the clouds, and visibility was reduced to zero. When the Hellcats reached 20,000 with no end in sight one pilot asked, "How high are we going, skipper?" Houck replied, "Looks like I can see the sun—we'll probably top out at about 25,000." Another squadron overheard this transmission and responded, "No you won't. I'm at 35,000 and haven't broken out yet."[11] Houck took his formation up to 25 grand just to be sure, but it was no use. He led his troops back to the task force.

Before Mitscher canceled further operations, a few sweep-strikes got through to their targets. Another 70 bandits fell to Hellcats and Corsairs, for a two-day total of nearly 320 fighter victories and 190 planes destroyed on the ground. Pat Fleming of VBF-80 repeated his previous day's performance by downing four more enemy fighters, raising his final score to 18. It was the highest personal tally in the task force at the time.

Carrier plane losses for both days amounted to 60 in combat, but some pilots were saved. One was Ensign R. L. Buchanan of VF-29. While escorting a strike against the Tachikawa Engine Plant, the *Cabot* Hellcats fought "a pitched battle over an airfield"[12] and claimed five kills and two probables. Buchanan, who had shot down five planes in one mission four months before, had to ditch near the mouth of Tokyo Bay.

Lieutenant A. J. Fecke and his wingman contacted the lifeguard submarine *Pomfret* 30 miles away, and established "a very lonesome air cover for both pilot and submarine for over an hour."[13] Despite the dangers of possible minefields, the extremely shallow water near shore, and a dozen Japanese airfields only 50 miles away, the *Pomfret* pressed on. Her gutsy skipper, Commander John Hess, scooped up Buchanan and a *Hornet* pilot of Air Group 17 in one of the most daring "zoomie" rescues of the war. Properly appreciative, VF-29 allowed as how the *Pomfret's* rescue would make Hollywood blush with envy.

By noon the strike planes were back aboard and the fast carriers steamed south to support the invasion of Iwo Jima.

And thus began the final six months of hostilities.

The month of March was an eventful one for the fighters of Task Force 58; it led up to the invasion of Okinawa. The fireworks began on the evening of the 11th, three days before the task force was to depart Ulithi. Sixteen fast carriers riding at anchor made an inviting target, even blacked out, and 24 Japanese twin-engine aircraft were sent from Minami Jima, 800 miles to the north. Only two Frances bombers got to Ulithi, and one of them crashed on the atoll. But the other—perhaps accidentally—flew into the *Randolph's* stern. Fire and explosions wracked the aft portion of her hangar deck, putting the ship out of action for almost a month, and nearly 30 men were killed. Air Group 12 would therefore miss the buildup to Operation Iceberg, the Okinawa invasion. But the CAG, Charlie Crommelin, ran true to form and got himself temporarily assigned to another carrier. He would perish in a mid-air collision on 28 March, three days before the invasion began.

Fighter sweeps were launched from 90 miles southeast of Kyushu early on 18 March, blanketing 45 enemy airfields. There were few planes on most fields, as they had been withdrawn north out of range, but *Hornet's* VF-17 found considerable activity around Kanoya. The skipper was Lieutenant Commander Marshall U. Beebe, a 31-year-old Californian who had led the Wildcats of escort carrier *Liscome Bay* until she was sunk in the Gilberts. Now, 16 months later, Marsh Beebe still had seven of his original pilots with him.

Approaching Kanoya and Kanoya East, the 20 Hellcats tally-hoed single Zekes, which were handled by Lieutenant Thomas S. Harris and his wingman. Between them, they scored two kills, two probables, and three damaged. Beebe took six planes down on Kanoya, where enemy aircraft were moving, and kept his other two divisions high as top cover. In a series of quick passes Beebe's Hellcats destroyed 15 planes on the ground, then were bounced by numerous Zekes, Franks, and Tonys. In the ensuing low-level hassle, Beebe dropped three Franks and two Zekes while one of his division leaders, Lieutenant Robert C. Coats, also made five kills, all Zekes. When airplanes quit falling, VF-17 had claimed 25 aerial victories and three probables without a loss.

Other Japanese aircraft were somewhat more successful. Conventional bombers and kamikazes made several attempts to hit the fast carriers, and TG-58.4 was the focal point. The *Enterprise, Intrepid,* and *Yorktown* all sustained minor damage.

Next day the Japanese came back. While carrier strikes were flown against enemy shipping, thereby reducing the number of CAP fighters over hostile airfields, Japanese bombers scored twice. About 0700 the *Wasp,* with Air Group 86 aboard, took a bomb which tore up her insides and left over 370 men dead or injured. Almost simultaneously another bomber hit the *Franklin* with two bombs, and the damage was appalling. "Big Ben" was turned into a ghastly floating oven as fires, explosions, and thick smoke almost obscured her from view. Though superhuman damage control eventually saved her, the *Franklin* and the re-formed Air Group Five were knocked out of the war. The ship's company and air group lost a combined total of 1,100 killed and wounded.

On the afternoon of 21 March a brand-new suicide threat appeared. It was the rocket-powered Ohka, or "Cherry Blossom" aircraft. The Americans had known of these "baka bombs" since February, and though "baka" was the Japanese word for fool, the design was ingenuous. A small, lightweight single-seater with twin rudders, the Ohka Model 11 carried 2,600 pounds of TNT in its pointed nose and could do 400 mph. Its vulnerability lay in its mode of transport; it was fastened to the belly of a Mitsubishi G4M Betty which took it within range of its target.

Eighteen Ohka-carrying Bettys escorted by 30 Zekes were plotted by TG-58.1 that afternoon, distance 70 miles. Two *Hornet* divisions, one each from VF-17 and VBF-17, were scrambled, while VF-30 dispatched eight Hellcats from *Belleau Wood.* Fighting 30 took on the Zekes while the *Hornet* fighters went for the Bettys. It was over in 20 minutes.

The F6Fs made repeated runs—some as many as a dozen each—methodically picking off the lumbering, laden bombers. Lieutenant Henry E. Mitchell, Jr., of VBF-17 splashed four Bettys, then saw another scooting for home at zero feet. Mitchell buzzed over the top of the bomber, forcing the enemy pilot to nose down. The Betty skidded into the water. Lieutenant Murray Winfield claimed four Bettys, and the other *Hornet* pilots accounted for the remaining nine. One VBF-17 plane was shot down, the only Hellcat loss against 18 Bettys, their Ohkas, and a dozen Zekes.

Ten days later the invasion of Okinawa began.

Okinawa is only 350 miles from the southern tip of Kyushu, placing it well within range of Japan-based aircraft. With the fast carriers that were supporting the invasion tied to a 60-square-mile area off Okinawa, the Japanese had no trouble locating their prime targets. And Task Force 58 remained in this precarious situation for two months—from mid-March to mid-May.

It was probably the most trying period of the Pacific war. Under constant threat of massed suicide and conventional air attacks, the fliers and ships' crews were worn down by the strain of operations—particularly the fighter pilots, whose responsibility was awesomely simple: shoot down the attackers before they could destroy the carrier decks.

This shot-up Hellcat was jettisoned from the escort carrier *Block Island* in May 1945, being too heavily damaged to repair.

To provide better advance warning, 16 radar picket stations were established around Okinawa. They were plotted in reference to "Point Bolo," the tip of land on Okinawa's west coast known as Zampa Misaki. The picket stations averaged 52 nautical miles from Point Bolo, with RP-13 being the closest, only 18 miles offshore, and RP-8 the farthest, 95 miles southeast. Each station was usually patrolled by two destroyers, which had highly trained fighter-director teams on board, and was supported by utility vessels.

The Japanese flung their first massed attack at the invasion fleet on D-Plus-Five, April sixth. It involved nearly 700 aircraft, including 355 kamikazes. Three squadrons of TG-58.1 were credited with nearly 90 kills among them, as Hellcats met succeeding waves of attackers.

A series of large battles was fought over Okinawa and the invasion fleet that afternoon and evening. Sixteen Air Group 17 Hellcats met "a swarm of kamikaze-bent Japs"[14] evidently headed for the landing beaches. The *Hornet* pilots barged in and gunned down 33 as other squadrons arrived on the scene. In this combat Lieutenant Willis E. Hardy was credited with a Zeke, two Judys, and a pair of Vals—the last with only one gun firing. Then later that afternoon, Marsh Beebe led two VF-17 divisions on CAP north of the force and bounced a formation of Val and Judy dive bombers, splashing eight. It brought the *Hornet* fighters' one-day total to 41½.

Fighting 30 had things entirely its own way in what it called "Turkey Shoot Number Two."[15] Over the island, 14 F6F-5s under Lieutenant R. F. Gillespie almost immediately contacted several small enemy groups when taking station at 1530. In a two-hour running battle, formations and singles of Vals, Zekes, and a handful of Tojos and Oscars were met— about 60 bandits in all. The Hellcats found their opponents inexperienced, unaggressive, and poor marksmen. Every *Belleau Wood* pilot scored, and upon return to the ship, the only damage VF-30 had suffered was 16 holes in one plane, put there by a "friendly" F6F night fighter.

Belleau Wood's 14 pilots accounted for 26½ Vals, 14 Zekes, 5 Tojos, and 2 Oscars. The top scorers were all ensigns, three of whom became "instant aces"; Carl C. Foster got six kills, Kenneth J. Dahms got five and one-half and Johnnie G. Miller bagged five. Michelle A. Mazzocco got three singles and three halves for a total of four and one-half, and three other ensigns each scored quadruples. The total of 47½ prompted *Belleau Wood*'s skipper, Captain W. G. Tomlinson, to query the task group commander, Rear Admiral Jocko Clark, "Does this exceed bag limit?" To which Clark replied, "Negative . . . . This is open season."[16]

The hunters of VF-83 certainly thought so; the *Essex* Hellcats claimed 56 kills from dawn to late afternoon. Four night fighter sorties contributed nine of this record total for 6 April, but the daylight F6Fs dropped 47 in

211

the course of two CAPs, an airfield strike, and a shipping search. The latter was a planned 300-mile mission to the northwest which included 15 Hellcats plus a dozen Corsairs of VBF-83, but few of the fighters got more than halfway outbound. The divisional search teams, flying ten-degree sectors, encountered widespread enemy planes and engaged 53 of them. Thirteen of the Hellcat pilots shot down 26 planes of six different varieties while losing one of their own and sustaining damage to eight more Grummans. The Corsairs added another half-dozen victories for a total of 32 on this mission.

An hour after the search-strike combats ended, a pair of *Essex* Hellcats on a special CAP near Yoro Shima sighted nine bomb-armed Zekes headed for the invasion force. The section leader, Lieutenant (jg) Hugh N. Batten, took advantage of the eight-tenth cloud cover and thick haze to approach undetected from astern. He and his wingman, Lieutenant (jg) Sam J. Brocato, dropped four Zekes between them before the others could take evasive action. In the brief dogfight that followed, the two F6Fs remained together even through violent aerobatics, splashing four more Zeros. Batten and Brocato had downed eight of the nine Zekes with barely 1,500 rounds of .50 caliber, all confirmed by gun-camera film or nearby witnesses.

In all, over 200 of the 350-odd victories claimed were credited to Mitscher's Hellcats during this, by far the largest one-day air attack of the campaign. Though the Japanese lost half of their committed aircraft, they succeeded in hitting 19 ships. Thirteen were destroyers on radar picket patrol, a foretaste of the ordeal to come.

The tempo increased, even if the weight of air attacks did not. Nine more massed suicide attacks were mounted against the invasion fleet and the carriers: three more in April, four in May, and two in June, each numbering from 45 to 185 planes. But by and large, the Hellcat and Corsair CAP handled these "smaller" raids.

Besides protecting the fleet and supporting the troops ashore, the fast carriers also launched further strikes against Japan. The *Hornet* fighters had another big day on 16 April when they knocked down 45 hostiles in the course of three CAPs, three scrambles, and a sweep. Marsh Beebe's pilots accounted for 31, including Lieutenant (jg) John Crosby, who got three Jacks, a Zeke, and a Val in an interception near the northern tip of Okinawa. The fighter-bombers dropped 14 more during the day, for a *Hornet* total of 45. Short, aggressive, Lieutenant John "Super Mouse" Johnston got four of the Zekes, doubling his previous score.

Next day Fighting Nine recorded another big success. Gene Valencia's division was vectored by *Yorktown*'s FDO onto a bogey about 60 miles north of the task group. At first the radar plot looked small, and the other two VF-9 divisions were not assigned. But when Valencia's sharp eyes detected the bandits, the situation changed rapidly. There were 38 bomb-carrying Zekes and Franks. While Lieutenant G. E. Phillips's division was racing to the scene, Valencia took his "Circus" into the enemy formation at 15,000 feet.

Outnumbered 38 to 4, Harris Mitchell on Valencia's wing recalled, "I discovered the true meaning of anxiety, but when I looked over at Gene his expression was that of a young child who had just spotted his favorite toy under the Christmas tree."[17] Valencia's first burst exploded a Frank, and all the others jettisoned their bombs. Then the two Hellcat sections took turns attacking while one stayed high to provide cover. It was sound doctrine; Mitchell shot two Zekes off Valencia's tail, and Gene got another Frank behind his number four, Clinton "Smitty" Smith.

The fight lasted 20 minutes, from 15,000 feet down to the deck, and ended as abruptly as it began. Valencia re-formed his division and circled the area, counting eight Japanese parachutes still in the air or on the water. The division accounted for 14 destroyed, three probables, and one damaged: six Franks for Valencia; three Zekes for Mitchell, four Zekes for Jim French, and a Frank for Clinton Smith. Phillips's division arrived late and splashed a Frank, an Oscar, and a Zeke. The only damage sustained was a few 7.7-mm holes in the wing of one of Phillips's Hellcats.

Though Japanese formations were flung at the invasion fleet in smaller numbers than before, they still came in infinite variety. On a "Barrier Cap" between Kyushu and Okinawa on 22 April, Lieutenant Rube Denoff, leading four VBF-12 divisions, saw about 50 mixed bandits at 16,000 to 18,000 feet. Before the hostiles pulled up into the overcast, Denoff caught a glimpse of an open-cockpit biplane among the fighters and dive bombers. Six or eight enemy planes then dropped out of the clouds and, though most were shot down, they gave the *Randolph* pilots a hard time. Denoff himself shot down a Jill, but Lieutenant (jg) Bob Drewelow's four Hellcats were so badly shot up they had to land at Okinawa where three were declared unflyable.

Meanwhile, the battle of the radar pickets continued. On 4 May Valencia and company knocked down 11 more bandits in a two-hour low-level combat over the destroyers. But one "can" was hit during this battle when the *Yorktown* division was forced to disengage and land at Okinawa with fuel gauges reading empty. Three easy-meat Vals were passed up en route to Yontan airfield, such was the critical gas shortage, and Harris Mitchell had to be towed off the runway when his engine quit.

One week later the Circus fought its last battle. The divisions of Valencia, Lieutenant Marvin Franger, and Lieutenant Bert Eckard took on at least 55 enemy fighters over the northern Ryukyus. The three flights were vectored separately to orbit 20 to 30 miles apart. Valencia's team fought 18 bandits in two groups, downing 9 without loss, although Valencia pressed his attacks so closely that his radio was jarred loose by an exploding Frank. It brought the Circus's total to 43 kills during the deployment, one-third of the squadron total, including 34 in the last three combats. With Valencia's previous tally of seven from the *Essex* cruise in 1943-44 it made a plump, comfortable 50 victories for no losses and only minor damage.

Bert Eckard and his wingman, Ensign J. Kaelin, tangled with 30 Zekes between 18,000 and 20,000 feet and harried them for 20 minutes. In that time the two VF-9 pilots hit 12 Zekes between them and definitely destroyed eight—five by Eckard and three by Kaelin. A Zeke and Frank splashed by the second section brought the division's total to ten, and Eckard became the 42nd and last Hellcat pilot to score five victories in one day.

Marv Franger's division saw only one hostile, a Tony which Franger quickly dispatched. It was his ninth and last victory of the war. And it had been a long war. Franger was undoubtedly the only fighter pilot to score on each of three successive tours with the same squadron. He had opened his string of victories by downing a Vichy French fighter while flying F4F-4s off the *Ranger* during the invasion of North Africa back in November of 1942. During the squadron's *Essex* tour he bagged five Japanese planes, and in 1945 he added the last three.

A former VF-9 squadron mate had almost as good hunting. Lieutenant Harold E. Vita was one of those transferred to form VF-12 when Air Group Nine was divided in late 1944. Handsome enough to make the cover of *Life*, "Honest Hal" Vita had been credited with one victory over North Africa but failed to score during the 1943-44 tour. The third time out was his lucky charm, however; while flying from the *Randolph* with Fighting 12, he knocked down five Japanese planes.

During this same period, a small ceremony marked a big achievement. In May, VBF-87 received some new F6F-5s. One of them was the 10,000th Hellcat delivered since December of 1942. As the fighter had progressed down the assembly line at Bethpage, a bucket was hung on its tail. Grumman workers dropped spare change into the bucket as a contribution to the welfare fund of the squadron which would eventually receive the new fighter. A check for several hundred dollars was made out, marked for delivery to the appropriate unit.

When Commander Porter W. Maxwell landed the special F6F aboard the *Ticonderoga*, Grumman's "tech rep" Ralph Clark was on hand to do the honors. Clark presented the check to Maxwell and VBF-87 on behalf of all Grumman employees. Hellcat production had peaked at 600 in March, but was holding steady at well over 400 per month. And the new fighter-bombers would soon be put to use, for Air Group 87 entered combat on 17 May.

The 10,000th Hellcat, an F6F-5, was delivered to VBF-87 aboard the USS *Ticonderoga* in May of 1945. From left to right are: Lieutenant Commander Charles Ingalls; Grumman tech rep Ralph Clark; Commander Porter Maxwell, the CO of VBF-87; and Commander Everett L. Phadres, CAG-87. Photo: Grumman

The carrier phase of the Okinawa Campaign lasted almost till the end of June. By that time another CV had been knocked out—the veteran *Bunker Hill* took two kamikazes on 11 May—but McCain's was "the fleet that came to stay." Some 3,000 enemy aircraft had attacked the task force, and nearly 1,700 were believed shot down by F6Fs and F4Us. Despite the handicap of operating in a restricted area in the face of massed land-based air assault, the fighters provided sufficient defense. Nine CVs and a CVL had been hit by kamikazes or bombs, and though none was sunk, some, like the *Franklin* and *Bunker Hill*, would not fight again.

Pilot fatigue was such that the normal six-month tour was reduced to four months at this time. Some second- and third-tour pilots found themselves questioning the need to chase a lone Japanese plane inland, weighing the risk against the benefit. Many others shared the feelings confided by a double ace years later, "I wasn't score happy, and I knew that one more kill wasn't going to end the war any sooner."

In defeating the kamikazes, three main factors were involved. One concerned the Japanese themselves. Lieutenant Commander Bill Leonard of McCain's staff summed it up: "Instead of the classic formations making their brave approach, we would have singles coming in on us from all directions, from all altitudes. It would have been much more hairy save for the fact that many of the kamikaze boys were pitifully short on flight experience, and got lost or fouled up. The few that did get through were bad enough."[18]

Secondly, there were the skilled, experienced fighter directors who were the key to handling suiciders, along with overlapping task group radar coverage. And finally, of course, there were the young men in Hellcat and Corsair cockpits. Their role in anti-kamikaze work was that of a high-priced CAP mission with a premium on good air and radio discipline, suspicion of every sighting, and reliance on sharp vision.

As the Okinawa Campaign began winding down, increasing attention was given to operations against the enemy home islands. Hellcats would finish the war over Japan itself.

Hellcat Squadrons in Combat: February to May 1945

VF-3	*Yorktown*	Lieutenant Commander W. L. Lamberson
VBF-3	*Yorktown*	Lieutenant Commander F. E. Wolf
VF-4	*Essex*	Lieutenant L. M. Boykin
VF-6	*Hancock*	Lieutenant Commander R. L. Copeland
VF-7	*Hancock*	Lieutenant J. A. Duncan
VF-9	*Lexington, Yorktown*	Lieutenant Commander H. N. Houck, Lieutenant J. S. Kitchen
VBF-9	*Lexington, Yorktown*	Lieutenant Commander F. L. Lawlor
VF-12	*Randolph*	Commander N. A. M. Gayler
VBF-12	*Randolph*	Lieutenant Commander E. Pawka, Lieutenant R. H. Denoff
VF-17	*Hornet*	Lieutenant Commander M. U. Beebe
VBF-17	*Hornet*	Lieutenant Commander H. W. Nicholson (KIA), Lieutenant E. S. Conant
VF-23	*Langley*	Lieutenant Commander M. Paddock
VF-29	*Cabot*	Lieutenant Commander W. E. Eder
VF-30	*Belleau Wood*	Lieutenant Commander D. A. Clark
VF-34	*Monterey*	Lieutenant Commander R. W. Conrad
VF-45	*San Jacinto*	Commander G. E. Schechter
VF-46	*Cowpens, Independence*	Commander C. W. Rooney
VF-47	*Bataan*	Commander W. Etheridge
VF-49	*San Jacinto*	Lieutenant Commander G. M. Rouzee
VF-53	*Saratoga*	Lieutenant Commander R. W. Conrad
VF-80	*Hancock*	Lieutenant Commander L. R. Keith
VBF-80	*Hancock*	Lieutenant Commander F. G. Gooding
VF-81	*Wasp*	Commander F. K. Upham
VF-82	*Bennington*	Lieutenant Commander E. W. Hessel
VF-83	*Essex*	Commander J. J. Southerland
VF-86	*Wasp*	Lieutenant Commander C. J. Dobson

10 Victory

And the combat ceased for want of combatants.
Pierre Corneille
El Cid

The Okinawa Campaign officially ended in the first week of June when TF-38 struck Kyushu again. Strikes were flown on the second, third, and eighth to destroy Japanese aircraft posing a threat to the invasion, but little aerial opposition was encountered. Hellcats and Corsairs claimed "only" 77 planes destroyed, while total fast-carrier losses amounted to 14. Again, the main cause was AA fire.

During one of these strikes, VBF-12 was certain it had lost its skipper over an airdrome near Hiroshima. Lieutenant Rube Denoff rolled into a steep strafing run and was instantly under heavy, accurate AA fire. After a bright explosion, his Hellcat was seen diving headlong at the ground, and the remaining 11 pilots sadly set course back to the *Randolph*.

Near the briefed rendezvous point a familiar F6 joined formation. The pilots were incredulous. "Rube, is that you?" queried one. "Hell, yes," came the reply, "where you been?"[1] Unknown to Denoff, the bursting flak had appeared to be a direct hit on his plane. But he had pressed his strafing attack on the airdrome, confident the squadron was following him down. Deprived of the element of surprise, VBF-12 abandoned its primary target and contented itself with shooting up about 20 suicide motor boats in Hiroshima Bay.

Back aboard the *Randolph*, Denoff speculated on the enemy gunners' opinion of the crazy American in the lone Hellcat who tackled an entire airdrome single-handed.

The fast carriers arrived at Leyte for replenishment on 14 June and remained for two weeks. While there, Air Group 12 was knocked out of the war—by a U.S. Army pilot. A pair of P-38 Lightnings buzzed the carriers riding at anchor, but one pilot misjudged his altitude and crashed into the *Randolph*'s flight deck. Eleven men were killed, 14 injured, and nine planes destroyed. Most of Commander Ed Pawka's airmen were ashore at the time, and commented on the strange plume of smoke rising out at sea. Not until their boats returned to the task group did they know it was their own unlucky "Randy." Rube Denoff found one of the P-38's Allison engines smouldering in his bunk. With no replacement carrier available, Air Group 12 ended its tour prematurely.

While the Navy fast-carrier Hellcats enjoyed a rest, the Marine escort-carrier F6Fs were hard at work. The first Marine carrier air group was composed of VMF-511 and VMTB-233, embarked aboard the second *Block Island* (CVE-106.) In combat since early May at Okinawa, the fighter squadron was led by Major Robert C. Maze with eight F4U-1Ds, eight F6F-5Ns, and two F6F-5Ps.

Three other Marine CVEs got into combat, but VMF-511 was the only Leatherneck carrier squadron to fly Hellcats. Lieutenant Chester Leo

Smith, a Californian, recalls the F6F's joint operations with the F4Us: "I flew fourth man on three Corsairs quite a lot from the *Block Island,* as spares were necessary. I checked out on the night fighter gear, and we used it in daytime occasionally, particularly in heavy weather. The Corsair had several knots on the night fighter F6F, and picked up speed a little faster in a dive, so formation flying had its problems."[2]

The *Block Island* shuttled between Okinawa and Formosa during May and June, flying more strike missions than the ground support sorties for which its pilots were trained. The CVE was then sent south to Borneo to help support the Australian landings at Balikpapan. During this operation VMF-511 scored its only aerial victory when Lieutenant Bruce J. Reuter's F6F-5N dispatched a Jake floatplane shortly after midnight, 3 July.

Task Force 38 sailed to war for the last time on 1 July, again bound for Japanese waters. As the conflict entered its last 60 days, the Tokyo area became the target for only the second time. Not since the original strikes in mid-February had carrier pilots been briefed to strike the airfields of the Tokyo plain.

The task force numbered eight CVs, including the night carrier *Bonhomme Richard,* and six CVLs. Six of these 14 air groups were embarked upon their second or third tour, including the indefatigable Air Group 27 under Fred Bardshar. Orphaned from the *Princeton* at Leyte Gulf only eight months before, the unit was now aboard the *Independence.* It was one of the quickest turn-arounds of the war. Recalled Bardshar: "We recommissioned at Sanford, Maine, on 1 January 1945 in 18° F below zero. . . . About half the pilots in VF-27 from the *Princeton* cruise made the *Independence* cruise. I remember stating that we were going back out with division and section leaders who had shot down at least two Japanese aircraft each."[3] It was further reason why assistant operations officer John Fitzgerald called VF-27 "the biggest little squadron in the war."[4]

The Tokyo strikes were launched shortly after dawn on 10 July, 170 miles offshore. The pilots assigned to fighter sweeps over Tokyo itself returned astonished and disappointed; there were no enemy aircraft. Low-flying fighter-bombers were completely unhindered from the air as they hunted for parked Japanese planes on the airdrome complexes around the capital. Few were found on the fields themselves. Instead, the enemy had reverted to their Philippine tactics of dispersing aircraft miles from any airfield. But it did little to prevent serious losses, as Hellcats and Corsairs destroyed 100 on the ground, all at least ten miles from their runways. The Japanese were hoarding their remaining planes in an effort to launch massive attacks against the anticipated invasion in the fall, but without airborne interceptors there was little to prevent the carrier pilots from having their way.

More unopposed strikes were flown on the 14th and 15th, against northern Honshu and Hokkaido. This time the fast carriers operated only 80 miles at sea. A lone Betty snooper was the only hostile plane to approach the force, and it was unsuccessful.

Poor weather had already forced a one-day delay in these strikes, and it only lifted enough to make flight operations difficult. Fighting 88's skipper, Lieutenant Commander Richard G. Crommelin, was leading a Hellcat squadron from the *Yorktown*, just as his older brother Charlie had done very nearly two years before. En route to his target on the 14th, flying formation in heavy clouds, Dick's plane was hit by another and he was killed in a mid-air collision—as his brother had been at Okinawa. It was one of those eerie, macabre incidents which was all the more difficult to accept because Dick Crommelin had been a combat fighter pilot since early 1942.

Most planes got through to their targets, however, and did considerable damage to Japanese shipping. Carrier planes sank 26 merchantmen, a destroyer, and three frigates on the 14th, and five more ships the next day. It was an indication of things to come, as aerial opposition remained nonexistent while shipping strikes increased.

On 16 July four carriers of the British Pacific Fleet joined the American fast-carriers as Task Force 37. They contained 112 Seafire or Firefly fighters, 73 Corsairs, and 62 Avengers. But the HMS *Formidable* also em-

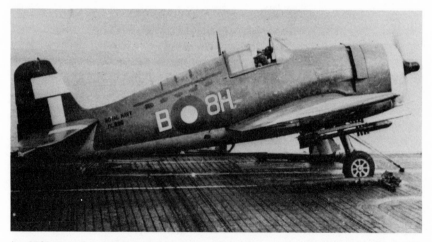

An 1839 Squadron Hellcat with rocket projectiles aboard the HMS *Indomitable* with the British Pacific Fleet. Photo: C. F. Shores

barked a detachment of Hellcats from the HMS *Indomitable*'s outstanding 1844 Squadron, Fleet Air Arm.

British use of Hellcats in the Pacific extended back to the fall of 1944. In a series of strikes on Sumatran oil fields in December and January, 1844 and 1839 Squadrons off the *Indomitable* had accounted for some 15 aerial victories with few losses. Then came the Okinawa Campaign where 1844 ran up the largest one-day score for British F6Fs by downing four Oscars, a Tony, and a Zeke over Formosa on 12 April. It was a mighty small bag by U.S. Navy standards, but proof the British could put the Hellcat to good use.

The Royal Navy put its F6Fs to a different use the night of 25 July. When a small Japanese formation was detected heading for the British task group, two of 1844's Hellcats were scrambled from the *Formidable* under a full moon. These were conventional Hellcat II's (F6F-5s) without radar, but their pilots had been trained in night flying and were vectored by the ship's FDO to an intercept position.

Lieutenant W. H. Atkinson, a Canadian, led the element and made contact. He identified the bandits as big, single-engine Grace torpedo planes and took his New Zealand wingman, Sub-Lieutenant R. F. Mackie, into the attack. Atkinson latched on to a pair of Graces and shot them both into the water while Mackie dumped a third. Then, in routing the other bandits, a fourth Grace was damaged and the attack was completely broken up.

It was ironic that the British, who led the Allies in night flying experience, should find themselves without their own carrier-based single-seat night fighters. Two Hellcat NF-II squadrons, 891 and 892, were forming with F6F-5Ns but would not become operational in time to fly combat.

These three victories raised the Hellcat's tally to 47½ under British colors in the Pacific. Not surprisingly, 1844 Squadron remained the most successful F6F unit in the Fleet Air Arm with 31½ of the Royal Navy total. It also produced the individual top scorer, Sub-Lieutenant E. T. Wilson, who claimed 4.83 victories flying from the *Indomitable* in the Sumatran and Okinawan operations.

The last week of July was devoted to heavy strikes on Kure, Kobe, and Nagoya. Many of the carrier pilots considered the big fleet base at Kure the most heavily defended. But Yokosuka was also loaded with heavy-caliber AA guns, and the air over both targets was frequently dotted with colored bursts as the Japanese gunners tried to get the range and altitude. Heavy strikes on the remaining capital ships at Kure were such that the concern with flak was overshadowed by fear of collision. The strikes were large and concentrated, but coordination was well executed, and they brought results. From the 24th to 28th, three battleships settled to Kure's shallow bottom while three carriers were heavily damaged by bomb-toting

Helldivers, Avengers, and Hellcats. There was little air combat, though VF-88 skipper Malcolm Cagle scored his squadron's first victory by downing a Jack and damaging another over Kure on the 24th.

Mainly the fighters went after smaller vessels operating within the confines of the Inland Sea. Bombing, strafing, and rocketing, the F6Fs and F4Us pounced on anything that moved, smoking their HVARs into thin-hulled vessels as .50-caliber bullets churned up the water in tall geysers. Commander Porter W. Maxwell's VBF-87 had already sunk a tanker, left a freighter burning dead in the water, and perforated the hulls of two flying boats, when he led his *Ticonderoga* Hellcats against airdromes of western Shikoku. In an extra low-level blitz at Niihama Airfield, Maxwell dived to 25 feet to get at a training plane. He set it afire where it sat, but the enemy gunners had his range. Unable to maintain control of his stricken F6F, Maxwell attempted to pull up over the water for enough altitude to bail out. His chute was seen to stream out just as the F6 went in, but it did not fully deploy. Another squadron commander gone.

The flak was just as intense elsewhere, and TF-38 lost 133 aircraft, mostly to AA fire, in the five days from 24 to 28 July. One of the few dogfights occurred near Nagoya on the 25th when VF-31 was jumped by a superior number of bandits while strafing on airfield. Flying his second combat tour was 24-year-old Lieutenant Commander Cornelius Nooy, who called a warning, turned into the attack, and promptly shot one Japanese off a *Belleau Wood* F6F. Nooy climbed to draw off the other hostiles, then rejoined his division and shot down two more with another claimed as a probable. It was a spectacular conclusion to an exceptional career. In only five combats during two tours with Fighting 31, Conny Nooy had scored 18 kills—never less than three in one engagement.

On 9 August, the same day the second atom bomb was dropped on Nagasaki, the fast carriers' main target was Misawa Airbase in northern Honshu. Some 200 twin-engine bombers were known assembled there, preparing for a desperate mass suicide attack on B-29 bases in the Marianas. Fully armed F6Fs and F4Us worked over the field to such an extent that nearly all the would-be suiciders were destroyed in their revetments.

The end was now very near, but still seemed acutely far off. Rumors were traded back and forth on the carriers that the Japanese were about to give in. It was bound to happen any day, now that two A-bombs had been dropped. But when the still-troublesome weather allowed, more strikes were scheduled.

On 13 August another 250 enemy planes were destroyed on the ground near Tokyo, including 61 by Fighting Six. The *Hancock* pilots claimed 49 of their total on Nagano Airfield alone, but spread a wake of destruction well beyond the airdrome. With 28 500-pound GPs, four 1,000-pounders, and 113 rockets they also wrecked two locomotives, an oil storage tank, several hangars, and inflicted heavy damage on other facilities.

Meanwhile, airborne hostiles put in a rare appearance near the task force. Eight different Japanese aircraft types were seen, including many single Jills and Judys. The CAP fighters saved 22 of them the trouble of a return trip.

Two more strikes were planned near Tokyo on the 15th. Strike Able launched at 0415, scheduled to arrive over the capital at dawn. At about 0635 the 103 planes of this mission were attacking their targets and the 73 of Strike Baker were approaching the coast when one of the carriers suddenly came on the air:

"All Strike Able planes, this is Nitrate Base. All Strike Able planes return to base immediately. Do not attack target. The war is over."[5]

The Japanese had agreed to unconditional surrender.

Some aviators penetrating Japanese airspace could hardly believe it. To Lieutenant (jg) Richard L. Newhafer of VF-6, the message brought "all the hope and unreasoning happiness that salvation can bring. It brought tears and laughter and a numb sense of unbelief. It was old news to most of the world by that time, but to us it was wonderfully new."[6]

For many airmen on both sides, however, the news came too late. Though the second strike jettisoned its ordnance and returned to the force, most of the first strike had already attacked. Probably the last bombs dropped in W.W. II were from 12 Hellcats of the *Ticonderoga*'s VBF-87, which had difficulty finding their briefed target on the Chiba Peninsula. Instead, Lieutenant Commander Charles W. Gunnels found a hole in the overcast which allowed his fighter-bombers to pounce on Choshi Airfield, a gunnery school, and a large industrial plant. Gunnels assigned one division to each target, and was just pulling out of his 60° dive when the cease-fire order came through. His other pilots were already committed to their dives, and made accurate drops on all three objectives. Lieutenant (jg) John McNabb, a 23-year-old Pennsylvanian, was the 12th man in the formation, and his 500-pounder was almost certainly the last one dropped on Japanese soil.

But the shooting was not yet over. Lieutenant Herschel Pahl's VF-6 division was returning to the *Hancock* when jumped by seven enemy fighters over Sagami Wan. In the short hassle which resulted, the four F6Fs shot down at least one Zeke and two Jacks without a loss. Other squadrons had similar experiences, but not all had such an easy time of it.

A fighter-bomber sweep over Choshi Point was led by Lieutenant Howard M. Harrison with 12 Hellcats of VF-88 and two dozen Corsairs from the *Shangri-La* and *Wasp*. The formation was dispersed by divisions while penetrating a cloud front, and upon emerging only six *Yorktown* F6Fs were together. Harrison was over Tokurozama Airfield when the cease hostilities order went out, but 17 Japanese pilots either lacked or ignored similar information. A mixed batch of Jacks, Franks, Georges, and Zekes bounced the six *Yorktown* Hellcats from above and behind at 8,000 feet.

Harrison turned his flight into the attack and opened fire. In that first pass four bandits went down. Then the formations were shredded in the head-on lunge.

Lieutenant (jg) T. W. Hansen, flying wing on Lieutenant (jg) M. Proctor, had exploded a Frank in the first pass and then splashed a second while Proctor shot the wing off another. The section turned starboard and saw a Jack on Lieutenant (jg) J. G. Shaloff's tail. Proctor fired at a range of 700 feet, and the Jack exploded. Shaloff's damaged F6F was smoking now and Proctor told him to head for the coast. It was Proctor's intention to escort Shaloff out of the area, but when tracers flashed past his wingtip, Proctor turned hard right and let Hansen shoot the troublesome Frank off his tail.

As Hanson weaved above Shaloff, Proctor reversed his turn and saw two more bandits in flames but did not know who was responsible. Then he was quickly boxed in by six of the enemy ahead and a Frank behind. Unaccountably, the front six pulled up, and Proctor got a good shot at the lone Frank, which split-essed burning. When the six enemy fighters turned towards him again, Proctor fled towards some clouds, slowly outrunning his pursuers. They put several holes in his Hellcat but failed to do any harm, and he remained in the clouds until out over the sea.

Once in the clear, Proctor tried to call the others but only Hansen responded. He had seen Shaloff clear the area, ducking in and out of clouds, but the smoking Hellcat apparently went out of control. It rolled twice and hit the water. Proctor and Hansen returned to base, reporting nine kills for the loss of four F6Fs and their pilots.

The last dogfight of W. W. II was over.

By mid-morning the last strike planes were back aboard, and confirmation of the cease-fire was obtained. The Navy was ordered to cease all offensive operations, but Admiral Halsey ordered his fighters to "investigate and shoot down all snoopers . . . in a friendly sort of way."[7] Dive bombers and torpedo planes were degassed, disarmed, and struck below to hangar decks while ForceCap was strengthened and additional fighters spotted for quick launch. There was no guarantee the Japanese would not attempt a final thrust against the carrier force.

During the rest of the morning and into early afternoon, eight lone hostiles were shot down near the task force. Still others were chased away by patrolling fighters. In the course of sweeps, strikes, and CAPs,

Hellcats claimed two dozen kills during the last day of hostilities. But there was still excitement to come.

The Hellcat's final appearance in the Second World War came on the morning of 2 September, the day of the formal surrender ceremony. General Douglas MacArthur, standing on the deck of the battleship *Missouri*, had barely said "These proceedings are closed," when 450 carrier planes flew overhead in Operation Airshow.

Looking down from their cockpits, the pilots could see Tokyo Harbor filled with the warships of many nations, both victors and vanquished. But they had little time for gawking. They were too busy keeping formation, jockeying the throttle, and watching for other aircraft.

Lieutenant Malcolm Cagle, leading Fighting 88, recalled the victory fly-over with ambivalence. It was a thrill and an honor to participate in such an historic moment, but there was also the constant threat of mid-air collision. Cagle remembered, "it was a full throttle-off throttle formation with no real order or organization."[8]

That same day, back across the International Dateline, the Navy canceled an order for 1,677 more F6F-5s.

Hellcat production dropped off drastically after V-J Day. None were delivered in September, and only 32 in October. The last 30 were completed in November. Of these, the 12,275th and final Hellcat was F6F-5 BuNo 94521, delivered not quite three years after that cold January day when Fighting Nine collected its first F6F-3s.

Like many W.W. II aircraft, the Hellcat had a long postwar career which included service with the French and Uruguayan navies. The hardworking Grumman remained in limited use with the U.S. Navy for eight years. Composite Squadron Four was the last American unit to operate Hellcats when it turned in its F6F-5Ns during August of 1953.

But the Hellcat justified its entire existence during the two years it was engaged in combat. U.S. Navy and Marine F6Fs were credited with 5,156 Japanese planes downed in the Pacific: 4,948 by carrier-based and 208 by land-based Hellcats. The British F6F toll of 47 raises the Pacific figure to 5,203. In Europe, British and American Hellcats claimed 13 German planes in the air—a grand total of 5,216 Axis aircraft credited from August 1943 to August 1945. About 270 F6Fs were lost in air combat during those 24 months, for a kill-loss ratio of 19 to 1.

But the mere statistical record cannot show what the F6F meant to America's war against Japan. The availability in large numbers of a rugged, versatile, easy-to-fly fighter-bomber had a tremendous impact in the Pacific. The F6F's high serviceability rate (often 95 percent) meant

Hellcats remained in postwar service among naval reserve squadrons. These are VF-695 aircraft of NAS Columbus, Ohio, in 1952. Photo: F. A. Bardshar

that near-maximum utilization could be achieved. This, combined with an efficient supply and replacement system, resulted in the one thing that mattered: sufficient numbers of fighter-bombers over the target or on station, when needed.

The Hellcat was not the fastest fighter in the Pacific. Nor did it attain the rate of climb many pilots desired. Other aircraft could perform specific missions somewhat better because they were built for those purposes. Only the Corsair matched the F6F in multi-mission versatility, but the F4U with its greater speed, ceiling, and payload was well over a year behind the Hellcat in operating from fast carriers. Nor did the F4U reach shipboard parity with the F6F. Even in the final weeks of the war, Corsairs represented less than half the embarked fighter-bombers in the Fast Carrier Task Force.

228

Perhaps the most impressive record the F6F left behind is not the number of enemy planes it shot down—for such figures are always subject to honest error—but its huge success in protecting U.S. Navy strike aircraft. The Hellcat proved to be a superb bomber escort—something more often attributed to the Army Air Force's P-51 Mustang. But official Navy records show that from 1943 to 1945, only 42 U.S. carrier-based dive bombers or torpedo planes were known lost to Japanese aircraft. This was, of course, the same period in which the F6Fs saw all of their combat. The angular Grumman fighters so completely controlled the sky with their Corsair stablemates that in the last eight months of the war, a mere seven carrier-based bombers fell to enemy aircraft.

For obvious reasons, fighter pilots weren't the only people who loved Hellcats.

Among the F6F's postwar roles was qualifying naval aviators for carrier operations. Here Navy Reserve pilots practice carrier landings aboard the USS *Monterey* (CVL-26) in June 1953. Photo: R. L. Lawson

VF-6	*Hancock*	Lieutenant Commander R. L. Copeland
VF-9	*Yorktown*	Lieutenant John S. Kitchen
VBF-9	*Yorktown*	Lieutenant Commander Frank L. Lawlor
VF-12	*Randolph*	Lieutenant Commander Fred A. Michaelis
VBF-12	*Randolph*	Lieutenant Reuben H. Denoff
VF-16	*Randolph*	Lieutenant Commander Charles S. Moffett
VF-17	*Hornet*	Lieutenant Commander Marshall U. Beebe
VBF-17	*Hornet*	Lieutenant Edwin S. Conant
VF-27	*Independence*	Lieutenant Commander Fred A. Barshar
VF-30	*Belleau Wood*	Lieutenant Commander D. A. Clark
VF-31	*Belleau Wood*	?
VF-34	*Monterey*	Lieutenant Commander R. W. Conrad
VF-46	*Independence*	Commander C. W. Rooney
VF-47	*Bataan*	Commander W. Etheridge, Lieutenant A. H. Clancy
VF-49	*San Jacinto*	Lieutenant Commander G. M. Rouzee
VF-50	*Cowpens*	Commander R. C. Kirkpatrick
VF-82	*Bennington*	Lieutenant Commander E. W. Hessel
VF-83	*Essex*	Commander J. J. Southerland
VF-86	*Wasp*	Lieutenant Commander Cleo J. Dobson
VF-87	*Ticonderoga*	Lieutenant Commander Charles E. Ingalls, Jr.
VBF-87	*Ticonderoga*	Commander Porter W. Maxwell (KIA), Lieutenant Commander Walter A. Haas
VF-88	*Yorktown*	Lieutenant Commander R. G. Crommelin (KIA), Lieutenant Malcolm W. Cagle
VF-94	*Lexington*	Lieutenant Commander R. J. Morgan

British F6F Squadrons in Combat: Pacific and Indian Oceans October 1944 to August 1945

800 Sqn.	*Emperor*	Lieutenant Commander D. B. Law, Lieutenant Commander H. DeWit (RNethN)
804 Sqn.	*Ameer, Empress, Shah*	Lieutenant Commander G. B. C. Sangster, Lieutenant Commander D. B. Law
808 Sqn.	*Khedive, Emperor*	Lieutenant Commander R. H. P. Carver, Lieutenant Commander O. F. Wheatley
885 Sqn.	*Ruler*	Lieutenant Commander J. R. Routley
888 Sqn.	*Indefatigable, Empress, Emperor, Ameer*	Lieutenant Commander L. Mann, Lieutenant B. A. McGraw
896 Sqn.	*Ameer, Empress*	Lieutenant Commander R. M. Morris, Lieutenant Commander G. J. Z. deBeyl (RNethN)
1839 Sqn.	*Indefatigable*	Lieutenant Commander D. M. Jeram, Lieutenant Commander S. F. F. Shotton
1840 Sqn.	*Speaker*	Lieutenant Commander B. H. C. Nation, Lieutenant Commander P. J. P. Leckie
1844 Sqn.	*Indefatigable, Formidable*	Lieutenant Commander M. S. Godson, (KIA), Lieutenant Commander P. J. P. Leckie

Appendices

Appendix A. The Prototype Hellcats

Over 35 years after the Hellcat first flew, neither Grumman nor the Navy can definitely confirm the real story behind the early experimental models. Grumman's historian, H. J. Schonenberg, believes the matter will never be fully explained, and his assessment is undoubtedly correct.

The Navy authorized two XF6F-1s, BuAer numbers 02981 and 02982, which received factory numbers 3188 and 3189, respectively. Grumman records indicate that for an unknown reason the BuAer numbers were exchanged on the XF6F-1s and that 02982, which became Grumman number 3188, was the sole test airframe. Reportedly, it was subsequently modified as the XF6F-3 with the adoption of the Pratt and Whitney R-2800 engine.

Presumably, then, the original prototype became the interim XF6F-4 between the two major variants. According to company records, this aircraft (now BuNo 02981, factory number 3189) was later delivered as a production F6F-3.

Robert L. Hall, the test pilot directly concerned, disagrees. His logbook shows two separate prototypes, an XF6F-1 (02981) and an XF6F-3 (02982). He contends that they could not possibly be the same airplane, since during the week of 25 July 1942 he flew both the -1 and -3. This contradictory evidence mystifies every researcher or historian who addresses the matter, and the puzzle is unlikely to be solved.

Overlooked among the Hellcat prototypes is the sole -2. The XF6F-2 was BuAer 66244, originally powered by a Wright R-2600-15. It was first flown in January 1944 by test pilot Carl Alber. Later modifications involved the Pratt and Whitney R-2800-16 and R-2800-21. Each of these engines utilized the Birmann turbo-supercharger.

Like many such experiments, the Birmann was highy promising but disappointingly erratic. It seemed capable of delivering sea-level performance at 20,000 feet, a potential advantage of extreme value in com-

XF6F-2 (BuNo 66244) with Wright R-2600-15 engine equipped with Birmann turbo-supercharger. It gave a sea-level performance at 20,000 feet but was never adopted because of fire danger. The name on the cowl is "Fuzzy Wuzzy," after the numerous felt tufts which provided aerodynamic information. Photo: Grumman

bat. But in-flight fires were a common occurrence due to the ignition of unburned fuel streaming from the supercharger near the engine's exhaust stacks. This ever-present danger was unacceptable, and the Birmann was never adopted as standard equipment. The XF6F-2 was eventually modified to -5 standards and delivered as such.

The last Hellcat model was the XF6F-6. Two examples (BuAer 70188 and 70913) were built, and the first was test-flown by Pat Gallo in July of 1944. The P&W R-2800-18 engine with water injection produced 2,450 horsepower which, combined with a 13 foot 2 inch Hamilton-Standard four-blade propeller, delivered a top speed of 425 mph, or 370 knots. This was 15 mph faster than the F6F-5, and rate of climb was marginally superior.

Further testing of the -6 continued as time permitted, but by mid 1944 Grumman was building nearly 500 Hellcats per month. With its energies devoted to production rather than additional experimentation, the factory did not put the ultimate Hellcat into manufacture before V-J day. Presumably the Navy felt no urgent need for an improved F6F, otherwise the -6 would have progressed further than it did.

Appendix B. Surviving Hellcats

Vintage aircraft are never easily documented. Papers and builders' plates are exchanged, aircraft are in and out of commission, are wrecked, restored, or retired. Very few people are in a position to keep a continuous record of each surviving warbird, even within specific categories.

By the latter part of 1977 about 15 Hellcat airframes remained intact in the United States. One had been destroyed in a crash earlier that year, and another was undergoing extensive repairs. Six F6Fs were being flown, with probably another three in airworthy condition.

Only three F6F-3s remained by the end of 1977, and five of the -5s were reconverted from F6F-5K drones. The only night fighter is the F6F-5N held by the Marine Corps Museum at Quantico, Virginia, though one privately owned -5N remains active as a "straight" -5.

In addition to the 15 surviving Hellcats in the United States, at least two are known to be preserved abroad. The Fleet Air Arm Museum at Yeovilton, Somerset, retains a Hellcat II, number KE209. It remains semiairworthy and is said to be in good condition. Less certain is the state of an F6F-5 still held by the Uruguayan Navy, which has been reported in storage for eventual display at Montevideo.

It is sadly unavoidable that as long as classic aircraft are flown, they will eventually be destroyed. Not even an easy-to-fly aircraft like the Hell-

Former Navy pilot Charles F. Willis, Alaska Airlines board chairman, flying his F6F-3 "Little Nugget" over Puget Sound in 1970. The airline's jets were emblazoned with "Golden Nugget," hence the Hellcat's name. Photo: F. A. Johnsen

The oldest remaining Hellcat is F6F-3 BuAer number 41476, a permanent exhibit in the Marine Corps Museum at Quantico, Virginia.

An oversized VF-16 insignia and curiously modified cowl mark the Confederate Air Force F6F-5, based at Harlingen, Texas. Photo: F. A. Johnsen

cat can remain active indefinitely. And while whole airframes can be assembled from bits and pieces, the day must inevitably come when the last active F6F makes its last flight. When that happens, however, there will still be room for cheer among those who care about historic aircraft.

The splendid restorations accomplished by the National Air and Space Museum, the Navy and Marine Corps museums, and a few private collectors will ensure that the F6F will never be gone or forgotten.

The following list is not comprehensive in that it includes only those Hellcats known to be intact or complete at the time of compilation. It is possible that one or two whole airframes have been assembled from parts during the interim. Almost certainly, the ownership of some of the individual planes has changed.

Type	BuAer	FAA Registry	1977 Owner and Location	1977 Status
F6F-3	41476	—	Marine Corps Museum—Quantico, Virginia	Airworthy
F6F-3	41834	—	National Air and Space Museum— Washington, D.C.	Storage
F6F-3	41930	N103V	Doug Champlin—Enid, Oklahoma	Flying
F6F-3	43014	—	D. B. Robinson—Miami Springs, Florida	Restoration
F6F-5	77722	—	Naval Section HQ—Andrews AFB, Washington, D.C.	Display
F6F-5	79192	—	Bradley Air Museum—Windsor Locks, Connecticut	Storage
F6F-5	79593	—	Battleship Memorial—Mobile, Alabama	Display
F6F-5	79683	N7968C	J. A. Ortseifen—Lexington, Massachusetts	Inactive
F6F-5	79863	N79863	Aerial Classics—Atlanta, Georgia	Flying
F6F-5	80141	N80142	T. H. Friedkin—Rancho Santa Fe, California	Flying
F6F-5	80166	N1078Z	Confederate Air Force—Harlingen, Texas	Flying
F6F-5	93879	N4994V	Planes of Fame—Chino, California	Flying
F6F-5	94203	N7865C	Naval Aviation Museum—Pensacola, Florida	Display
F6F-5	94204	N4998V	M. E. Coutches—Hayward, California	?
F6F-5N	94263	—	Marine Corps Museum—Quantico, Virginia	Restoration
F6F-5	Royal Navy KE209		Fleet Air Arm Museum—Yeovilton, Somerset	Display

Appendix C. Specifications

	F6F-3	F6F-5	Mitsubishi A6M5 Zeke 52
Wing area	344 sq. ft.	344 sq. ft.	229.2 sq. ft.
Wing span	42 ft. 10 in.	42 ft. 10 in.	36 ft. 1 in.
Length	33 ft. 7 in.	33 ft. 7 in.	29 ft. 9 in.
Height	11 ft. 1 in.	11 ft. 1 in.	9 ft. 2 in.
Empty weight	9,023 pounds	9,238 pounds	4,167 pounds
Loaded weight	12,415 pounds	12,483 pounds	6,035 pounds
Wing loading	37.17 lbs./sq. ft.	38.17 lbs./sq. ft.	26.3 lbs./sq. ft.
Engine	Pratt & Whitney R-2800-10	Pratt & Whitney R-2800-10 W	Sakae 14-cyl. radial
Engine rating	2,000 horsepower	2,000 horsepower	1,130 horsepower
Speed at altitude	388 mph (335 knots) /25,000 ft.	400 mph (348 knots) /20,000 ft.	350 mph (305 knots) /19,700 ft.
Speed at sea level	312 mph (270 knots)	318 mph (275 knots)	297 mph (258 knots)
Initial climb rate	3,650 feet per minute	3,200 feet per minute	4,500 feet per minute
Time to altitude	7 min. 0 sec. to 20,000 ft.	7 min. 30 sec. to 20,000 ft.	7 min. 1 sec. to 19,700 ft.
Service ceiling	35,500 feet	36,000 feet	38,500 feet
Maximum range, clean	1,085 st. miles (945 n. mi.)	1,300 st. miles (1,115 n. mi.)	1,190 st. miles (1,030 n. mi.)
Internal fuel	250 gallons	250 gallons	150 gallons
External fuel	150 gallons	150 gallons	85 gallons
Armament (standard)	Six .50-cal. machine guns	Six .50-cal. machine guns	two 20-mm cannon two 7.7-mm machine guns
Number manufactured (excludes prototypes)	4,403	7,868	10,094 all Zekes

Kawasaki N1K2 George	Kawasaki Ki.61-I Tony	Nakajima Ki.43-II Oscar	Nakajima Ki.84-I Frank
253 sq. ft.	215.2 sq. ft.	236.8 sq. ft.	226 sq. ft.
39 ft. 3 in.	39 ft. 4 in.	37 ft. 6 in.	36 ft. 10 in.
30 ft. 8 in.	29 ft. 4 in.	29 ft. 2 in.	32 ft. 6 in.
13 ft. 0 in.	12 ft. 2 in.	10 ft. 2 in.	11 ft. 1 in.
5,860 pounds	5,800 pounds	3,812 pounds	5,864 pounds
9,040 pounds	7,650 pounds	5,320 pounds	7,965 pounds
33.07 lbs./sq. ft.	35.53 lbs./sq. ft.	22.44 lbs./sq. ft.	35.15 lbs./sq. ft.
Nakajima 18-cyl. radial	Kawasaki V-12	Nakajima 14-cyl. radial	Nakajima 18-cyl. radial
1,990 horsepower	1,160 horsepower	1,100 horsepower	1,900 horsepower
370 mph (320 knots) 18,300 ft.	348 mph (300 knots) /16,400 ft.	320 mph (258 knots) /19,700 ft.	388 mph (335 knots) /19,700 ft.
——	302 mph (260 knots)	288 mph (250 knots)	320 mph (255 knots)
——	——	3,240 feet per minute	——
7 min. 22 sec. to 19,700 ft.	7 min. to 16,400 ft.	5 min. 50 sec. to 16,400 ft.	5 min. 54 sec. to 16,400 ft.
39,700 feet	32,800 feet	36,800 feet	34,450 feet
1,070 st. miles (930 n. mi.)	1,180 st. miles (970 n. mi.)	1,006 st. miles (870 n. mi.)	1,025 st. miles (885 n. mi.)
190 gallons	145 gallons	148 gallons	220 gallons
105 gallons	106 gallons	105 gallons	105 gallons
four 20-mm cannon	two 20-mm cannon two 7.7-mm machine guns	two 12.7-mm machine guns	two 20-mm cannon two 12.7-mm machine guns
1,435 all N1Ks	2,803 all Ki.61s	5,751 all Ki.43s	3,577 all Ki.84s

Appendix D

The following document was prepared in December 1944 by the Royal Navy for distribution to its Hellcat pilots. It was appended to Naval Air Tactical Note Number 106, and was provided by British aviation historian David Brown.

Comparative Combat Evaluation Trial between a Hellcat and a Zeke 52

Introduction

1. The following is the summary of a report on comparative performance trials between an F6F-5 and a captured Zeke 52 undertaken by Technical Air Intelligence Centre at N.A.S. Patuxent River, Maryland.

Brief Description of Aircraft

2. *Hellcat* F6F-5 with 250 gals. fuel, guns and ammunition, All-Up Weight 12,285 lbs.

3. *Zeke 52* with Nakajima Sakae 31A Engine, not equipped with water injection. Armament consisted of two Mk.II 20-mm M.G.s and two 7.7-mm M.G.s. The all-up weight of the aircraft as flown: 6,094 lbs.

Results of Trials

Climbs

4. The Zeke 52 climbed about 600 ft./min. better than the F6F-5 up to 9,000 feet, after which the advantage fell off gradually until the two aircraft were about equal at 14,000 feet, above which altitude the F6F-5 had the advantage, varying from 500 ft./min. better at 22,000 feet to about 250 ft./min. better at 30,000 feet.

The best climbing speeds of the F6F-5 and Zeke 52 were found to be 130 and 105 knots indicated, respectively. (150 m.p.h. and 120 m.p.h. respectively)

Speeds

5. The F6F-5 was much faster than the Zeke 52 at all altitudes.
At sea-level the F6F-5 was 41 mph faster than the Zeke 52.
At 5,000 feet the F6F-5 was 22 mph faster than the Zeke 52.
At 10,000 feet the F6F-5 was 45 mph faster than the Zeke 52.
At 15,000 feet the F6F-5 was 62 mph faster than the Zeke 52.
At 20,000 feet the F6F-5 was 69 mph faster than the Zeke 52.
At 25,000 feet the F6F-5 was 75 mph faster than the Zeke 52.
At 30,000 feet the F6F-5 was 66 mph faster than the Zeke 52.

Top speeds attained were 409 mph at 21,600 feet for the F6F-5, and 335 mph at 18,000 feet for the Zeke 52.

Rolls

6. Rolls of the Zeke 52 were equal to those of the F6F-5 at speeds under 200 knots (230 mph) and inferior above that speed, due to high control forces.

Turns

7. The Zeke 52 was greatly superior to the F6F-5 in slow speed turns at low and medium altitudes, its advantage decreasing to about parity at 30,000 feet. In slow speed turns it could gain one turn in three and one-half at 10,000 feet.

Dives

8. Initial dive accelerations of the Zeke 52 and F6F-5 were about equal, after which the F6F-5 was far superior.

The F6F-5 was slightly superior in zooms after dives.

Vision

9. The Zeke 52 was considered to permit better vision in all respects, the rear vision being good due to the use of a bubble canopy and the complete absence of armor behind the pilot's head. There was no rear vision mirror installed in the Zeke 52 tested. The small gun sight did not interfere with forward vision.

Maneuverability

10. The maneuverability of the Zeke 52 is remarkable at speeds below about 175 knots (200 mph), being far superior to that of the F6F-5. Its superiority, however, diminishes with speed, due to its high control forces, and the F6F-5 has the advantage at speeds above 200 knots (230 mph).

Suggested Tactics

11. The following tactics are suggested for use against the Zeke 52 by the F6F-5:

Do not Dog-Fight with the Zeke 52.

Do not Try to Follow a Loop or Half-Roll with Pull-Through.

When attacking, use your superior power and high-speed performance to engage at the most favourable moment.

To evade a Zeke on your tail, roll and dive away into a high-speed turn.

Naval Staff
Admiralty (A.W.D.742/44)

241

Appendix E. The Top Hellcat Aces

Name	Unit	Carrier	Aerial Victories	Comments
Commander David McCampbell	AG-15	*Essex*	34	Medal of Honor
Lieutenant Eugene A. Valencia	VF-9	*Essex, Lexington, Yorktown*	23	
Lieutenant Cecil E. Harris	VF-18	*Intrepid*	22	Plus 2 in F4F
Lieutenant Alexander Vraciu	VF-6 VF-16, VF-20	*Independence, Intrepid Lexington*	19	9 with VF-6 10 with VF-16
Lieutenant Patrick D. Fleming	VF-80 VBF-80	*Ticonderoga Hancock*	18	10 with VF-80 8 with VBF-80
Lieutenant Cornelius N. Nooy	VF-31	*Cabot, Belleau Wood*	18	
Lieutenant (jg) Douglas Baker	VF-20	*Enterprise, Lexington*	16	KIA 14 December 1944
Lieutenant Arthur R. Hawkins	VF-31	*Cabot, Belleau Wood*	14	
Lieutenant John L. Wirth	VF-31	*Cabot*	14	
Lieutenant Commander George C. Duncan	VF-15	*Essex*	13.5	
Lieutenant (jg) Roy W. Rushing	VF-15	*Essex*	13	
Lieutenant John R. Strane	VF-15	*Essex*	13	
Lieutenant (jg) Wendell Van Twelves	VF-15	*Essex*	13	
Lieutenant Daniel A. Carmichael	VF-2 VBF-12	*Hornet Randolph*	12	8 with VF-2 4 with VF-12
Lieutenant Clement M. Craig	VF-22	*Independence, Belleau Wood, Cowpens*	12	
Lieutenant Commander Hamilton McWhorter	VF-9 VF-12	*Essex Randolph*	12	10 with VF-9 2 with VF-12
Lieutenant James A. Shirley	VF-27	*Princeton*	12	
Lieutenant George R. Carr	VF-15	*Essex*	11.5	
Commander Fred E. Bakutis	VF-20	*Enterprise, Lexington*	11	
Commander William A. Dean, Jr.	VF-2	*Hornet*	11	
Lieutenant James B. French	VF-9	*Lexington, Yorktown*	11	
Lieutenant Commander Charles M. Mallory	VF-18	*Intrepid*	11	

Name	Unit	Carrier	Aerial Victories	Comments
Lieutenant Harvey P. Picken	VF-18	*Intrepid*	11	
Lieutenant (jg) James V. Reber, Jr.	VF-30	*Belleau Wood*	11	
Lieutenant Richard E. Stambook	VF-27	*Princeton*	11	
Lieutenant Commander Marshall U. Beebe	VF-17	*Hornet*	10.5	
Lieutenant William E. Henry	VF (N) -41	*Independence*	10.5	
Lieutenant Armistead B. Smith, Jr.	VF-9 VBF-12	*Essex* *Randolph*	10.5	6 with VF-9 4½ with VBF-12
Lieutenant Robert E. Murray	VF-29	*Cabot*	10.33	
Lieutenant Robert H. Anderson	VF-80	*Ticonderoga, Hancock*	10	
Lieutenant Carl A. Brown, Jr.	VF-27	*Princeton*	10	
Lieutenant Commander Thaddeus T. Coleman	VF-6 VF-83	*Intrepid, Princeton* *Essex*	10	2 with VF-6 8 with VF-83
Lieutenant William J. Masoner	VF-19	*Lexington*	10	Plus 2 in F4F
Lieutenant (jg) Harris E. Mitchell	VF-9	*Lexington, Yorktown*	10	
Lieutenant (jg) Arthur Singer	VF-15	*Essex*	10	
Lieutenant Charles R. Stimpson	VF-11	*Hornet*	10	Plus 6 in F4F

Top F6F Night Fighter Scores

Name	Unit	Base	Night	Day	Comments
Lieutenant William E. Henry	VF (N) -41	*Independence*	6.5	4	
Captain Robert Baird	VMF (N) -533	Okinawa	6	0	
Lieutenant (jg) John Orth	VF-9	*Yorktown,* *Lexington*	6	0	
Ensign Jack S. Berkheimer	VF (N) -41	*Independence*	5.5	2	KIA Dec. 1944
Lieutenant Robert J. Humphrey	VF-17	*Hornet*	5	.33	
Lieutenant Donald E. Umphres	VF-83	*Essex*	4?	2?	
Ensign Robert L. Bowman	VF-6	*Hancock*	4	0	
Lieutenant John W. Dear	VF (N) -76	*Hornet*	4	3	
Lieutenant Fred L. Dungan	VF (N) -76	*Hornet*	4	3	
Ensign Philip T. McDonald	VF (N) -91	*Bon Homme* *Richard*	4	0	All 13 Aug. 1945
Lieutenant (jg) Kenneth D. Smith	VF (N) -90	*Enterprise*	4	1	

Appendix F. U.S. Navy Escort Carrier Hellcat Squadrons in Combat in the Pacific, 1943–45

Unit	Carrier	In Combat	Squadron Leaders
VF-24	*Santee*	March to July 1945	Lieutenant Commander R. J. Ostrom (KIA) Lieutenant P. N. Charbonnet
VF-25	*Chenango*	April to July 1945	Lieutenant Commander R. W. Robinson (KIA) Lieutenant B. Phillips
VF-26	*Fanshaw Bay*	July to August 1945	Lieutenant Commander H. N. Funk
VF-35	*Chenango*	Nov. 1943 to Oct. '44	Lieutenant Commander F. T. Moore
VF-37	*Sangamon*	Nov. 1943 to Oct. '44	Lieutenant Commander S. E. Hindman
VF-40	*Suwannee*	March to August 1945	Lieutenant Commander R. D. Sampson (KIA) Lieutenant Commander J. C. Longino
VF-60	*Suwannee*	Nov. 1943 to Oct. '44	Lieutenant Commander H. O. Feilbach
VF (N) -33	*Sangamon* *Chenango*	March to July 1945 July to August 1945	Lieutenant Commander P. C. Rooney
VMF-511	*Block Island*	May to August 1945	Major R. C. Maze (KIA) Captain J. L. Secrest

Notes

Chapter 1

1. Correspondence with Robert L. Hall, March 1977.
2. Ibid.
3. The usually quoted figure is 664, but Navy acceptance records show six fewer.
4. Richard Thruelsen, *The Grumman Story* (New York: Praeger, 1977) , p. 53.
5. Robert A. Winston, *Fighting Squadron* (New York: Holiday House, 1964), p. 78.
6. Thomas G. Miller, *The Cactus Air Force* (New York: Harper and Row, 1969), p. 156.
7. Correspondence with Chester Leo Smith, December 1975.
8. Interview with W. Ralph Clark, April 1978.
9. Interview with Ken Jernstedt, June 1976.
10. Thruelsen, *The Grumman Story*, p. 206.

Chapter 2

1. Interview with Reuben H. Denoff, 12 February 1977.
2. "Air Group Nine Comes Home," *Life* magazine, 1 May 1944, p. 92.
3. Interview with Alexander Vraciu, March 1977.
4. Oliver Jensen, *Carrier War* (New York: Simon and Schuster, 1945), p. 53.
5. Ibid.
6. Correspondence with William N. Leonard, 1976.
7. VF-12 action report, 5 November 1943.
8. Samuel Eliot Morison, *A History of U.S. Navy Operations in W.W. II*, Vol. VI (Boston: Little, Brown & Co., 1969), p. 333.
9. Denoff interview, 12 February 1977.
10. Raymond F. Toliver, *Fighter Aces* (New York: Macmillan, 1965), p. 158.
11. Ibid.
12. Correspondence with Bernard M. Strean, November 1976.
13. Ibid.
14. Papers of Robert M. Duncan.
15. Ibid.

16. Ibid.
17. Jensen, *Carrier War*, p. 80.
18. Ibid.

Chapter 3

1. Correspondence with Sam L. Silber, January 1976.
2. Correspondence with Edward M. Owen, February 1976.
3. Silber correspondence, 1976.
4. Conversation with E. A. Valencia, San Diego, June 1971.
5. Robert D. Loomis, *Great American Fighter Pilots of W. W. II* (New York: Random House, 1961), p. 135.
6. Owen correspondence.
7. Jensen, *Carrier War*, p. 119.
8. Interview with Armistead B. Smith, February 1977.
9. Correspondence with E. S. McCuskey, February 1977.
10. Correspondence with Francis M. Fleming, March 1975.
11. VF-32 action report, 29 April 1944.

Chapter 4

1. VF-2 action report, 11 June 1944.
2. David Wittels, "4-F Hero," *Saturday Evening Post*, 14 April 1945.
3. VF-2 action report, 15 June 1944.
4. W. G. Land and A. O. Van Wyen, *Naval Air Operations in the Marianas*, 1944.
5. Thomas L. Morrissey, *Odyssey of Fighting Two* (Privately printed, 1945), p. 135.
6. VF-15 action report. 19 June 1944.
7. Correspondence with Fred A. Bardshar, 25 March 1977.
8. VF-2 action report, 19 June 1944.
9. Correspondence with David McCampbell, 1 November 1976.
10. Ibid.
11. Ibid.
12. Clark G. Reynolds, *The Fast Carriers* (New York: McGraw-Hill, 1968), p. 193.
13. Air Group One action report, 20 June 1944.
14. J. Bryan and Philip Reed, *Mission Beyond Darkness* (New York: Duell, Sloan & Pearce, 1945), p. 84.
15. Telephone conversation with Bernard M. Strean, September 1976.
16. Ibid.

Chapter 5

1. Ian Cameron, *Wings of the Morning* (New York: Morrow, 1963), p. 16.
2. Fighter-Observation Squadron One history.

3. John G. Norris, "Hellcats over France," *Flying* magazine, January 1945.
4. Morison, *History,* Vol. XI, p. 281.

Chapter 6

1. Morrissey, *Odyssey,* p. 190.
2. Ibid, p. 179.
3. VF-15 action report, 12 September 1944.
4. VF-15 action report, 13 September 1944.
5. Morrissey, *Odyssey,* p. 190.
6. Correspondence with Carl A. Brown, 18 July 1977.
7. Ibid.
8. Toliver, *Fighter Aces,* p. 191.
9. Ibid., p. 192.
10. Morrissey, *Odyssey,* p. 198.
11. VF-18 action report, 12 October 1944.
12. Interview with H. B. Moranville, 1976.
13. Interview with Charles R. Stimpson, March 1977.
14. VF-14 history.
15. VF-19 action report. 24 October 1944.
16. Brown correspondence, 18 July 1977.
17. Ibid.
18. Ibid.
19. Telephone conversation with John Fitzgerald, 21 June 1977.
20. Ibid.
21. Brown correspondence, 18 July 1977.
22. Ibid.
23. Correspondence with Fred A. Bardshar, 29 March 1977.
24. VF-15 action report, 24 October 1944.
25. Ibid.
26. Ibid.

Chapter 7

1. VF-14 history.
2. Ibid.
3. VF-15 action report, 11 November 1944.
4. Correspondence with E. S. McCuskey, 14 July 1977.
5. Ibid.
6. Correspondence with W. N. Leonard, 10 January 1977.
7. Interview with Alexander Vraciu, March 1977.
8. Ibid.
9. Ibid.
10. Barrett Tillman, "A Sundowner's Adventure," *AAHS Journal,* Winter, 1975.
11. Correspondence with E. G. Fairfax, 10 December 1975.

12. Ibid.

13. Norman Polmar, *Aircraft Carriers* (New York: Doubleday, 1969), p. 422.

14. Correspondence with Robert E. Clements, 31 January 1976.

15. Ibid.

16. Ibid.

Chapter 8

1. Turner F. Caldwell, "We Put the Flattops on the Night Shift," *Saturday Evening Post*, 11 August 1945, p. 26.

2. Ibid.

3. Correspondence with William E. Henry, 8 January 1975.

4. Ibid.

5. Interview with William E. Henry, March 1976.

6. Correspondence with James S. Gray, 14 October 1976.

7. Henry correspondence, 8 January 1975.

8. Reynolds, *Fast Carriers*, p. 330.

9. VF (N) -90 history.

10. Interview with R. B. Porter, October 1976.

11. VMF (N) -533 action report, 22 June 1945.

12. Correspondence with Robert Baird, March 1976.

13. Ibid.

Chapter 9

1. Interview with James B. French, June 1976.

2. Morison, *History*, Vol. XIV, p. 22.

3. Private papers of Harris E. Mitchell.

4. VF-80 history.

5. Mitchell papers.

6. Ibid.

7. VF-80 history.

8. Interview with Reuben H. Denoff, February 1977.

9. Ibid.

10. Mitchell papers.

11. Ibid.

12. VF-29 history.

13. Ibid.

14. Toliver, *Fighter Aces*, p. 183.

15. VF-30 action report, 6 April 1945.

16. Reynolds, *Fast Carriers*, p. 341.

17. Mitchell papers.

18. Correspondence with W. N. Leonard, 14 December 1976.

Chapter 10

1. Denoff interview, 12 February 1977.
2. Correspondence with Chester Leo Smith, December 1975.
3. Correspondence with Fred A. Bardshar, 19 April 1977.
4. Fitzgerald phone interview, 21 June 1977.
5. R. L. Newhafer, "I'll Remember," *Naval Aviation News*, December 1976.
6. Ibid.
7. Polmar, *Aircraft Carriers*, p. 464.
8. Correspondence with Malcolm Cagle, 20 May 1977.

Sources

Official

Official research sources usually begin and end at Building 210 of the Washington Navy Yard. There Dr. Dean C. Allard and his helpful staff run the Operational Archives which contain most of the squadron, air group, and ship action reports for W. W. II. Numerous mail transactions and a personal visit yielded the largest share of original research material, and the assistance of the archives personnel has been consistently outstanding. Two types of primary sources were consulted: after-action reports and unit histories. The former were compiled immediately after each combat mission by squadron intelligence officers and then typed on a standard Air Combat Action report form. These ACA-1 forms contain a wealth of tactical, technical, and operational details. Unit histories, when available, were the second source consulted. Many are fairly detailed but some are sketchy or incomplete. In the few instances where conflicts arose between the two, I have favored the ACA reports.

The squadron after-action reports consulted were for Fighting Squadrons 1, 2, 6, 9, 11, 15, 16, 17, 18, 19, 20, 24, 29, 32, 33, 51, 74, 76 (N), 77 (N), 78 (N), 83, and 88.

Squadron histories were obtained for VF-5, VF-6, VF-9, VF-11, VF-15, VF-16, VF-19, VF-29, VF (N)-41, VF-83, VF (N)-90 and VF (N)-91.

The U.S. Marine Corps Audio-Visual Branch provided night fighter action reports, not previously available to the public. The squadrons concerned were VMF (N)-533, VFM (N)-541, VFM (N)-542, and VFM (N)-543.

Additionally, two official studies conducted during the war proved useful. These were *Naval Air Operations in the Marianas* and *Aviation Statistics of W. W. II*. The former is a not entirely complete summary of the "Marianas Turkey Shoot," but is a good starting point. The latter included valuable information on aerial defense against kamikaze attacks.

Thanks is also due the staff of the Inactive Ship Facility at Bremerton,

Washington, for allowing me aboard the mothballed USS *Hornet* (CV-12). Commander Bob Pettyjohn kindly showed me around the old carrier, upon which he made the 83,000th landing.

Unofficial

Only a handful of single volumes can be properly termed invaluable to researching naval aviation during the Pacific War. They include *Aircraft Carriers* by Norman Polmar, the definitive work on the subject, and Dr. Clark G. Reynolds's detailed, scholarly study, *The Fast Carriers*. Between them, these two volumes contain more than most enthusiasts and some students of the subject will require, and I have relied upon them heavily for background material. Samuel Eliot Morison's 14-volume history of U.S. naval operations in W. W. II is often weak on aviation, but remains an essential research tool for anyone dealing with the U.S. Navy from 1941 to 1945.

On a smaller scale, unofficial ship and unit histories helped round out much of the text. Foremost among these is Edward P. Stafford's *The Big E*, the standard by which all subsequent ship histories must be measured.

Privately published squadron histories offer an insider's look at the units which produced such volumes. *The Odyssey of Fighting Two* is an excellent example, as is *Another Light, Please: The Story of VBF-87*. In the absence of both official and semiofficial unit histories, particularly that of VF-27, direct contact with former squadron personnel has substituted for previous documentation.

Perhaps the Grumman Corporation should not be listed as an unofficial source, but by any interpretation it offers a wealth of information. And Grumman has two marvelous representatives in Herman J. Schonenberg, its historian, and W. Ralph Clark, director of Washington, D.C., operations. Both these gentlemen were informed of the project late in its progress, but their enthusiasm, knowledge, and willingness to help are unsurpassed. They even took time to show me through Plant Number 3, which now produces components for A-6s and F-14s. Ralph Clark's recollections of his wartime service as a TBF and F6F tech rep were particularly helpful. And as a combat P-51 pilot, "Schony" Schonenberg knows the fighter plane business both as a participant and as an enthusiast.

While mentioning Grumman, I would be amiss in not thanking Mr. Andre Hubbard, the corporation's former historian. He answered many of my initial questions, and dug out several factory photos.

I am bound to salute the long-suffering efforts of those other individuals who contributed to the completion of this project. Richard M. Hill of Milwaukee, Wisconsin, is a former F8F pilot with a wealth of information and trivia on the Hellcat. His generosity and enthusiasm have been truly exceptional, and I could not exaggerate the importance of his assistance with documentation and photos. Others who figured in the photo department were Harold Andrews, Rowland P. Gill, Frederick A. Johnsen, and Christopher F. Shores in Britain.

William N. Hess of Houston is one of my oldest friends—and one of the most put-upon. He is also secretary and historian of the American Fighter Aces Association, the erstwhile B-17 gunner who holds that elite organization together. His wholehearted support and his numerous contacts were both major factors in completion of the Hellcat story.

Sergeant Lowell Thompson of Fairchild Air Force Base earns a dip of the wing in salute to his detailed knowledge of surviving W. W. II aircraft. Robert C. Mikesh of the National Air and Space Museum was equally generous with his information. And two sources of hard-to-find foreign information were most helpful: Mannosuke Toda of Japan's renowned *Koku-Fan* magazine, and David Brown in England who knows almost everything there is to know about the Royal Navy's Fleet Air Arm.

At this printing, few F6F combat pilots remain on active duty. Almost none of those consulted for this history still fly. They pursue other careers and interests ranging from teaching and banking to golf and gardening. But each of those listed below took time to talk or write about their affiliation with the Hellcat. Those who were enthusiastic enough or tolerant enough to perform special services "above and beyond" included:

Gene Fairfax, Dave McCampbell, Blake Moranville and Alex Vraciu who all read portions of the early manuscript and made corrective suggestions.

Bill Leonard and Hank Rowe provided more information on Task Force 38 operations and fighter direction than could be used in this volume.

Harris Mitchell allowed access to his unpublished recollections of VF-9, and Scotty McCuskey provided detailed information on VF-8's G-suits and activities in general.

Bill Henry and Chick Harmer were the main sources of information on Navy night fighters. Bob Baird wrote at length on his days—and nights —with VMF (N)-533. And Bruce Porter earned my thanks for his continuing assistance on the Marines, not to mention access to his backyard whirlpool bath.

Charlie Stimpson is the wonderful host of The Inn at Rancho Santa Fe, California. He made it possible to meet several other naval aviators, in addition to discussing his own colorful career.

Finally, I must acknowledge the collective assistance of the alumni of

Fighting Squadrons 9, 11, and 27. Twenty-eight squadrons are represented among the nearly 50 contributors, but these three units provided an unusual degree of response. I would be proud to fly with any of them in any sky.

None of the contributors listed here remain on active duty. The ranks listed are those held at time of retirement.

Colonel Robert Baird, USMC, VMF (N) -533, Okinawa
Vice Admiral Frederick A. Bardshar, Commander Air Group 27, the *Princeton* and *Independence*
Lieutenant James A. Barnett, VF (N) -41, the *Independence*
Captain Marshall U. Beebe, CO VF-17, the *Hornet*
Commander Carl A. Brown, VF-27, the *Princeton*
Vice Admiral Malcolm W. Cagle, CO VF-88, the *Yorktown*
Mr. Ralph Clark, Field service representative, Grumman
Captain Robert E. Clements, XO VF-11, the *Hornet*
Captain Richard L. Cormier, VF-80, the *Ticonderoga*; VBF-80, the *Hancock*
Commander Reuben H. Denoff, VF-9, the *Essex*; CO VBF-12, the *Randolph*
Commander William Devaney, Plane captain, VF-31 and 29, the *Cabot*
Captain Robert M. Duncan, VF-5, the *Yorktown*
Rear Admiral Eugene G. Fairfax, CO VF-11, the *Hornet*
Lieutenant John D. Fitzgerald, Asst. Ops. Officer VF-27, the *Princeton*
Commander Francis M. Fleming, VF-16, the *Lexington*
Lieutenant James B. French, VF-9, the *Lexington* and *Yorktown*
Captain James S. Gray, CO VF (N) -78 and VF-20, the *Enterprise*
Mr. Robert L. Hall, Grumman test pilot
Captain Richard G. Hanecak, VF-7, the *Hancock*
Captain Richard E. Harmer, CO VF (N) -101, the *Enterprise* (F4Us)
Captain Harry W. Harrison, Jr., CO VF-6, the *Intrepid*
Commander William E. Henry, XO VF (N) -41, the *Independence*
Lieutenant Paul F. Irvine, VF (N) -91, the *Bon Homme Richard*
Rear Admiral William N. Leonard, Operations staff, Task Force 38
Captain David McCampbell, Commander Air Group 15, the *Essex*
Commander E. Scott McCuskey, VF-8, the *Bunker Hill*
Commander W. Robert Maxwell, VF-51, the *San Jacinto*
Commander Richard H. May, VF-32, the *Langley*
Commander Harris E. Mitchell, VF-9, the *Lexington* and *Yorktown*
Lieutenant Commander H. B. Moranville, VF-11, the *Hornet*
Captain Edward M. Owen, CO VF-5, the *Yorktown*
Colonel R. B. Porter, USMC, CO VMF (N) -542, Okinawa
Rear Admiral Emmett R. Riera, Commander Air Group 11, the *Hornet*

Captain Henry A. Rowe, Fighter Director, Task Force 38

Captain Jimmie E. Savage, VF-11, the *Hornet*

Lieutenant (jg) John G. Selway, VF(N)-53, the *Saratoga* and VF(N)-91, the *Bon Homme Richard*

Captain Seth S. Searcy, Jr., Commander Air Group 88, the *Yorktown*

Commander Sam L. Silber, CO VF-18, the *Bunker Hill*

Captain Armistead B. Smith, Jr., VF-9, the *Essex*; XO VBF-12, the *Randolph*

Lieutenant Chester Leo Smith, USMC, VMF-511, the *Block Island*

Captain Richard E. Stambook, VF-27, the *Princeton*

Captain Edgar E. Stebbins, Commander Air Group Five, *the Yorktown*

Commander Charles R. Stimpson, VF-11, the *Hornet*

Rev. Elmer G. Stratton, Photo Recon Unit 1, the *Hancock*

Vice Admiral Bernard M. Strean, CO VF-1, Tarawa and the *Yorktown*

Commander Alexander Vraciu, VF-6, the *Independence* and *Intrepid*; VF-16 and 20, the *Lexington*

Lieutenant Bruce W. Williams, VF-19, the *Lexington*

Lieutenant George D. Wood, VBF-87, the *Ticonderoga*

Bibliography

Belote, J. H. and W. M. *Titans of the Seas*. New York: Harper & Row, 1975.

Bryan, Joseph, III. *Mission Beyond Darkness*. New York: Duell, Sloan, & Pearce, 1944.

Buchanan, A. R., ed. *The Navy's Air War*. New York: Harper, 1947.

Cameron, Ian. *Wings of the Morning*. New York: Morrow, 1963.

Green, William. *Famous Fighters of the Second World War*. Garden City: Doubleday, 1962.

Grumman Aircraft Company. *Grumman at War*. New York, 1945.

Hill, Richard M. *Grumman F6F-3/-5 Hellcat*. New York: Arco-Aircam Series No. 23, 1971.

Hill, Richard M. *Markings of the Aces, Part 2*. Australia: Kookaburra Publications, 1968.

Jensen, Oliver. *Carrier War*. New York: Simon and Schuster, 1945.

Morison, Samuel Eliot. *A History of U.S. Naval Operations in W. W. II*. Boston: Little, Brown and Co., 1969.

   Vol. VI   *Breaking the Bismarcks Barrier*
   Vol. VIII *New Guinea and the Marianas*
   Vol. XI   *The Invasion of France and Germany*
   Vol. XII *Leyte*
   Vol. XIV *Victory in the Pacific*

Morrissey, T. L., ed. *The Odyssey of Fighting Two*. Privately printed, 1945.

Mosier, David W., ed. *Another Light, Please*: the Story of VBF-87, circa 1946.

Okumiya, Masatake, et al. *Zero!* New York: Ballantine, 1971.

Polmar, Norman. *Aircraft Carriers*. New York: Doubleday, 1969.

Reynolds, Clark G. *The Fast Carriers*. New York: McGraw-Hill, 1968.

Sherrod, Robert. *History of Marine Corps Aviation in W. W. II*. Washington, D. C.: Combat Forces Press, 1951.

Stafford, Edward P. *The Big E*. New York: Dell, 1964.

Thruelsen, Richard. *The Grumman Story*. New York: Praeger, 1976.

Toliver, R. F. and Constable, T. *Fighter Aces*. New York: Macmillan, 1965.

Winston, Robert A. *Fighting Squadron*. New York: Holiday House, 1946.

257

Articles

Life staff. "Air Group Nine Comes Home," *Life*, 1 May 1944.

Caldwell, Turner F. "We Put the Flattops on the Night Shift," *Saturday Evening Post*, 11 August 1945.

Maisel, Albert Q. "Zoot Suits that Save Fliers' Lives" *Readers Digest*, May 1945.

Miller, Thomas G. "Anatomy of an Air Battle," *AAHS Journal*. Summer 1970.

Newhafer, Richard L. "I'll Remember," *Naval Aviation News*, December 1976.

Norris, John G. "Hellcats Over France." *Flying* Magazine, January 1945.

Shores, C. F. and Brown, J. D. "Fleet Air Arm Fighter Operations in WW II," *Air Pictorial*, October, November, 1967, and April 1971.

Tillman, Barrett. "A Sundowner's Adventure," *AAHS Journal*, Winter 1975. "Hellcat," *Wings*, October 1974. "Hellcats Over Truk," USNI *Proceedings*, March 1977.

Wittels, David G. "4-F Hero," *Saturday Evening Post*, 14 April 1945.

Index

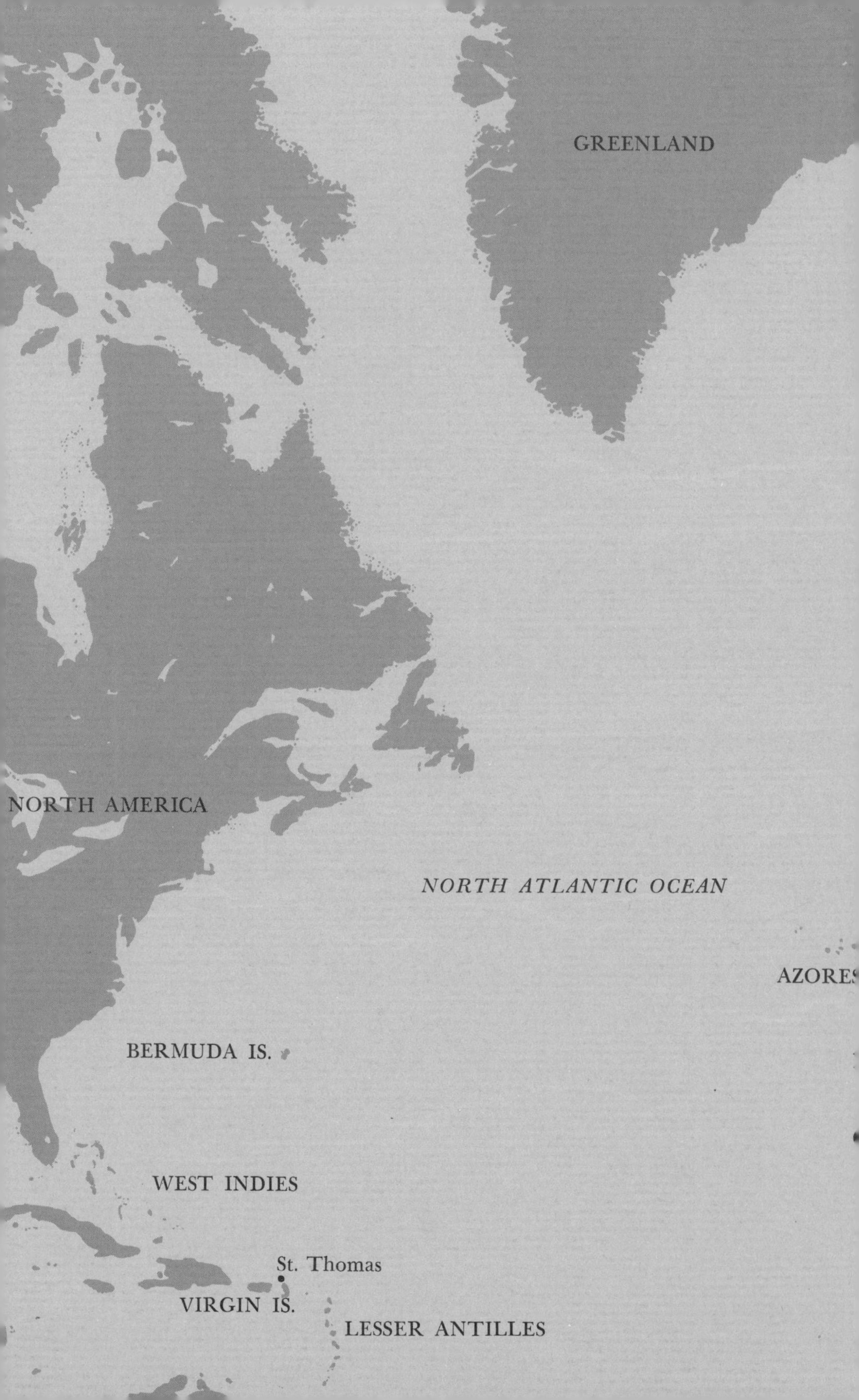
GREENLAND
NORTH AMERICA
NORTH ATLANTIC OCEAN
AZORES
BERMUDA IS.
WEST INDIES
St. Thomas
VIRGIN IS.
LESSER ANTILLES